Silas Talbot

*Captain
of Old Ironsides*

By William M. Fowler, Jr.

William Ellery: A Rhode island Politico and Lord of Admiralty
Rebels Under Sail: The American Navy During the Revolution
The American Revolution: Changing Perspectives (edited with Wallace Coyle)
The Baron of Beacon Hill: A Biography of John Hancock
Jack Tars and Commodores: The American Navy, 1783-1815
Under Two Flags: The American Navy in the Civil War

Silas Talbot

 *Captain of Old Ironsides*

By
William M. Fowler, Jr.

Mystic Seaport Museum
Mystic, Connecticut

1995

Printed in the United States of America
ISBN 0-913372-73-0

Cataloging-in-Publication Data:
Fowler, William M., 1944-
     Silas Talbot—captain of Old Ironsides / by William
M. Fowler, Jr. — 1st ed. — Mystic, Conn. : Mystic Seaport Museum, c1995.
     xvip. 233:ill.,1 port. ;   26 cm.
     Includes bibliographical references and index.

     1. Talbot, Silas, 1751-1813. 2. U.S. - History -
Revolution, 1775-1783 - Biography. 3. U.S. Navy -
Biography. 4. Constitution (Frigate). I. Title.

E207.T13F68

Book design by Caroline Rowntree
Typeset in Stone Informal
Printed by Courier Companies Inc.

Published by Mystic Seaport Museum, Inc.
75 Greenmanville Avenue
Mystic, Ct 06355

Raymond Henry Robinson

Abbreviations

DBW   *Naval Documents Related to the United States Wars with The Barbary Powers.* Dudley W. Knox, ed., 6 vols. Washington: United States Government Printing Office, 1939-45.

DQW   *Naval Documents Related to the Quasi War Between the United States and France: Naval Operations from February 1797 to December 1801.* Dudley W. Knox, ed., 7 vols. Washington: United States Government Printing Office, 1935-9.

JCC   *Journals of the Continental Congress, 1774-1789.* W. C. Ford, ed., 34 vols. Washington: United States Government Printing Office, 1904-12

MHS   Massachusetts Historical Society, Boston, Massachusetts.

NDAR   *Naval Documents of the American Revolution.* William B. Clark and William James Morgan, eds., 8 vols. Washington: United States Government Printing Office, 1964-

NEHGS New England Historic Genealogical Society, Boston, Massachusetts.

NYHS   New-York Historical Society, New York, New York.

PCC   Papers of the Continental Congress, Microfilm Edition, National Archives, Washington, D.C.

RIHS   Rhode Island Historical Society, Providence, Rhode Island.

STP   Silas Talbot Papers, G.W. Blunt White Library.

Contents

Foreword

I never met my fourth great-grandfather, of course, but his eyes followed me whenever I was around him as I was growing up. He watched—taking my measure, perhaps—from his portrait on our dining room wall. I came to know Silas Talbot, however, from my own father, William Richmond Talbot, learning from the stories he told me through my childhood, seeing Silas through my father's eyes.

This foreword, then, is not about Silas Talbot. You will meet him in the excellent narrative by William M. Fowler, Jr. that follows. Instead, these few words are in the way of a dedicatory tribute to my father, who sought some forty years ago to bring Silas back to life—phoenix-like out of the ashes of unsung Revolutionary War heroes.

After dinner each weeknight, Dad would pull out the metal file boxes and begin laying out the copies of Silas Talbot's original correspondence, commissions, and records. With all the lights blazing and under the watchful eye of the Lieutenant Colonel and Commodore, Dad would catalogue and cross-reference the papers. Although acutely myopic, Dad's vision was to research and ultimately write an accurate biography that would acknowledge Silas' role in the beginning years of the republic and his legacy to future generations.

As he pursued this goal, my father continued his commitment to promoting the goals of the New York State Society of the Cincinnati, founded to preserve inviolate those principles for which Silas and his fellow officers fought and died. My father served as President of the New York State Society of the Cincinnati for two months before his untimely death in 1966. As an aside, I served as President when the New York State Society hosted the General Society of the Cincinnati's Bicentennial meeting in May, 1983. There is continuity from Silas.

But back to my father. I will never forget those hours long into the night as he pored over those papers, often having trouble deciphering some detail even with the help of a large magnifying glass. Nor will I forget the look in his eyes when the *USS Talbot*—originally a Guided Missile Escort

Destroyer—was christened in 1966 in Bath, Maine. He told me this was actually the second ship named for Silas. The first was sent to the Russians via lend-lease during World War II, having been decommissioned previously. This second ship was named in Silas Talbot's honor in large part because of my father's persistent research with the Navy Department. And we had tears in our eyes (my father had died by then) when the *USS Talbot* was commissioned in Boston's Charlestown across the pier from Old Ironsides, our ancestor's old command. *USS Talbot* subsequently became classified a frigate. How Silas must have enjoyed that.

Now forty years later my father's vision is being realized. Ralph Earle's portrait of Silas shows the eagle of the Society of the Cincinnati. Organized more than 200 years ago, this "one Society of Friends" continues today to perpetuate that spirit. And it is that spirit that brought together my father; Alexander Vietor, also a member of the Society of the Cincinnati; Mystic Seaport Museum's Library; and this book. I am indebted to Mr. and Mrs. Vietor; to Mystic Seaport Museum, especially Joseph Gribbons, Director of Publications; and to Professor Fowler.

More especially I am grateful to Silas for his legacy. And most of all I pay tribute to my father, whose dedication gave birth ultimately to this volume. He would have been proud of the result.

William Richmond Talbot, Jr.

Introduction

Gerry Morris, former Librarian at the G. W. Blunt White Library at Mystic Seaport Museum, introduced me to Silas Talbot, although I had been acquainted with him long before Gerry formally presented him. A portrait of Silas Talbot is a prominent feature of an upstairs reading room in the library, and anyone entering that room can't avoid the hard stare of Talbot, nor the vivid red of his uniform waistcoat. Frankly, I never paid much attention. The only thought that ever crossed my mind was a question. What did a Rhode Island hero of the Revolution, congressman from New York, and commander of the frigate *Constitution* in the Quasi War have to do with Mystic Seaport? I never asked. I thought it might have been one of Gerry's endearing idiosyncrasies. He has many.

My relationship or non-relationship with Talbot changed abruptly one afternoon when Doug Stein, Curator of Manuscripts in the library, mentioned the existence of the Talbot papers. That piqued my curiosity about the man on the wall. Mild interest turned to fascination when Doug reached to the top of the card catalog and pulled down a thick loose-leaf notebook marked "Calendar of the Silas Talbot Papers." What a treasure. In 1961 Alexander Vietor purchased a collection of letters, daybooks and assorted documents once owned by Silas Talbot. Mr. Vietor was not only an astute collector but a fine judge of libraries as well. He was confident that the staff at Mystic Seaport Museum's library would recognize the value of this collection for the study of America's early maritime and naval history. He also appreciated that Talbot's close ties to New England and the sea made this library the proper place for such a collection.

Early in 1962, Alexander Vietor donated his collection of approximately 2000 Talbot items to the G. W. Blunt White Library. In the winter of 1963-64, Mrs. John Talbot Curtis of Southport, Connecticut, gave an additional 900 Talbot items to the library. A further gift of Silas Talbot materials and a reproduction of the Silas Talbot portrait by Ralph Earle came to the library in 1964 from William Richmond Talbot of Philadelphia. It was William Richmond Talbot and his wife Emily who initiated discussions with Mystic

Seaport Museum for the publication of a Silas Talbot biography, and it was William Richmond Talbot who undertook the first research for this project.

The years since Alexander Vietor's initial donation have shown the wisdom of his decision and the wisdom and generosity of subsequent donors of Silas Talbot material. Since its arrival at Mystic the Talbot collection has been carefully arranged and calendared. Its historical importance has been attested by the numerous scholars who have come to use the papers. Oddly enough, although several scholars had made their way through the collection to learn about events around Talbot, and some to write the lives of his associates, none had focused on the man himself. There have been only two book-length biographies of Talbot, both hagiographic in the extreme and both published before the Civil War.

This neglect of Silas Talbot is easily understood. His accomplishments during the Revolution, particularly those at sea, have been ignored largely because they took place at sea. Very little attention has been paid to the roles of the American Navy and privateersmen in the struggle for independence, and when scholars do pay attention they hardly ever get beyond John Paul Jones. Those Americans, Talbot included, who served at sea were truly part of the silent service. The same claim, of course, can be made for the Quasi War, although here it is even more true. In American history textbooks, the Revolution is discussed at some length. The Quasi War rarely gets a paragraph.

Talbot deserves attention not only for brave service creating and defending the republic but for a life that illuminates his time. Biographies are prisms, translucent devices through which we may view past times and events. By knowing Silas Talbot we become acquainted with his world and the people he knew. Talbot's life is particularly instructive, for his trajectory between 1751 and 1813 carried him through a variety of universes: rural and urban, military and naval, east and west, poverty and wealth, and home and abroad. In each of these worlds he knew and was known by the great, the near-great and the forgotten. To travel with Silas Talbot is to better understand these worlds and these people.

In my own travels I have been assisted by a legion of Samaritans. Already mentioned is Gerry Morris, under whose direction the G. W. Blunt White Library at Mystic Seaport has become home for the premier collection of materials relating to American maritime history. His associates at the library, particularly Curator of Manuscripts Doug Stein and Paul O'Pecko, formerly Reference Librarian and now Gerry's successor as Director, deserve special thanks. So, too, do my colleagues in the Munson Institute at Mystic: Ben Labaree, Ted Sloan, John Hattendorf and Jeff Safford. While I cannot claim to have sought their advice in matters relating to Talbot, I can say that their conviviality and example helped create an atmosphere in which I could work with great ease and pleasure.

Mystic has by far the largest collection of Talbot papers; but other caches exist, and I am grateful to several institutions that have cared for these manuscripts and made them available to me. Among these are the Rhode Island Historical Society; the United States Naval Academy Museum; the New-York Historical Society; the Massachusetts Historical Society; the Bristol County Court; the New England Historic Genealogical Society; the Old Colony Historical Society; USS Constitution Museum; the Boston Athenaeum; the Peabody Essex Museum, and the Clements Library of the University of Michigan. All of these institutions and their amiable and helpful librarians and scholars deserve my hearty thanks.

Along the path many individuals have gone out of their way to extend a helping hand. Kate Viens, Roger Joslyn and Maria Melchiori have provided invaluable information and insight concerning the Talbot family genealogy. In family matters two descendants of the Commodore, Thomas Talbot and Alice Niles, have been particularly helpful.

What better way for a biographer to imagine his subject than to visit the place where he or she lived? My visit to Talbot's home, Johnson Hall, an historic site administered by the State of New York, was a delight. The state should be congratulated for its care of so important a place. Ms. Wanda Burch, director of Johnson Hall, was generous with her time and information. I wish that I could have visited Bardstown. It was not to be—perhaps some day. Fortunately, I was able to contact Lillian H. Ockerman of Bloomfield, Kentucky. I am indebted to Ms. Ockerman for sharing with me the information she obtained from the Nelson County records concerning the Talbots in Bardstown.

In the course of my investigations I had need of legal and medical advice to help explicate certain documents in the Talbot papers. Ray Harrington kindly shared his knowledge of law, and Dr. Worth Estes entertained and graciously answered my medical questions. In the same light I am indebted to Alan Taylor for providing me with a copy of his important essay on Judge William Cooper, which at the time of this writing has not yet appeared in print.

My deepest gratitude must go, as it has for more than two decades, to Northeastern University. I am particularly grateful to the staff at Snell Library who in every way have always been both cheerful and helpful. Their role in making the University's new library the centerpiece of our campus deserves great praise. Others deserve thanks as well, including President John Curry, whose public and private support has long meant a good deal to me and many other faculty. Nor should I fail to mention the support I received from the Provost's Research and Development Fund.

Authors need publishers, and I have been favored with a very fine one. Joe Gribbins, the Director of Publications at Mystic, and Andy German, Editor of Publications, have both been very patient and kind.

My colleague Linda Smith Rhoads, Associate Editor of *The New England Quarterly*, continues to patiently teach me about scholarly publishing. Her knowledge and her skills are unsurpassed. Somehow, at the same time, she manages to oversee the journal and direct the efforts of our able editorial assistants.

Finally, although in order of importance first, I turn to my wife and children. It is they who remind this biographer of the preeminent importance of family in everyone's life—and so I thank Marilyn, Alison, and Nathaniel for being so rich a part of mine.

William M. Fowler, Jr.

This shews the Schooner Baltick

coming out of St Eustatia ye 16, of Nov, 1765

*S*ILAS TALBOT MANAGED *his escape
from Dighton in a vessel much like
this New England topsail schooner of
the colonial period. Sloops and
schooners like* Baltick, *shown here, a
45-ton vessel built in Newburyport in
1763, carried goods up and down the
coast from Canada to Georgia and
traded with the West Indies in
Talbot's time.*

(Courtesy Peabody Essex Museum, Salem, MA)

Chapter One

Dighton Beginnings

From the muddy waters of Hockomock Swamp, the Taunton River meanders through southeastern Massachusetts toward Mount Hope Bay, a small appendage to its greater and more famous neighbor, Narragansett Bay. The stream, tidal for a good deal of its length, seems barely to move. Three centuries ago the countryside along its low banks was tidewater woods broken by an occasional open field or deer meadow and crisscrossed by creeks and rivulets making their own way to the Taunton. Today the region is part of Bristol County, Massachusetts, but from its first settlement until 1691 it was part of Plymouth Colony.

Taunton, known to the Wampanoags as Cohannet, was the chief town of a frontier region populated in 1639 by settlers hiving out from Plymouth. Despite the settlers' kinship ties and political connections to the Old Colony, distance strained their attachments. Plymouth town was more than twenty miles away, linked to Taunton by lonely paths. Not surprisingly, the people of Taunton found it safer and easier to sail their river down to the Narragansett country than to make an overland journey east. This is the river Jared Talbot, most recently of Barbados, sailed up sometime in the early 1660s to make his home in Taunton.[1] He may have been one of the many agricultural refugees who left that tobacco and sugar island in the West Indies in the middle of the seventeenth century—a white worker displaced in Barbados by black slaves.[2]

Some of the displaced laborers returned to England, but most remained in the western hemisphere. Either they struck out for another island in the West Indies or they took passage for one of Britain's North American colonies. Jared Talbot may have chosen Rhode Island. He most likely landed at Newport and, not finding much in that town, made his way inland up Mount Hope Bay and the Taunton River.

Talbot did well with what he had, in a community that valued hard work and ingenuity. In 1662 he married Sarah Andrews, daughter of one of the town's founders and richest citizens. Jared and Sarah's first child, a son named Jared for his father, arrived in March 1666.

Talbot and his Taunton neighbors were farmers, and it was a difficult business. Clearing woods, ditching boggy land and then coaxing crops from their small holdings offered little in the way of reward. Adding to their woes was a scarcity of good pasture for their animals. Small wonder that Talbot and his neighbors eyed with interest a large open tract of land along the river in the direction of the Narragansett country. The land was owned by the Wampanoags whose chief, Metacomet, or King Philip as he was called by white men, was anxious to strike a bargain with his land-hungry neighbors. After considerable negotiation, Talbot and 87 other farmers bought the land, henceforth to be known as the South Purchase, from Metacomet in 1672.[3]

Each spring as the ice melted on the ponds and the fields turned to mush, Jared Talbot and his neighbors made plans to drive their livestock to the pastures in the South Purchase. During the warm months of spring and summer the animals grazed freely and fattened on the rich marsh grass. In the fall these same pastures yielded a harvest of hay to be cut, stored and then parceled out to animals brought home to winter in crude barns and shelters. For the Talbots and their neighbors, these summer sojourns in the South Purchase must have been delightful, and the temptation to make a permanent settlement there must have been great. There were reasons, however, to dismiss such a thought. There was talk that Metacomet was becoming increasingly angry with his white neighbors. There was even suspicion that a plot might be afoot to drive the whites out of Wampanoag country. Such uncertainty made it unwise to stray too far or too long from the safety of Taunton's stockade.

Given this state of affairs it seems strange, indeed foolish, that in June 1675 Talbot, as had been his custom, took his wife and four children, including a son barely four months old, down to the South Purchase. Talbot could not have been unaware of a series of violent events earlier in the year that made such a move very risky.

In January the body of John Sassamon had been found under the ice in Assawompsett Pond not far from Taunton. Just before his disappearance, Sassamon, a Christian Wampanoag, had been in Plymouth where he reportedly informed the authorities about an Indian conspiracy to wipe out the English settlements. The skeptical authorities did not heed Sassamon's warning; but his death refocused their attention, particularly when an autopsy revealed that Sassamon had died of a broken neck, not drowning. After a brief investigation three Wampanaogs were arrested, tried and convicted. No one doubted for a moment that these men were agents of Metacomet. On 8 June they were hanged.

Anger that had been smoldering for years amongst the Wampanoags burst forth. Under Philip's leadership they prepared for war. Talbot knew of the executions in Plymouth. Indeed, scarcely had the bodies been taken down from the gallows than reports circulated in his neighborhood that armed bands of Wampanoags were about. Notwithstanding these warnings Jared Talbot, his wife and children, remained in the South Purchase grazing their animals.

One night, late in June, as they all lay sleeping, a friend came charging into their camp with the alarm that only a few minutes away was a Wampanoag war party. With barely enough time to awaken his family Talbot quickly and quietly moved them through the brush to the river and into a small boat. He pushed off from the shore and pulled into the stream. The family reached Taunton shortly after dawn.

Talbot and his family had escaped from the beginnings of what soon became known as King Philip's War, the most destructive conflict colonial New England ever faced. Twice during the war Taunton was attacked, surviving both times. King Philip and his people were not so fortunate. English manpower, organization and weapons took a fierce toll on the Wampanoags and their allies. In August of 1676 Metacomet and the remnants of his followers were tracked to the Great Swamp. There they were surrounded and butchered. Metacomet's mangled body was quartered; his severed head was carried off to Plymouth where it was skewered on a pike and given public display as a warning to remaining Wampanoags.[4]

The War was a calamity for the Native Americans but a blessing for the English, including Jared Talbot. With the Wampanoag menace removed he and his family could move permanently into the South Purchase. Talbot became the first settler and built a small frame house near the river close to where Sunken Brook River joins the main stream. Although the Talbots were soon joined by others, the growth of this isolated community was slow. By the time of Jared Talbot's death in 1686 there were probably fewer than twenty families in the South Purchase.[5]

Talbot's eldest son, Jared, inherited most of his father's land, and the other children had little to share beyond a few household belongings. Their fortunes and that of the Purchase were unaffected in 1691 when Plymouth Colony was absorbed by its larger and more prosperous neighbor, the Massachusetts Bay Colony. Aside from the fact that the government of all of Massachusetts was in Boston, and the Plymouth settlers were no longer their own colony, there was little alteration in the patterns of life. The Old Colony died with barely a whimper and few regrets. The rhythms of farming life were interrupted occasionally in the countryside by a bit of boatbuilding, brick-making, timber-cutting, iron-forging—but these were all peripheral to the raising of crops and families.

Taunton's peace and harmony were shaken in 1708 by a character-istically New England disturbance—controversy over the location of a church. Since the first settlement of the South Purchase, its people had traveled seven miles to Taunton in order to worship. It was always inconvenient, and tolerated only because the Purchase did not have enough worshippers to establish a separate congregation. Believing that they now had a sufficient body, in October 1708 the churchgoers of the South Purchase petitioned the Massachusetts General Court for permission to form a new congregation. Recognizing the threat this represented (i.e., loss of parish income), the stable members of the Taunton congregation issued a strong dissent and asked the Court to deny the petition. After years of disagreement the issue was finally resolved in 1712 when the South Purchase was incorporated as a new town—Dighton.[6]

The new town was home to successive generations of Talbots who remained struggling farmers, perhaps because there was too little land and too many Talbots. For example, Samuel Talbot, grandson of the founder, had eight children. Small wonder that a history of Dighton refers to his situation as "modest." Upon his death he left his house to his son Benjamin, who in turn had fourteen children by two wives.

Despite their lives of toil and isolation the people of Dighton did enjoy the advantage of a connection to the sea. Although quite a small one, Dighton was a seaport. Along its river sloops, schooners and flat-bottomed scows and barges came and went hauling cargo and bringing strangers with tales of faraway places. Even if those places were only Newport and Providence, the boys on the town wharf who listened to sailors' tales would have found those places as romantic as Brazil or Zanzibar. One of the boys who came to listen and wonder was Silas Talbot, Benjamin's youngest son, born in Dighton on 11 January 1751.

Vessels that brought sailors with tall tales could also deliver lethal cargo such as smallpox. No seaport in America, including little Dighton, could escape this disfiguring and often fatal disease. The winter of 1763-64 was particularly severe. Remembered by the people of Dighton for its blustery cold and heavy snow, the season was cursed even more by the arrival of the dreaded pox. Among those struck was Benjamin Talbot.

Through the unusual cold of that winter he grew weaker, and as his life ebbed away, in the presence of his wife and eldest sons Zephanias and Samuel, he dictated his will. He had little to leave. In land he owned less than a hundred acres; it was divided between Zephanias and Samuel. Zephanias was also to inherit his father's yoke of oxen. To his daughter Hannah he gave his bed. His remaining possessions, such as they were, he distributed among his fourteen children. For two months after signing his will Benjamin Talbot remained "in languor and pain." In February, having made his peace with the probate court and the Lord, Benjamin died.[7]

To Zephanias and Samuel fell the task of seeing to the care of their stepmother, Mary, and the minor children. Among the youngsters was Silas, age twelve. Zephanias and Samuel appear to have dealt with Silas in a time-honored way. They indentured him to a local stonemason, from whom he might acquire a useful trade. It is a matter of record that Silas learned the skills of a bricklayer, and his later life testifies that he was a good one. But bricklaying afforded too confining and mundane a life for someone of Silas Talbot's ambition, a thing he seems to have determined even as a boy. So too did Dighton. The best route out of town was down the river. Silas Talbot signed aboard a small coaster and headed for the Bay. For the next few years he spent his time as a sailor on sloops ferrying cargo up and down Narragansett Bay, over to Long Island and along the coast to Virginia and the Carolinas.[8]

Coasting out of New England was a prosperous business. Enterprising Yankees sent barrel staves, cod and foodstuffs south and came back with tobacco, rice, sugar and molasses. Sloops and schooners, small and cheap to build, dominated the trade and there were hundreds of them. Even without experience Talbot would have had no trouble finding a berth.

Life was exciting for this vigorous and handsome young man. In 1768, as a lusty seventeen-year-old, he met a woman a bit younger than he, Lydia Arnold of Warwick, Rhode Island. Just how and where the two met is not certain; but whatever the circumstances they had a child, a daughter Elizabeth. Silas and Lydia never married. Perhaps her family would not permit it. Both were young, and Talbot's prospects were anything but promising. The child stayed with Lydia, and her older brother, Israel, took charge of his sister and illegitimate niece.[9] It may have been this personal crisis that persuaded Talbot to leave the coasting business and settle ashore. Since there was nothing in Dighton to draw him home, he decided to seek his fortune in Rhode Island. He made a wise choice.

Rhode Islanders were proud of their radical past. Founded by Roger Williams and other religious renegades, the colony had earned a reputation for being a disputatious place and a haven for groups with obnoxious religious principles. Indeed, in many ways Rhode Island and Providence Plantations never quite shed the image conjured up by John Winthrop and the Puritan oligarchy that the Narragansett country was a moral sewer. In the generations since its first settlement, time and prosperity had muted a good deal of the colony's legendary dissent, but not the energy of the inhabitants, who had gradually turned their attention away from God and toward Mammon.

By the middle of the eighteenth century Rhode Island, with its face set to the sea in trade and commerce, was a thriving, cosmopolitan corner of colonial America where two communities, Newport at one end of the Bay and Providence at the other, fought over every political, social and economic issue. This rivalry enlivened Rhode Island politics to the point where on occasion chaos seemed to reign. Such apparent disorder masked what was arguably the most democratic colony in America. It was a world in flux, where a young ambitious man might grasp political and economic opportunity. Not yet twenty years old, Talbot had neither capital nor family to establish himself in business; he did, however, have a skill. He was a bricklayer and stonemason.

His craft was an urban one. To practice it he would have to live in either Newport or Providence. At first glance Newport might seem the better choice. By nearly every measure this city that faced the Atlantic was richer and of greater eminence than its rival up Narragansett Bay. Newport had more than twice the population of Providence, and its harbor, nestled behind the protective rise of Goat Island, was deep, spacious and dotted with vessels from all over the growing British Empire. The town's merchants trumpeted their prosperity, not an insignificant amount of it from the slave trade, by constantly building impressive houses, churches, a synagogue and even a library. There were lots of possibilities for a young bricklayer. But what made Newport so pleasing and promising also made the town vulnerable. It was, after all, on an island. It was a port without a secure hinterland. Should there be any disruption of trade on the Bay or along the coast, Newport would suffer more than Providence.[10]

While Providence might lack the gentility, apparent prosperity and worldwide connections of Newport, it enjoyed the advantage of a sizable hinterland from which products might be drawn and an energetic merchant elite led by the redoubtable Brown brothers. By 1770 Providence was living up to its name. Fed by an influx of young artisans and laborers, the population was growing at a rate four times that of Newport. Among those who had abandoned the countryside for the streets of Providence was Benjamin, one of Talbot's older brothers. He moved from Dighton sometime in the mid-1760s and was working in the town as a laborer. Even that lowly existence was preferable to poverty in Dighton, and Benjamin's "success" helped bring young Silas to this city-in-the-making where a growing population required construction of homes, churches and commercial buildings. It was the right place for a bricklayer. It may also have been the right place for a father who wanted to be close to his new daughter living in nearby Warwick.[11]

Sometime in 1769-70 Silas Talbot settled in Providence. He came with some advantages. His family and friends back in Dighton, with whom he always kept in contact, could supply him with at least two of the essential materials for his trade, bricks and lath. Then there was Benjamin, his brother. Although he seems not to have had any special skills, he could assist his younger brother as a friend and laborer.[12]

Earning five to six shillings per day, the average wage for skilled artisans, Talbot put aside enough money in two years to purchase a lot of land from Job Olney on Weybosset Street, in one of the town's less fashionable, and hence less expensive, neighborhoods. In this small way Silas Talbot launched his lifelong pursuit of property, a land quest that would take him from Rhode Island, to New York, Philadelphia, Vermont and eventually to the Kentucky frontier. Land meant security. It guaranteed that he would never again be poor and without prospects.[13] And land meant something more than security. It meant status. Land ownership, even in small amounts, held out the promise that someday he would be known as a gentleman.

One of Talbot's neighbors was Barzillai Richmond, known in Providence as the Deacon or Colonel. Richmond was one of the founders of the Benevolent Congregational Society, a group that had split off from the First Congregational Church of Providence during the Great Awakening. The Awakening, America's first great revival, was in part a conservative reaction to the stale liberal theology that had grown so common in eighteenth-century America. In the case of the Church in Providence some members, Richmond among them, became convinced that their pastor, Josiah Cotton, was too fond of "damnable good works." Disgusted with him they left and founded what they called, ironically, the Benevolent Society. In 1752 they built their own meetinghouse on the west side of the river in the same area where Talbot and Richmond now lived. Richmond was known not only for his religious conservatism but also for service in the French and Indian War, in which he had risen to the rank of Lieutenant Colonel. While no one would suggest that the Richmonds belonged to the elite of Providence—they did not sup, for example, with the Browns—nonetheless they were several rungs higher on the social ladder than this newly-arrived bricklayer/sailor from Dighton.[14]

Throughout his career Silas Talbot would manage to marry well, and in Providence he took an interest in the Colonel's daughter. Whatever the Colonel might have thought about the advances of this rough-hewn young man toward his daughter, on 7 March 1772 Silas Talbot and Anna Richmond were married. Although there is no reason to suspect that Silas did not love Anna, it was a union blessed with great social advantage.

Within a few days of his marriage Talbot bought more land. He made the purchase from his father-in-law with the intention of building a home close to the Richmonds. It took slightly more than a year to finish the job, but in November 1773 Talbot noted proudly in his daybook, "moved into my house." The transition came none too soon. He needed space for his growing family. In the summer of 1773, while his house was yet unfinished and he and Anna were living with the Richmonds, his son Cyrus was born. And by the time the Talbots packed to move into their new home Anna was pregnant again.

The Talbot household was joined by another person as well—a young male slave named Primus, bought late in December 1772 from Kezia Carew. Primus was the first of many slaves that Talbot would own during his career. Indeed, whenever he lived where slavery was legal Talbot owned a slave. This is hardly surprising since Talbot's world tolerated slavery and many Rhode Islanders, both in Providence and Newport, were deeply entangled in the trade. Furthermore, owning a black servant was a mark of status.[15]

Talbot did well in Providence, and by early 1774 he had built a prosperous construction business. At various times he had as many as four men working for him, and judging by his account book there were dozens of chimneys, plaster walls and stone structures in Providence that bore the mark of his craftsmanship. Keen to advance his enterprise and influence, Talbot invested his profits in other businesses. His account books reveal ventures in selling general merchandise, including rum, molasses and other such commodities, as well as lending money out at interest. By buying property and slaves, and moving beyond manual labor into trade and "banking," Silas Talbot had advanced a long way from his Dighton beginnings.[16]

His increasing prosperity in Providence was accompanied by family tragedy. In the winter of 1773-74, shortly after the Talbots crossed the threshold of their new home, Cyrus, less than a year old, took sick and died. In the midst of their grief the parents found ready distraction, for barely had the death been recorded than a new son was born. The baby was named Cyrus after his unfortunate brother.[17]

Conspicuous by her absence in Talbot's growing family was his illegitimate daughter Betsey. She continued to live in Warwick with her mother and uncle. Although her thoughts on this matter have gone unrecorded, it seems unlikely that Anna could have been unaware of Betsey's existence. For his part Talbot recognized his responsibility and sent money to Israel for Betsey's support. For the time being, however, it must have seemed best for everyone that Betsey remain in Warwick. Her presence in Providence would be an embarrassment for all.

By most calculations, at age twenty-three Silas Talbot was a man with a promising future. It had been eleven years since his father's death and the orphaned boy's sudden apprenticeship to the world beyond the Dighton farm. In that time he had learned a trade, been to sea, bought property and married well. Talbot must have appreciated his good fortune, and perhaps he also understood that his prosperity and future were tied to that of

THIS DRAMATIC DEPICTION of the burning of the Gaspee, *an engraving based on an oil painting, was published in 1856. The real event may have been this dramatic, although the raiders, men from the Providence waterfront, were not dressed as Indians—a detail borrowed from the Boston Tea Party.*

Providence. Here he could take comfort, for the town was thriving and bid well to surpass Newport in population and wealth. According to the census of 1774 Providence's population stood at 4321 and was growing rapidly. There were in the town 655 families, 370 horses and 278 shops and stores. Providence could boast of a half-dozen distilleries as well as several tanneries, sugar houses, grist mills, chocolate houses and two spermaceti-candle works. Stretched out along both sides of the Providence River for more than a mile, the town had a pleasing prospect in every sense of the word. Ironically, though, it was not trade and industry that would secure Providence's future. It was politics.[18]

From the very moment they came into existence as outposts and resources of England, Rhode Island and her sister colonies had faced a persistent problem that threatened to divide them from the mother country. The issue was the nature of representative government and what sovereignty Parliament and King might exercise over the American colonies. For most people the issue, when recognized at all, was distant and philosophical. The British Empire was, after all, barely a century old. Despite the establishment of colonies in the early seventeenth century, the concept of empire did not emerge until the period of the Restoration. The economic and political relationships of colonies to the mother country, particularly those settlements that predated 1660, were by no means clear. Unless there was some practical issue, all parties were in implicit agreement that the matter was worth avoiding. Sir Robert Walpole's notion of "salutary neglect" is a glib reminder of British policy of the time and testimony to the triumph of expediency over principle. Despite the impression it gave of unity and strength, at its core the Empire was a fragile creation. Just how fragile became apparent in the wake of the Treaty of Paris in 1763.

Everywhere in the Empire, from Providence to Calcutta, news of the Treaty was received with great joy. By its terms the long war with France was over. England was victorious. The Empire had been enlarged. For Americans in particular the news was good, for by the terms of the Treaty Canada was now British. No longer would New Englanders fear being attacked by, in the words of the great Boston divine Cotton Mather, "half-Indianized French and half-Frenchified Indians." In Boston, Providence and elsewhere bonfires were lit in celebration, parades mustered, church bells rung and barrels of rum tapped. Such rejoicing proved premature. The former Prime Minister, William Pitt, whose policies had guided the King's forces to victory, expressed his doubts when he described the treaty as "The Peace that Passeth Understanding." His skepticism was born of experience, for while the treaty brought vast new territories into the King's realm it brought not a farthing into the treasury. If ever the treasury needed money it was in the mid-1700s after years of war had saddled the kingdom with huge debts and burdensome taxes. For the young King George III and his ministers there was no task more urgent nor more difficult than finding ways to replenish the nearly empty coffers of an Empire close to bankruptcy.

It was the quest for revenue that would lead Britain into the troubled waters of debate over authority and rights in the colonies. From 1763 to the rupture in 1776 the King and his ministers stumbled blindly ahead seeking ways to get revenue out of their overseas settlements. Each new measure— Sugar Act, Stamp Act, Townsend Duties and others—brought with it a dearth of revenue and a wealth of opposition.[19]

As a people dependent upon trade and long accustomed to independent behavior, Rhode Islanders detested the new revenue measures. They saw them as unconstitutional invasions of their rights as free-born Englishmen. They took every opportunity to express their opposition, not only by normal political action but also with an occasional violent outburst. The burning of the *Gaspee* was one of these outbursts.

His Majesty's schooner *Gaspee* arrived in Narragansett Bay in March 1772 at the opening of the colony's trading season. Her commander, Lieutenant William Duddington, held orders to enforce the laws on trade, with a particular charge to halt the outrageous smuggling activities of the Rhode Island merchants. Duddington took his job seriously, and seems to have disliked the Rhode Islanders as much as they disliked him. More than once he overstepped his bounds—by boarding vessels, many of which were obviously engaged in legitimate trade, by stealing cattle and supplies from local farmers, and in general by being an arrogant intrusion into the life of the colony. On the afternoon of 9 June Duddington, to the glee of those who watched from shore, failed to heed his chart and an ebbing tide. He ran his schooner hard aground on Namquit Point (now called Gaspee).

Not a moment was to be lost. John Brown, Providence's most important merchant and a notorious smuggler, organized a party to visit the distressed *Gaspee*. With Brown along, but led actually by Abraham Whipple, a party of thirty to forty men, recruited hastily from the waterfront, rowed quietly down the Bay. As they drew near the grounded vessel Duddington called for them to identify themselves. With a bravado characteristic of the men of the Bay, Whipple hollered back: "I am the sheriff of the county of Kent, G-d d—n you. I have got a warrant to apprehend you, G-d d—n you; so surrender, G-d d—n you." Duddington answered in kind and a melee followed as Whipple's men scrambled aboard the schooner. One of the Rhode Islanders fired at the Lieutenant, hitting him in the groin. Duddington fell to the deck murmuring "Good God, I am done for." He was wrong. The wound may have been excruciating, but it was not fatal. While Duddington lay in agony, Whipple pushed towards him and, with a belaying pin held high, shouted out, "Stand aside; let me dispatch the piratical dog." Duddington, according to reports by Rhode Islanders, begged for his life. Whipple spared the Lieutenant's life, but put him and the rest of his crew into a small boat which was set adrift. Once rid of the crew Whipple set *Gaspee* on fire.[20]

The wounding of a King's officer and the destruction of a Royal Navy vessel was no small matter. The ministry in London ordered a special commission to Rhode Island to take evidence for a prosecution. Should the culprits be found it was the intention of the government to remove them from the colony for trial elsewhere. Ignoring the cause of the action, the patriot faction in Providence and elsewhere pointed to these unusual proceedings as examples of dreadful tyranny. The Providence *Gazette* protested the coming of the commission, and the town meeting denounced it as well.

The commissioners arrived in Rhode Island in January 1773, presented their commission to the local authorities, and then tried to go about their business. It was all a farce. Little evidence could be found, and amnesia spread among potential witnesses. No one in Providence seemed able to recall the event. The commission's conclusion, as stated by one of the commissioners, Judge Daniel Horsmanden of New York, was that the *Gaspee* was destroyed by "a number of bold, daring, rash, enterprising sailors, collected suddenly from the neighborhood."[21]

Whether Silas Talbot was one of those sailors is uncertain. It is curious that shortly after the event, as the investigation was beginning and suspects were being sought, Talbot went "sick to Dighton" for sixteen days. Whether or not he ever boarded the *Gaspee*, Talbot, like other patriots in Providence, was incensed by all the recent intrusions of the British government into their lives. It is likely that in matters of sovereignty and natural rights Silas Talbot was an intellectual onlooker. He was never much concerned with abstract issues. When it came to the practical affairs of Providence, however, Talbot had every reason to be concerned, and he would have been quick to defend those interests closest to his life and his enterprises.

While the aftermath of the *Gaspee* incident continued to stir passions in Providence, events taking place in Boston aroused fear and anger among Rhode Islanders. Through newspapers, committees of correspondence and a loose association of groups variously described as "Sons of Liberty," people in all the colonies were being kept informed of developments in Boston, the capital of sedition. By the early 1770s Boston was seething with discontent. Bostonians, organized in their town meeting and led by Hancock, Adams and others, were ready to express themselves. And although the "bold, daring, rash, enterprising sailors" of Providence had already expressed their discontent on the decks of the *Gaspee*, and though local pride might not allow them readily to admit it, the Rhode Islanders looked to Boston to show them the way.

Boston showed the way on the evening of 16 December 1773, when a group of patriots, lightly disguised as Indians, dumped several hundred chests of British East India Company tea into the harbor. In Providence the action was celebrated. In London the emotion was horror. His Majesty's government reacted with a series of intemperate acts that proved very unwise. They first closed the port of Boston and then added to the insult by arbitrarily altering the colony's form of government. They also required that troops be housed in private homes and that officers accused of capital offenses be tried elsewhere at the discretion of the governor.[22]

The alarm from Boston struck a resonant chord in Rhode Island, and by the spring of 1774 Rhode Islanders were organizing with a martial spirit to defend their rights. The colony did have a regular militia organization, but it was small and suspect. A good many of its senior officers were alleged to have Tory sympathies. Furthermore, the old militia organization, hardened by tradition and smacking of elitism, could not accommodate the swell of new volunteers. Everywhere throughout the colony independent military companies were formed. Providence led the way, and Silas Talbot rushed to join one of the new companies. It was an opportunity not to be missed. In ordinary circumstances this Providence bricklayer could have aspired to little more than a non-commissioned rank in the old militia; the new companies, anxious to fill their ranks, were less encumbered by the old social standards and more generous in granting officer commissions. Generous enough, in fact, to commission Talbot a Lieutenant.[23]

Three nights a week Talbot and his company drilled in a Providence sugar house. By candlelight and under the watchful eye of an old British army veteran, the company learned the rudiments of drill, tactics and weapons. The people of Providence took pride in their companies, the *Gazette* noting proudly that "the several military companies in and near this Town have been indefatigable in their Endeavors to obtain perfect Knowledge of the Art military."[24]

As the political crisis deepened, the need for intercolonial coopera-tion became more apparent. On 17 May 1774, the freemen of Providence, Talbot among them, called for a convention to consider the rights of Americans. Others followed, and when the First Continental Congress assem-bled in Philadelphia, on 5 September 1774, Rhode Island was present. The Congress adjourned on 26 October after passing resolutions condemning the actions of the British government and calling for a boycott of British trade. Before leaving Philadelphia the delegates agreed to reassemble on 10 May the following year. Many left the meeting, however, believing that reconven-ing would not be necessary. They were confident that King and Parliament would listen to American grievances and cease burdening the colonies with troops, taxes and high-handed acts.

Whether Talbot believed this would happen is uncertain; neverthe-less, the news from the Congress would likely have done nothing to lessen his determination to stand ready to fight. He and many others were already "the young men of the Revolution," whether they realized it or not. Shortly after the Continental Congress adjourned, the Newport *Mercury* remarked that "there is now such a martial spirit running through the country that tis thought by next April North-America will be the best disciplined of any country in the world." The comment was prophetic.

Within hours of the events of 19 April, 1775, news of the battles at Lexington and Concord arrived in Providence. Immediately the call went out for the militia to assemble. Talbot's company, along with the others, assem-bled but did not march. It was best, in their judgment, that the company remain in Rhode Island. The colony was deeply split. Ships of the Royal Navy were in the Bay and the governor, Joseph Wanton, had shown himself a Tory. For the moment at least the company was needed at home.

Notes

1 For the early history of Taunton and Bristol County see Samuel Hopkins, *History of Taunton, Massachusetts, From Its Settlement to the Present Time* (Syracuse: D. Mason, 1893) and Duane Hamilton Hurd, ed., *History of Bristol County, Massachusetts* (Philadelphia: J. W. Lewis, 1883). For the history of Dighton see Helen M. Lane, *History of the Town of Dighton* (Taunton:Published by the Town of Dighton, 1962). There are several Talbot genealogies. The best is Thomas W. Talbot, "Jared Talbot of Taunton," typescript at New England Historic Genealogical Society, Boston.

2 Richard S. Dunn, *Sugar and Slaves: The Rise of the Planter Class in the English West Indies* (Chapel Hill: University of North Carolina Press, 1973), 111-16.

3 Plymouth Colony Records.

4 There is a considerable literature on King Philip's War. Douglas Edward Leach, *Flintlock and Tomahawk: New England in King Philip's War* (New York: W. W. Norton, 1958) remains among the best. See also Russell Bourne, *The Red King's Rebellion: Racial Politics in New England, 1675-1678* (New York: Oxford University Press, 1990); Alden Vaughan, New England Frontier: Puritans and Indians, 1620-1675 (Boston: Little Brown, 1965) and Philip Ranlet, "Another Look at the Causes of King Philip's War," *New England Quarterly 61* (March 1988): 79-100.

5 Lane, *History of Dighton*, 24.

6 *Historical Data Relating to Counties,* *Cities and Towns in Massachusetts* (Boston: Secretary of the Commonwealth, 1975), 25; Lane, *History of Dighton*, 24; and Carl Boyer, *Brown Families of Bristol County* (Newhall, California: C. Boyer, 1981), 134-36.

7 Bristol County Court, Probate Records. Benjamin Talbot, Book 18:316.

8 *Historical Sketch To The End of Revolutionary War of the Life of Silas Talbot, esq. of the State of Rhode Island, Lately Commander of U.S. Frigate Constitution and of the American Squadron in the West Indies* (New York: H. Caritat, 1803). This is the memoir Talbot gave to Samuel Taylor. See below.

9 Receipt signed by Israel Arnold, 30 January 1776, B1 F2 STP. The evidence for the above statement concerning the identity of Elizabeth's mother is circum-stantial but persuasive. Although Talbot freely admitted to the illegitimacy of Elizabeth's birth he left no record identifying her mother. A search of the vital records of Providence for the late 1760s and early 1770s revealed an Elizabeth Arnold born in 1768. Curiously, no parents were listed. A search of the same records did not ind-icate a brother and sister Israel and Lydia. However, such a combination did show up in the Warwick, Rhode Island, records. This Israel was born in 1749 and his sister Lydia in 1752. Lydia did not marry until she was in her late twenties. It is my belief that she is Elizabeth's mother. I am indebted to Katherine

Viens for this information.

10 For descriptions of Newport in the eighteenth century see "Newport Historical and Social," *Harpers New Monthly Magazine* 9 (1854): 289-317; see also William B. Weeden, "Ideal Newport in the Eighteenth Century," *Proceedings of the American Antiquarian Society* 18 (1906): 106-7; and Weeden, *Early Rhode Island* (New York: Grafton Press, 1910.) 270-72.

11 Lynne Withey, *Urban Growth in Colonial Rhode Island: Newport and Providence in the Eighteenth Century* (Albany: State University Press of New York, 1984), 15.

12 Talbot's name first appears on the Providence Colony Tax in 1771, leading me to believe, given the lag time in tax assessing, that in all likelihood he was in the town the year before. Providence Colony Tax, RIHS.

13 Deed, 18 February 1772, B1 F1 STP.

14 Sidney V. James, *Colonial Rhode Island* (New York: Charles Scribner's Sons, 1975), 204-5; Gertrude S. Kimball, *Providence in Colonial Times* (Boston: Houghton Mifflin Co., 1912), 194.

15 Deed, 29 December 1772, B1 F1 STP.

16 Daybook, STP

17 Talbot, "Talbot Genealogy."

18 Rhode Island Census 1774, RIHS; Providence *Gazette*, 28 May 1774.

19 For an overview of Rhode Island during this troubled period see David Lovejoy, *Rhode Island Politics and the American Revolution* (Providence: Brown University Press, 1958).

20 John R. Bartlett, *A History of the Destruction of His Britannic Majesty's Schooner Gaspee* (Providence: A. Crawford Greene, 1861); and Bartlett, ed., *Records of the Colony of Rhode Island and Providence Plantations in New England,* 10 vols. (Providence: A. G. Greene, 1856-1863), 3:70-72, 82-86.

21 Quoted in James, *Colonial Rhode Island*, 342.

22 See Benjamin W. Labaree, *The Boston Tea Party* (New York: Oxford University Press, 1964).

23 *Historical Sketch ... of the Life of Silas Talbot*, 11.

24 Lovejoy, *Rhode Island Politics*, 174; Providence *Gazette*, 18 June 1774.

*T*HE BATTLE OF Bunker Hill as engraved
by Bernard Romans in 1775 shows
Charlestown burning and a furious
face-to-face engagement typical of
eigteenth-century warfare. Silas Talbot
was with his regiment in Providence on
June 17, 1775, but soon would be on
the hills overlooking Boston, dug in for
the winter of 1775-6 to watch British
activity in the town and harbor.

(Courtesy Massachusetts Historical Society)

Chapter Two

The Revolutionary Years:

Boston to Philadelphia

By the time the Second Continental Congress assembled, the spirit in the country was more martial than peaceful. Indeed, on the day delegates took their seats, 10 May 1775, Ethan Allen and his Green Mountain Boys seized Fort Ticonderoga and its store of cannon "in the name of the Great Jehovah and the Continental Congress."

It took a few days for the news from Ticonderoga to reach Philadelphia, and in the meantime the delegates had a stack of reports to read. Most of these were depositions from people who had been at Lexington and Concord. Some of the accounts were accurate, others were simply false, but in either case they served the purpose of exciting the Congress and stiffening their resolve to resist the "tyranny" of King and Parliament.[1]

Mixed in with the emotional and lurid accounts of events in Massachusetts was a formal request from that colony's Provincial Congress. They wished to know if the Continental Congress would take direction of the army then collecting around Boston. The Massachusetts authorities were fearful that the thousands of militia that had gathered, many from other colonies, would look to them for support. Who would sustain these troops was one issue, another was the confusion of command. No one was certain for how long militia from other states would abide the authority of Massachusetts officers. It seemed to the Massachusetts Provincial Congress that, lest this gathering of militia disappear, or worse yet become a mob, the gentlemen in Philadelphia ought, in the name of all the colonies, to take charge.[2]

When presented with the offer of an army, not all members of the Congress wished to accept. On 2 June the Massachusetts request was placed on the agenda and then quickly hustled off to committee. Events around Boston, however, overcame whatever unwillingness might have been present in the body, and in the week following receipt of the Massachusetts petition Congress moved toward adopting the army at Boston. This "Continental Army" needed a commander, a person of repute and a man who could symbolize national unity. In one of the wisest moves ever made by an American Congress, the delegates on 15 June elected George Washington, a Virginian, to command a Yankee army.[3] As Washington was accepting the good wishes of his congressional colleagues, events in Boston were beginning to swirl around a place called Bunker Hill.

Two small hills rose from the Charlestown peninsula across the Charles River from Boston. Although a tangle of brush here and there and some wooden fencing were part of the landscape, for the most part the hills were sloping, open pasture. The one farthest west, and closest to the American main camp in Cambridge, was Bunker's Hill. The easternmost was Breed's Hill. Recognizing the importance of holding this high ground, the Massachusetts Committee of Safety ordered Colonel William Prescott to march by dark and entrench on Bunker's Hill. On 16 June after sunset Prescott led his men onto the peninsula. In a blunder that has never been explained Prescott, contrary to his orders, bypassed Bunker's Hill and instead established a series of positions on Breed's Hill. Through the night British sentries on the Boston shore could hear the clanking of shovels and picks as they heaved up earth into ramparts. In the light of morning British officers atop Copp's Hill could clearly see the American fortifications.

For the British there was no choice. The new commander in Boston, General Sir William Howe, gave orders for an attack. Somberly and in good order trains of barges crossed the Charles on the morning of the 17th bearing the regiments of the King. In preparation for the attack the ships of the Royal Navy laid down a barrage. Their shots were foolish and cruel. Unable to elevate their cannon to an angle sufficient to heave round shot at Prescott, their guns dropped missiles like rain into the town hugging the shore. The houses splintered and burned.

By midday the redcoats were ready. So were the Americans. Twice the red lines managed to make their way through the brush and over the fences in the heat and dust and smoke. Twice they came within range of American muskets. Each time the men behind the ramparts waited to fire at close range. Each time American fire tore through the redcoat ranks leaving gaping holes where men once stood. The field was littered with dead and dying soldiers. On the third assault the soldiers put their packs on the ground. Reserves were summoned. Once more they marched in cadence up the hill. The Americans remained silent again, this time less by plan than from a shortage of powder and ball. They fired again but with less ferocity and force. With the honor of the Empire and their regiments now at stake, the redcoats did not falter. They came over the ramparts, and in revenge for their fallen comrades they took a fearful toll of the American defenders. Nevertheless there were more than a thousand British casualities in the battle, prompting Nathanael Greene, the Quaker general from Rhode Island, to offer to sell the British more hills at the same price. The Americans who stood, fought and died on Breed's Hill had proven beyond a doubt that the colonists could and would stand against the King's army.[4]

Silas Talbot did not fight at Bunker Hill. For the time being at least he and his company remained in Providence. Other Rhode Islanders, however, were not content to wait. Already the Assembly had stretched the colony's resources by ordering the militia to Boston, but in light of the new and more threatening situation some members demanded that additional measures be taken. On 28 June the Assembly called for six additional companies to be formed and sent north. Talbot stepped forward, offered to join and was quickly made a Lieutenant in the ninth company. He bade farewell to his wife, then seven months pregnant, made his last entry in his daybook, and marched with his men to Boston to join the second Rhode Island regiment commanded by Colonel Daniel Hitchcock. This regiment was taken into the pay of Congress, and on the first of July Talbot received another commission, this one signed by John Hancock, President of the Continental Congress, making him a Captain of the second regiment of Rhode Island.[5]

Talbot's regiment was camped outside Boston on the third of July when Washington took formal command of this new army on Cambridge Common. The new Commander-in-Chief had to make sense out of what until then had been an ad-hoc organization. He divided his army into three brigades and stationed them in positions surrounding the British—a rough semicircle from Medford in the north around to Roxbury in the south. The first and second Rhode Island regiments, commanded by James Varnum and Hitchcock, respectively, were brigaded together and placed under the command of Nathanael Greene. Washington ordered them to dig in at the Charlestown-Cambridge line near Greene's headquarters on Prospect Hill. From there they could block any attempt by the British to sortie out of Boston via Charlestown.[6]

Siege warfare is tiresome for armies on both sides of the lines, and Boston was no exception. Aside from an occasional artillery exchange or some sporadic fire between pickets, very little happened. Inside the town British soldiers idled away their time while their commanders pondered the situation. Fortunately for the King's troops the winter of 1775-1776 was rela-

*A*RCHIBALD ROBERTSON WAS a British
soldier and artist in Boston in the winter of 1775-6. This is his sketch of the
heights of Charlestown as seen from
British fortifications on the Boston side
of the Charles.

(The New York Public Library)

tively mild. Bivouacked in private homes, some of them left vacant by patriots who had fled the town, as well as in some public buildings, the British soldiers spent a reasonably comfortable winter. Major General John Burgoyne, "Gentleman Johnny," an officer as skilled in courtly manners as in battle tactics, found time to put on a stage play in Faneuil Hall. He did this as much to anger pious Bostonians, who viewed the theater as the work of the devil, as to entertain his fellow officers. Other officers pursued less civilized amusements. One group actually tore the pews out of the Old South Meetinghouse and covered the floor with dirt so they might have a riding academy.

For the Americans the situation was less cozy. Talbot and his company, like virtually all the colonial militiamen, had little military experience. Drilling in the Providence sugar house might have fostered comradeship and boosted morale, but it bore little resemblance to the routines of warfare and camp life. For the 1200 men in the Rhode Island brigade, life watching over the redcoats soon centered on guard duty, sleep, food and maintaining camp hygiene. Greene, Hitchcock and Varnum were stern disciplinarians who brooked no nonsense in the ranks. Nonetheless, keeping novice soldiers busy was a chore. It was a relief in late fall when the order came down for the regiments to turn to and build barracks on Prospect Hill. Talbot's masonry skills were appreciated, and the exercise kept both him and his men usefully occupied.[7]

Surprised by the resolute behavior of Washington's army, and recognizing that they were outnumbered by a ratio of almost four to one, in late winter the British pondered withdrawing from the town. After informal assurances from Washington that the Americans would not attack while they were withdrawing, the British agreed that they would not burn Boston to the ground. The soldiers boarded their ships on 17 March and sailed off for Halifax, Nova Scotia. Washington entered the town and almost immediately began preparations to move his army to New York City where he rightly suspected the British would next move.

Greene wasted no time breaking camp and moving his brigade. The route of march to New York went through Providence, and by 2 April the Rhode Island regiments were back home, temporarily at least. In the meantime Washington was on his way south right behind them. On 4 April Greene sent orders to Hitchcock "to turn out tomorrow Morning to Escort His Excellency into town."[8]

It was a proud moment for Silas Talbot. Dressed in the uniform of his regiment—"a Brown frock Fringed"— Talbot led the ninth company to the outskirts of Providence to greet the Commander-in-Chief. Joined by other Rhode Island units, they led Washington into town. All of Providence turned out, including Anna with Cyrus and her youngest, George Washington Talbot, born the previous September.[9]

Washington's stay in Providence was brief; so, too, was Talbot's. Greene marched his men to Norwich, Connecticut, at the head of the Thames River. From there he intended to take them downriver to New London and thence by transports to New York. Washington arrived in New London on the eighth. Almost immediately he was visited by Esek Hopkins, Commander-in-Chief of the Continental Navy. Commodore Hopkins had a problem.

Not long after creating a Continental army Congress faced the need for a navy. During the siege of Boston, Washington had engaged a few armed vessels to attack and capture inbound British supply ships. Their success inspired some members of Congress to more ambitious plans, and on 13 October 1775, acting on a proposal from the Rhode Island delegates, Congress authorized the outfitting of two vessels. This date marks the birth of the Continental Navy. A few weeks later, on 2 November, eight additional vessels were purchased, and in an act of fantasy and hubris on 22 December Congress authorized the construction of 13 frigates. Experience would prove that the men in Congress were woefully ignorant of the huge task they were assigning themselves and their nascent navy. To command this navy Congress had commissioned Hopkins, a member of a powerful Rhode Island clan. Hopkins was a former West Indies trader, privateer and brother to Stephen Hopkins, a Rhode Island delegate to the Congress and member of the Naval Committee.

The problem Commodore Hopkins brought to the Commander-in-Chief was a consequence of one victory and one defeat in the recent past. In February of 1776 Hopkins had sailed with a squadron composed of nearly the entire Continental Navy, eight vessels, to the Bahamas. There he managed to surprise a weak enemy garrison and force them to surrender. He then stripped the fort of cannon and other munitions, loaded the booty aboard his vessels, and headed for Providence. It was an unlucky voyage. Near home his squadron came upon a small British frigate, HMS *Glasgow*. By every measure Hopkins should have had no trouble dispatching this single ship. That, however, was not what happened, for little *Glasgow* bested her enemies and sailed to safety. Hopkins then elected not to try for Providence but scurried with his damaged ships to the sanctuary of New London harbor. Dropping anchor at

New London only increased his difficulties. He still needed to get his squadron home to Providence, but the smell of land was too much for his crew and they began to desert in droves. It was in these circumstances that he visited Washington to ask for help.[10]

In order to bring his squadron home to Providence, Hopkins needed crewmen. Not anticipating any immediate engagement with the enemy, Washington offered to loan Hopkins 200 men to be drawn from the Rhode Island regiments. Greene passed the word that "All those acquainted With Sea Service that have a mind to join the Admiral as Volunteer have Liberty" to assist. Greene underscored that he expected the men to be gone for only a few days and then rejoin their regiments.[11]

For Silas Talbot this was a chance, albeit a brief one, to go home and visit, and so he eagerly stepped forward to join the Commodore's eight ships for what would be a short jaunt up the coast. Talbot and his shipmates soon found themselves sharing the Commodore's bad luck. First it took Hopkins until the 19th to ready his ships; then, as the squadron headed out of New London, Hopkins brought his flagship *Alfred* up on a ledge at the mouth of the harbor. Although he got off on the next tide, with no apparent damage, everyone had to return to port. It was not until the end of April that Hopkins and his ships, with Talbot aboard, finally came alongside the wharf in Providence.[12]

While Talbot was at home his brigade made its way to New York. They took the water route via Long Island Sound and then down through Hell Gate. It was a cold and stormy passage. When the Rhode Islanders finally landed on Manhattan more than a few green-faced soldiers hurried ashore. Since Washington had immediate need of the soldiers lent to Hopkins, it is likely that Talbot did not linger long in Providence. When he rejoined his comrades he found them billeted in various homes in Manhattan. By early May the weather had improved enough that Washington ordered his troops out of the city and into the field. Greene's brigade was sent over to Long Island with Hitchcock's regiment and ordered to encamp on Brooklyn Heights.[13]

Washington's plan was simple, if flawed. He rightly anticipated that the British would soon launch an attack on New York City with the strategic goal of seizing control of the Hudson River Valley and thereby isolating New England. Should they succeed the colonies would be split and the American cause doomed.

In 1776 the City of New York hugged the southern tip of Manhattan, and its only link to the mainland was Kingsbridge at the very northern end of the island. An enemy with control of the water around the island could, therefore, cut off any force that might choose to stand on Manhattan.

Across the East River lay Brooklyn Heights, Greene's position. It was a commanding place from which an enemy could easily dominate the tip of Manhattan. Washington decided that he must hold Manhattan and that to do so he must also hold Brooklyn Heights. Contrary to all military wisdom,

*I*N THE MIDDLE OF July, 1776, a huge British fleet gathered in New York Harbor with troops whose mission was to drive the rebels out of Manhattan and Brooklyn. Here is Archibald Robertson's sketch of that gathering, something like what Silas Talbot saw from Brooklyn Heights.

(*The New York Public Library*)

in the face of a superior enemy he divided his already inferior force into two weaker elements. For a clever enemy Washington was offering a classic military opportunity. On 25 June just such an enemy arrived.[14]

One can only imagine the reaction of Silas Talbot and his fellow soldiers as they looked down the harbor to the lower bay and across to Sandy Hook. Beginning on the 25th and for each day thereafter the forest of masts grew more dense. By mid-July there were more than 250 of His Majesty's ships riding at anchor and disgorging a seemingly endless stream of soldiers, horses, cannon and other equipment. Under the command of the Howe brothers, General Sir William Howe and Admiral Lord Richard Howe, the force landed unopposed on Staten Island.[15]

General Howe spent several weeks carefully preparing his troops. On Long Island Greene kept his men busy digging and drilling. A bit of excitement came early in July when Admiral Howe sent two frigates, *Rose and Phoenix*, accompanied by three smaller auxiliaries, up the Hudson to test American defenses and annoy Washington. To the great embarrassment of the Americans the two ships sailed through the gauntlet with very little damage and dropped anchor 30 miles above the city at Tappan Zee.[16]

The presence of the frigates behind the American lines was both shameful and threatening. Without ships of their own or powerful shore batteries, the Americans could only strike at the frigates with clumsy fireships. Fireships were a common tactic employed to attack vessels at anchor. After stripping a vessel of all her useful appurtenances, she was crammed to the gunwales with combustibles. At night a small crew of daring men with the help of a fair tide or current piloted the fireship as close as possible to an unsuspecting enemy. When close aboard they set her afire and then escaped as best they could, hoping that the flames would engulf the enemy. While a standard tactic, it was rarely successful and always desperate.

When the call went out for men to man fireships Talbot stepped forward. Fortunately he was too late. Another officer from Rhode Island, Ensign John Thomas, got there before him. Thomas took command of a fireship, failed in his mission and died in the inferno.

In the brigade camp at Brooklyn Heights there was no such excitement. Each day fatigue parties were formed up and marched off to dig more fortifications. Sentries were posted and patrols sent out. Boredom and idleness soon produced mischief. Some Rhode Island soldiers took to swimming naked in the mill pond in full view of the local women. Others plunged into the bay's waters and stole oysters planted there by Long Island oystermen. Such behavior caused Greene to ask in a general order, "Is not the Crime of Indecency a sufficient Vice, but Robbery must be added to it?" Soldiers were caught deserting, stealing and fighting among themselves. Talbot, as bored and irritable as the rest, stepped out of line himself. Late in July he and another officer, Lieutenant Dunworth, fell into a dispute. Dunworth challenged Talbot to a duel. When the matter came to Greene's attention he sought Washington's advice—not exactly a matter the Commander-in-Chief wanted to be bothered with at such a time. Meanwhile, tempers must have cooled; to everyone's relief the duel did not come off. Dunworth was cashiered from the army.[17]

Having gathered his troops (more than 30,000), General Howe was ready to move by the middle of August. Through a series of well-planned maneuvers, and taking advantage of Washington's divided force, Howe launched a spirited attack on 22 August and broke the American lines on Long Island. Routed, they fled toward Brooklyn Heights and took refuge with the Rhode Islanders. Had Howe been a more aggressive commander, he would have pressed on, and in all likelihood the redcoats would have captured the entire American force on Long Island, nearly 10,000 men. Instead, Howe took up positions outside the Brooklyn Heights entrenchments (perhaps all that digging had served a purpose) and prepared a conventional eighteenth-century siege. Facing disaster, Washington ordered a withdrawal. On the night of 29 August the entire army was silently ferried across the East River in small boats manned by men from Colonel John Glover's Marblehead, Massachusetts, regiment. Glover's web-footed soldiers saved the day for Washington and his army.

Once the Americans were massed on Manhattan Island, Howe's conservatism saved them again. Not until Sunday 15 September did he launch an attack against Manhattan. He landed 4000 men at Kips Bay behind American lines. Had he moved more quickly across the island he might have trapped a large portion of Washington's army. But Howe delayed long enough for the Americans to escape, marching north along the Hudson. Although Washington and his men had suffered another defeat, the army was still intact and the cause of American independence was still alive. They took up strong positions at Harlem Heights.

At the very moment that British soldiers were landing on the east side of Manhattan at Kips Bay, three British vessels, *Renown, Repulse* and *Pearl*, were ranging their guns to pummel the American retrenchment from the Hudson. As part of securing his new position on the Harlem Heights, Washington had to rid himself of this naval nuisance. Once again he turned to the only useful weapon at hand—fireships. Talbot volunteered to command one of them. The next morning before dawn four American fireships, taking advantage of an ebbing tide, slowly floated down on their three targets. The Royal Navy was not caught unawares. In the early morning light picket boats spotted the Americans and sounded the alarm. Officers barked orders and sailors ran forward to cut anchor cables and quickly free the ships. Men took positions on the bowsprits and in the forechains in the hope of being able to fend off the blazing hulks. Three of the fireships drifted aimlessly and went aground to burn themselves out. Talbot's command was the only one to even come close. Having torched his vessel Talbot came down on *Renown* close enough to heave a grappling hook. It was a good effort but the British freed their vessel with little damage. As soon as the hook thumped over the bulwark *Renown's* crew cut the line and let the fireship pass to leeward. The British vessel was scorched but otherwise little damaged. Talbot himself was not so lucky.

Hoping to con the fireship into *Renown*, Talbot stayed on deck too long. Finally, with his clothing aflame, he leaped over the side and struggled to swim to land. Ashore he realized his eyes had been seared and he could not see. Fortunately, some Americans who had gathered on the beach to watch the fiery scene found him and carried him to a nearby house, where for two weeks he lay in bed in pain and blindness. William Eustis, a senior surgeon with Washington's army, visited Talbot and described him as being "burnt in a most shocking manner." He was lucky to be alive.[18]

Talbot's recovery was slow, but at the end of two weeks he had strengthened sufficiently, including regaining his sight, and he was able to travel. He asked for leave to return to his family in Rhode Island and the leave was granted. While Talbot was at home Washington managed once more to play the fox to Howe's lethargic hounds. He took his army out of New York, through New Jersey and across the Delaware. Then, in one of the most daring ventures in American military history, he recrossed the Delaware and in a brilliant tactical move fell on the Hessians at Trenton while they were busy celebrating Christmas. One week later he hit the enemy again at Princeton. From there he took his army into a winter encampment at Morristown, New Jersey.

ONE OF THE FIRESHIPS *sent against* HMS Phoenix *and* HMS Rose *is shown here on the night of August 16, 1776. This episode, the predecessor to Silas Talbot's escapade, was famous enough to have produced several variations of this engraving, which appeared in editions of* The Atlantic Neptune, *an elephant folio of charts and engravings produced by J.F.W. Des Barres in London for the use of the British Admiralty.*

(*The New York Public Library*)

Talbot's convalescence went well. At home with his family—Anna, Cyrus and George Washington—he gradually recovered his health. By Christmas he was well enough to throw himself into the business of recruiting soldiers. Resplendent in his Captain's uniform, this wounded hero of the Rhode Island troops, this man who had survived the fireships on the Hudson, had no trouble signing men on for the American cause.

Recruiting soldiers, managing his property and caring for his family (Anna was pregnant again), kept him busy. And yet there was time—and will—for further adventures. In a somewhat bizarre twist of fate, this man who barely missed death on one fireship and was seriously injured on another stepped forward to do it all again. Brave or foolhardy, two days before Christmas Silas Talbot and Joseph Brown were appointed by the Rhode Island Assembly to procure two fireships with Talbot in command. The Assembly planned to run them down the Bay at the British fleet anchored around Newport. As it happened, and for the moment at least, the Assembly came to its senses and canceled the attack.

With Washington wintering at Morristown, Talbot decided not to return to the army until spring when the campaign was likely to be renewed. In winter encampment he would simply be another mouth to feed. There were personal reasons that kept him home, too. Sometime during the winter or spring of 1777 Talbot and Anna lost another infant son named Barzillai after his grandfather. Talbot stayed in Providence to grieve with his wife.

By June the 1777 campaign season was underway. Talbot bade farewell to his family and rode to rejoin the army. During his absence over the winter the Rhode Island regiments had been reduced from four to two (and were now called battalions). As a result Talbot was assigned to a battalion commanded by Lieutenant Colonel Christopher Greene and brigaded under Brigadier General James Varnum. He knew and liked both men, having served with them during the campaigns around Boston and New York.[19]

Having kept his army in comfortable winter quarters in New York City, General Howe was considering his next move. He had at least two options. He might march north toward Albany or he might resume his move toward the south and Philadelphia. Washington was uncertain of Howe's intentions. To the north General John Burgoyne was preparing to invade from the St. Lawrence via the Lake Champlain/Hudson River corridor. Might not Howe march out of New York and link up with Burgoyne? On the other hand there was the possibility that Howe might leave Burgoyne to his own devices and march his army on the American capital at Philadelphia. Until he was certain in which direction to move, Washington positioned his main body at Middlebrook, New Jersey, where he could move to block Howe whether he headed south or north. At the same time he detached Varnum's brigade to Peekskill on the east side of the Hudson to block any British advance up the river.

Gradually as the weather warmed the two armies woke from their winter slumber. In good eighteenth-century military fashion neither side rushed to action. Through June and July Howe and Washington played a cat-and-mouse game, watching and probing one another. In August Howe embarked his regiments aboard transports in New York. He was bound down the coast and thence up Chesapeake Bay, where he intended to land his army for an overland assault against Philadelphia. As soon as he was certain of Howe's intentions Washington broke camp and marched to defend the city.

Fully recovered from his wounds, Talbot joined his brigade at Peekskill in July. It was dull duty, waiting and watching on the Hudson. Most of the day was spent drilling and listening to rumors. From upstream stories filtered into camp that General Horatio Gates and his army of militia and Continentals were preparing to welcome the British army coming down from Canada under General Burgoyne. In August joyous news arrived that a strong detachment of British sent out by Burgoyne on a massive foraging expedition had been beaten and captured at Bennington, Vermont. A few days later more good news arrived, this time from the west. Colonel Barry St. Leger, who had been marching through the Mohawk Valley to join Burgoyne, had been turned back at Fort Stanwix. Everyone at Peekskill understood that the noose was tightening on Burgoyne.

Harassed by local militia as they slogged their way through brush and mud, Burgoyne's army was dwindling rapidly. The news from Bennington and Stanwix only added to the demoralization. Realizing how precarious his situation was, Burgoyne sent messages to New York asking for help. Howe, by this time nearing Philadelphia, was too far away to lend assistance. Sir Henry Clinton, the man left behind by Howe to command the city, had neither the will nor the force to alter Burgoyne's fate. He made a gesture upriver, more to salve his conscience and please his superiors than from any realistic hope of saving the doomed Burgoyne. It was hopeless. First at Freeman's Farm and then at Saratoga the armies engaged. Burgoyne surrendered. He and his soldiers went off to Boston as prisoners.

Talbot and his Rhode Islanders were spectators in the Saratoga campaign. Of more immediate concern to them than a distant threat of redcoats, either in Canada or New York City, was the well-founded suspicion that spies and traitors were in their midst. The region around southern New York and Connecticut was home to a worrisome number of Tories. In July Lemuel Ackely of Westchester County was arrested and charged with being a robber and a spy. At the time of his arrest Ackely was carrying a weapon and explained that he was a soldier and had been separated from his unit. No one believed this story—but since he claimed to be a soldier he was hauled before a court martial at Peekskill. Talbot sat on the court. It was a quick business and a unanimous decision. Ackely was sentenced to death.[20]

Ackely's trial and hanging brought some excitement to the Peekskill camp, but it was quickly past and July and August dragged on. The watch on the Hudson was a boring and frustrating business made even more so by the knowledge that the rest of Washington's army was in a great campaign that would decide the fate of Philadelphia. Washington's defense of Philadelphia was not a success. While it may be true that at both Brandywine and Germantown his troops acquitted themselves well, and the commander himself could not be faulted, in the end Howe and his redcoats took Philadelphia. In the Philadelphia campaign the British General finally found opportunities for his tactical skills. The British army met the Americans at Brandywine and Germantown and beat them twice. Nonetheless, while Washington and his army were defeated they were intact. Frustrated at his inability to finish the job, Howe took his troops into Philadelphia for the winter.

Although they held the capital the British did not control the countryside. To provision their troops they depended on a logistics line that stretched back to New York. With Washington's army in the neighborhood this overland line of communication and supply was precarious. Howe could only supply his forces by sea, down the coast and up the Delaware to Philadelphia, and on the Delaware the Americans had wisely fortified several places from which they could hinder British access to Philadelphia. With some difficulty Howe's forces had pushed most of these obstacles aside by mid-September. The Americans still held two key positions on the river—Forts Mercer and Mifflin. The former, under the command of Nathanael Greene, was on the east side of the Delaware River below Philadelphia. Fort Mifflin was located on Mud Island along the same stretch of river. Because of its

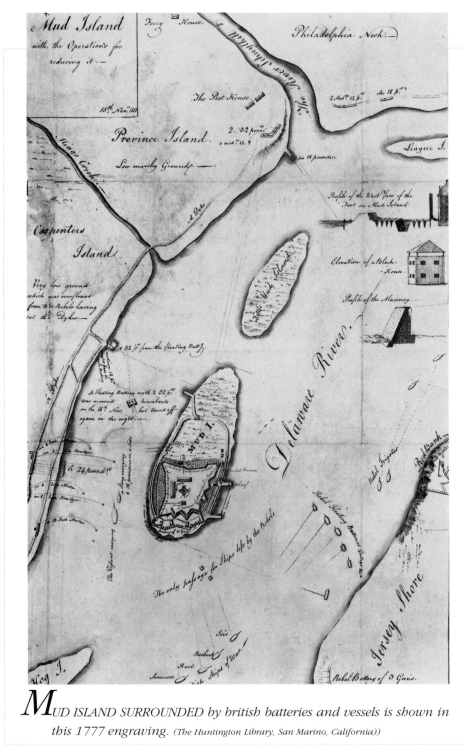

*M*UD ISLAND SURROUNDED *by british batteries and vessels is shown in this 1777 engraving.* (The Huntington Library, San Marino, California))

exposed location on an island, Fort Mifflin could survive only as long as it could be reinforced and supplied from the mainland garrison. So over-whelming was the constant bombardment that Greene kept men there on a 48-hour rotation. Every other night small boats brought fresh troops in and took off exhausted veterans.[21] Nevertheless, the men held the fort, and the fort held off Howe's supply vessels.

Washington moved to reinforce the Delaware forts. On 4 November he ordered Varnum's brigade, including Silas Talbot, to march to Woodbury, New Jersey, to take a position close enough to reinforce Greene. Talbot rejoiced that his unit would finally be part of the battle. He had another rea-son to be pleased as well. In recognition of his bravery on the Hudson the President of the Continental Congress, John Hancock, had promoted him to the rank of Major.[22]

By mid-October Talbot was at the Delaware with his brigade. There he saw a scene that instantly impressed and horrified him. Fort Mifflin had been under near-constant bombardment since 10 October. Its defenses had been poorly constructed and were too extensive for the number of men try-ing to keep them intact. Mifflin's strongest point faced south, but elsewhere the fort was vulnerable, particularly on the north where an active enemy battery was not more than 500 yards away. Fort Mifflin's men recognized their weakness, and at the center of the fort the defenders had built a small redoubt where they planned to make their last stand.

On 22 October a force of 2000 Hessians made an attack against Fort Mercer. They advanced after dark in two columns. It was a poor plan made worse by faulty reconnaissance. The northern column charged over a ram-part only to run smack against an unexpected wall recently thrown up by the Americans. Their comrades in the other column came up against similar unexpected obstacles. All this time Greene's men held their fire. When they had the enemy in confusion and in close range, they poured down a wither-ing fire of ball and grapeshot. The Germans went reeling back.

As the Hessians were faltering, so too was the Royal Navy. A squadron had tried to force its way between Forts Mifflin and Mercer, but the Americans had prepared the way with a chevaux-de-frise that restricted nav-igation and forced the ships to come within range of American batteries from which they took a severe drubbing. Adding to the navy's woes was shallow water. Five of the squadron ran aground. Three managed to escape, but *Augusta*, 64 guns, and the smaller *Merlin*, 10 guns, were not so fortunate. At ten o'clock on the morning of 23 October, *Augusta* blew apart with a thundering roar. Whether this was a result of American fire or some other cause is not certain. *Merlin* had to be abandoned.[23]

The repulse at Fort Mercer offered the Americans respite from a grim defense campaign, but time and force were on the side of the British. On 10 November the pounding of Fort Mifflin began again. Talbot was inside the crumbling fort. He was there as part of the Rhode Island reinforcement drawn from Varnum's brigade. Neither he nor anyone else in the fort had experienced anything like what they now suffered from British cannon and small arms. In nearby Philadelphia people reported that the roar of cannon sounded like constant thunder. On 8 November during the bombardment the fort's commander, Lieutenant Colonel Samuel Smith, was consulting with his engineer, Lieutenant Colonel François Fleury. Their conversation was interrupted by a flying splinter that came tearing across the fort, killing Fleury and seriously wounding Smith. As the officers fell, Talbot came rushing to their side only to be hit himself in the leg and arm by enemy grapeshot. Smith's injuries were serious enough to force him to turn command over to Lieutenant Colonel Simeon Thayer.

The enemy showed no sign of letting up, and because there seemed to be no means to force their withdrawal the situation on the Delaware was hopeless. Inside the fort the men had not slept for days. In the lower portions of Mifflin the cold water of the Delaware was at two feet and rising. On 15 November the British launched a furious attack. Nearly 3000 shot per hour were raining in on the Americans. At the same time British ships were close enough so that marine sharpshooters in the rigging could take careful and effective aim on Americans. For the defenders all hope was gone. In the dark Thayer quietly passed the order to abandon the fort. Talbot commanded the force in the redoubt and remained to cover the withdrawal. In the noise and darkness Thayer managed to evacuate his men. Silas Talbot was one of the last to leave Fort Mifflin.[24]

It was one of the most gallant actions of the American Revolution, and although they had been driven out the defenders of Fort Mifflin earned the thanks of Washington and the respect of General Howe. With Mifflin gone Fort Mercer was next. Rather than sacrifice more men in what surely would be a defeat, the Americans abandoned their positions on the New Jersey shore of the river. The British were now in control of the Delaware from Philadelphia to the sea.

With winter near, the campaigning season was over for both sides. While Washington and his Continentals retired to Valley Forge, Talbot returned to Providence for his second convalescence. He found Anna and his sons faring well. For Rhode Island as a whole, however, the situation was less secure. Since late 1776 the British had occupied Newport. Their original intention had been to hold a base in New England from which they might harass the coast. Over time, as British strategy tended more and more to focus on areas outside of New England, Newport became less important in their plans. Nevertheless, they continued an occupation largely confined to the environs of the town itself, and by early 1778 the British force numbered about 3000 men under the command of General Sir Robert Pigot.[25]

For political reasons Washington could not disregard the British presence in Rhode Island, although there was no military reason to be alarmed. The Rhode Island delegation, joined by their New England neighbors, were incessant in their demands that the enemy be driven out, and to please the politically powerful New Englanders Washington sent a force of 1000 troops to Providence under the command of General John Sullivan. Their presence was reassuring—they demonstrated the concern of the Continental Congress for Rhode Island's distress—but it was also frustrating. There were too few of them to have any chance of dislodging the enemy but too many to be comfortably housed in Providence. In point of fact there was very little for Sullivan's troops to do, and underemployed soldiers have a natural inclination to mischief. The citizens of Providence were soon complaining to the General about the misbehavior of his men.

Although he lacked sufficient force to drive the enemy out, Sullivan was not without a plan. There were ways to make life unpleasant for Pigot and his men, and perhaps to prepare the resources to drive them out. During the spring he turned to Silas Talbot to lend a hand. He asked Talbot to prepare a large number of flat-bottomed craft to be used in an assault when, as he devoutly hoped, enough troops might be sent to him to launch such an attack. The scheme suffered a minor setback when the British launched a surprise raid against Bristol and destroyed several barges abuilding,[26] but the loss was made up when Sullivan arranged to borrow 11 barges from Massachusetts. These were brought down the Taunton River and sailed over to Howland's Ferry in Tiverton. At the same time Sullivan ordered Talbot to prepare 86 more, each barge intended to carry 100 men.

Talbot took up the task with gusto and soon had his crews working by candlelight nailing and caulking and sawing wood. But no matter how many barges, or even how many men Sullivan assembled, there still remained a flaw in the American plan. As long as the British controlled the water approaches to Aquidneck Island an American force fortunate enough to get onto the island in the face of naval opposition would almost certainly find itself cut off and cut down.

Sullivan saw new hope in this situation when on 4 May Congress ratified a treaty of alliance with France. America's new ally had a powerful navy, and if some of those ships could be brought to Newport Sullivan would have the support he needed for a successful attack. It was this message Sullivan entrusted to Talbot when in early June he ordered him to visit Congress.[27] Talbot rode out of Providence west to Hartford, then west again across the Hudson and south towards York, Pennsylvania, where the Congress had fled after the fall of Philadelphia. Enroute to York Talbot got the good news that the British had evacuated Philadelphia and were marching back across New Jersey to New York. He and Congress arrived back in Philadelphia at about the same time.

Sullivan's message was not the only piece of business Talbot carried to Philadelphia. There was also a personal and financial matter. Congress owed him several hundred dollars. From his own pocket he had paid all of his medical expenses after the fireship disaster. More than a year before he had presented a careful record of these expenses to Congress, but they had yet to respond. Tired of writing, tired of waiting, Talbot used this opportunity to see to the business in person.

Silas Talbot's stay in Philadelphia was brief. He delivered the message from Sullivan and made the rounds trying to collect his overdue reimbursements. But instead of cash Congress gave him a promise that as soon as possible they would examine his accounts. As for Sullivan's hope of help Congress responded that, although both they and General Washington were sensitive to the situation in Rhode Island, strategic concerns dictated that New York City was a far more promising target for a Franco-American attack than Newport.

On 8 July, Charles Hector Theodat Comte d'Estaing arrived with his fleet off the Delaware Capes. After consulting with his American allies, the Admiral laid a course for New York and a rendezvous with Washington's army. What greeted d'Estaing was a sight fit for King Tantalus himself. From off Sandy Hook French lookouts could make out the topmasts of the British fleet. They counted nine British ships of the line. D'Estaing had twelve. With the odds so greatly on his side a French victory was nearly assured. Off Sandy Hook, however, d'Estaing received disturbing news. The American pilot who had promised to guide the French through New York's tricky waters had reneged on his agreement. For several days the Admiral and his captains consulted with other pilots who agreed that the deep-draft French vessels could only cross the bars "when a northeast wind coincided with a strong spring tide." On the 22nd, although the wind and tide were right, "D'Estaing's heart failed him under the discouragement of the pilots." He judged the situation too dangerous to risk his fleet. Having wasted two weeks off New York the Admiral ordered a course set for Newport.[28]

Events now moved rapidly. Washington ordered Sullivan to request "in the most urgent manner" that the states of Rhode Island, Massachusetts and Connecticut raise 5000 men for the Newport adventure. The Commander-in-Chief himself sent the Marquis de Lafayette to lead two of his army's best brigades—Varnum's Rhode Islanders and Glover's web-footed Marbleheaders. Major Talbot was ready as well, but instead of posting him back with his own unit in Varnum's brigade Sullivan assigned him to Colonel John Laurens' light infantry, a move probably intended to provide the South Carolina Colonel an officer with local knowledge of Rhode Island's terrain and people.

The New England states responded with despatch. From Massachusetts John Hancock, former president of the Continental Congress and now Major General of militia, arrived. Soon Sullivan had enough troops to make an advance possible. Victory, however, still required seapower. Victory required the French fleet, which arrived off Point Judith on 29 July. After some consultation d'Estaing and Sullivan agreed that the French would proceed up the west side of Aquidneck Island and land troops north of Newport. Simultaneous with the French movement Sullivan promised to bring his forces down from Providence and cross over to the northern end of the island from Tiverton.

It was a good plan but one that required coordination. On 8 August Sullivan got underway too soon and crossed over to the island ahead of the French. Admiral d'Estaing, a man of considerable rank and even greater pride, was furious at his American ally for launching an attack without consulting him and in advance of his own movement. The Admiral had little time to pout, for the next day word arrived that a British squadron was off

Point Judith. D'Estaing immediately signaled his own fleet to get underway and to sortie towards the enemy at sea. Sullivan was left to deal with the enemy ashore.

For the next few days the British and French fleets toyed with one another. Bad weather prevented decisive combat, although a few vessels managed to engage one on one. D'Estaing returned to Newport—not with any intent to continue the battle but only to take on board his disembarked troops and to bid farewell to Sullivan, an ally for whom he had little liking. At midnight on 21 August the French hauled down Narragansett Bay on a course for Boston. News of the French withdrawal put Sullivan's militia detachments in great anxiety, a condition they cured by leaving as quickly as they could. Within a few days 5000 American militia had taken their own form of French leave. Sullivan's position was now impossible; instead of attacking Pigot he now had to devise a withdrawal.

The British, understanding their advantage in men and mobility, did not plan to let Sullivan disengage with impunity. On the night of 12 August Sullivan ordered a retreat towards Tiverton. He posted Laurens' light infantry to cover the withdrawal on the west side of the island. Initially forced back by a spirited British attack, Laurens was reinforced and managed to hold his line and prevent Sullivan's main body from being outflanked. Pigot, determined to break the American line on the right, ordered another move forward. Supported by artillery as well as naval gunfire, Pigot's men pressed the assault. Again Laurens and his men stood their ground. Laurens and Talbot held the enemy at bay long enough for Sullivan to ferry his army over to Tiverton. Satisfied at having driven the Americans off the island, Pigot stopped at the water's edge, regrouped and took his army home to the safety of Newport. On the mainland Sullivan ordered a few militia units to dig in and watch the ferry points while he took his own Continentals back to quarters in Providence.

Silas Talbot returned to Providence with Sullivan, but his stay was brief. On the very day that he came home to Weybosset Street more distressing news came up from Newport. Eight regiments of His Majesty's infantry, a battalion of grenadiers, and one of light infantry, altogether 5000 men, had just arrived by sea under the command of Sir Henry Clinton and Major General Charles Grey.

Disappointed at having come too late to dispatch Sullivan and his troops, Clinton and Grey decided on a major raid against Dartmouth (present-day New Bedford, Massachusetts). This port, only a short sail up Buzzards Bay, was home to a number of American privateers and reportedly had several British prizes at the wharf. Grey embarked his infantry and sailed for Dartmouth.[29]

Since Dartmouth was so close to Dighton, Talbot either on his own or at Sullivan's orders, but in either case with the General's blessing, rode to help in the town's defense. It was a disaster. Saturday afternoon 5 August the British fleet dropped anchor in Clark's Cove, at the entrance to Dartmouth harbor. They hoisted out the small boats, and when they landed they proceeded to destroy everything they could find for six miles up both sides of the Acushnet River. There were 2000 local militiamen with a few small artillery pieces for the town's defense, but against regulars they were amateurs fighting professionals. By the time Talbot arrived on Monday morning it was desolation. He reported the grim scene to Sullivan:[30]

> *Twelve shops and stores in town are burnt, together with*
> *ten dwelling houses, 12 houses standing around the cove*
> *and eight shops are also burned; and all the shipping belonging*
> *to the inhabitants of these states, except a very few are burnt.*

Most likely Talbot carried his own dispatch back to Providence. When he arrived an important request from General Lafayette awaited him.

Notes

1   For examples of these accounts see PCC roll 79, item 65. Some of these reports are also printed in the JCC 2.

2   PCC roll 166, item 152, vol. 1:67. See also Edmund C. Burnett, *The Continental Congress* (New York: W. W. Norton,1965), 65.

3   JCC 2:79, 84, 85, 89, 91; Christopher Ward, *The War of the Revolution*, 2 vols. (New York: Macmillan, 1952), 1:99.

4   There are several accounts of the battle of Bunker Hill. Among the best are Allen French, *The First Year of the American Revolution* (Boston: Houghton Mifflin, 1934), and Richard M. Ketchum, *The Battle for Bunker Hill* (Garden City, New York: Doubleday, 1962).

5   Silas Talbot Daybook, STP; Talbot's commissions may be found in BI F2 STP and in the Silas Talbot Papers, Rhode Island Historical Society.

6   French, *The First Year*, 269n.

7   Nathanael Greene to Governor Nicholas Cooke, 5 November 1775. Richard K. Showman, ed., *The Papers of General Nathanael Greene*, 6 vols, (Chapel Hill: University of North Carolina Press, 1976), 1:148.

8   General Greene's Orders, 4 April 1776. *The Papers of Nathanael Greene*, 1:208.

9   General Greene's Orders, 4 April 1776. *The Papers of Nathanael Greene*, 1:208n; Talbot Genealogy, typescript at New England Historic Genealogical Society.

10 Commodore Esek Hopkins to John Hancock, 9 April 1776, NDAR 4:736; William M. Fowler, Jr. *Rebels Under Sail:*

The American Navy in the Revolution (New York: Charles Scribner's Sons, 1976), 99. William James Morgan, *Captains to the Northward: The New England Captains in the Continental Navy* (Barre, Vermont: Barre *Gazette*, 1959), 139.

11 General Greene's Orders, 9 April 1776. *The Papers of Nathanael Greene*, 1:209.

12 Journal of Continental Brig *Andrew Doria*, Captain Nicholas Biddle, 19 April 1776. NDAR, 4:1163.

13 General Greene's Orders, 29 April 1776. *Papers of Nathanael Greene*, 1:211n.

14 For an analysis of the New York campaign see Bruce Bliven, Jr., *Under the Guns: New York 1775-1776* (New York: Harper and Row, 1972) and Ward, *The War of the Revolution*, 1:202-74.

15 For a discussion of the Howe brothers in the Revolution see Ira D. Gruber, *The Howe Brothers and the American Revolution* (New York: Athenaeum, 1972).

16 William M. Fowler, Jr. "The New York Frigates," *The American Neptune* 38 (1978): 21-22; Richard Koke "The Struggle for the Hudson: The British Naval Expedition Under Captain Hyde Parker and Captain James Wallace, 12 July-18 August 1776, New-York Historical Society, *Quarterly Bulletin*, 40:114-75.

17 Greene to Washington, 25 July 1776. *Papers of Nathanael Greene*, 1:262

18 Silas Talbot to Congress, October 1777. PCC roll 56 item 42, 7:334; Certificate of William Eustis, Senior Surgeon, 26

September 1777. PCC roll 56 item 42, 7:342.

19 Silas Talbot Commission, 5 January 1778. Silas Talbot Papers, RIHS.

20 Army General Court Martial, 29 July 1777. PCC roll 178, item 159, 83.

21 For a general description of the campaign see John W. Jackson, *The Pennsylvania Navy, 1775-1781* (New Brunswick, New Jersey: Rutgers University Press, 1974), 120-281.

22 Commission, 10 October 1777, Talbot Papers, RIHS.

23 "The Siege of Fort Mifflin," *Pennsylvania Magazine of History and Biography,* 11: 82-88.

24 John Laurens to Henry Laurens, 15 November 1777. *Pennsylvania Magazine of History and Biography,*

65 (1965): 357-58.

25 For an overview of the situation in Rhode Island see Paul F. Dearden, *The Rhode Island Campaign of 1778: Inauspicious Dawn of Alliance* (Providence: Rhode Island Bicentennial Foundation, 1980).

26 Dearden, *Rhode Island Campaign,* 51.

27 Thomas Greene to Silas Talbot, 13 June 1778, B1 F3 STP.

28 Stephen Bonsal, *When the French Were Here* (Port Washington, New York: Kennikat Press, 1968), 45, 360-61.

29 Daniel Ricketson, *The History of New Bedford* (New Bedford: The Author, 1858), 265-99.

30 Silas Talbot to John Sullivan, 7 September 1778. Sullivan Papers, MHS.

*T*HE INFAMOUS PRISON *bulk* Jersey,
one of a fleet of prison vessels anchored
in New York harbor, is depicted here in
a wood engraving published in
Harper's Weekly *in 1873. Silas Talbot*
was captured by the Royal Navy in
October 1780 and spent nearly two
months aboard Jersey *before making a*
transatlantic passage with 70 other
American officers to be put into Mill
Prison in Plymouth, England.

(The New York Public Library)

Chapter Three

The Revolutionary Years:
Service at Sea

Lafayette was in a tough position. As the resident Frenchman he was left to defend d'Estaing's apparent desertion of his American allies. No one, least of all the Marquis, was happy at the Admiral's hasty departure and the consequent collapse of the Rhode Island campaign. His unhappiness, however, was nothing like the resentment felt by New Englanders who were heard to use the word betrayal in describing the actions of the French. In the midst of this acrimony Lafayette hit upon a plan, a kind of *beau geste,* that he hoped would divert attention from the failed campaign and focus it against the common enemy still entrenched at Newport. Silas Talbot was essential to the plan.[1]

What Lafayette had in mind was a daring scheme to free Narragansett Bay of the troublesome schooner *Pigot*. For weeks this British impediment, named appropriately for His Majesty's commander in Newport, had been harassing and effectively blocking trade coming down the Bay's Eastern Passage. Lafayette saw the wisdom of capturing or destroying this vessel, restoring faith in the Continentals and alarming the redcoats. To accomplish this he needed a daring commander, a man experienced in night attacks and a seaman who knew these local waters. What he needed was a local hero. Talbot was the very man, and Lafayette had no trouble persuading the Major to lead the attack.

Like most of his fellow revolutionaries, Silas Talbot often mixed public and private motives and saw nothing amiss in using the former to advance the latter. In this he was a typically enterprising New England man, and his actions were within the ethics of the time and in keeping with the business arrangements of privateering. As he prepared for the attack, Talbot sought out Nicholas Cooke, Governor of Rhode Island. Cooke owned the sloop *Hawke*, then idle at a Providence wharf. With the help of other Providence merchants, Cooke fitted out and armed *Hawke* and Talbot agreed to command. Sullivan gave permission to recruit soldiers from the Continental battalions to fill the crew. Despite the obvious public support and public—indeed, patriotic—interest, this was a private venture and the partners agreed to share fifty-fifty. One half the value of the capture would go to Talbot and his men and one half to Cooke and his associates; nothing was planned as a contribution to Sullivan's troops or to fill the public coffers.[2] The public, of course, would benefit in other ways from *Hawke's* success.

On Sunday 25 October *Hawke* eased away from her Providence berth and rode the tide down the Bay. By evening the wind had died and the tide turned. Unable to make way, Talbot anchored at Rocky Island near Bristol. The next day a fair breeze carried *Hawke* through Bristol Ferry to a point near Mount Hope just north of Portsmouth. There in a secluded anchorage Talbot waited until Wednesday night. At ten in the evening he quietly passed the word to take in the anchor and get underway. With a fair tide *Hawke* drifted past Bristol Ferry, and as they glided through the darkness Talbot called forward and ordered the mainsail and jib lowered so that *Hawke's* silhouette would be only a low hull and bare poles. No one spoke as the sloop passed the enemy cannon and the slumbering sentries on Newport's island. But the game was up when a lookout spied the sloop and shots boomed from an enemy battery. They missed their mark, but now the hunter was the hunted. Talbot took *Hawke* six miles up the familiar Taunton River so that he might do a bit of reconnoitering. At first light Talbot took a small boat down the Sakonnet River and landed at a point not far from *Pigot's* anchorage. From there he could make out the schooner. What he saw caused concern. To protect against boarding, the British had erected netting along the bulwarks. Talbot took note of the nets and laid plans to overcome them. When he returned to *Hawke* he ordered the kedge anchor lashed to the jib boom. His plan was to jam the boom, with the anchor at its tip, through the netting.

After dark *Hawke* got underway again. She came out of the river and glided unseen past the batteries at Fogland Ferry. By one-thirty in the morning Talbot had sight of his prey and was moving to close on the schooner. Finally, sleepy *Pigot* came alive. From her quarterdeck a marine sentry hailed *Hawke*. When no response came back he fired his musket at the stranger. *Hawke*'s men replied with a hail of shot that sent *Pigot*'s deck watch scurrying below. Talbot ordered his sloop onto a heading that brought his jib boom and kedge anchor through the netting and into the fore shrouds of the enemy. Within an instant *Hawke*'s men were swarming forward across the boom and onto *Pigot*'s deck. The enemy crew, bewildered and in fear, stayed below. The only person to resist was *Pigot*'s Captain, but within minutes he was overwhelmed and pinned to the deck. Talbot put a prize crew aboard the vessel, locked the prisoners below, and set a course south and then southeasterly around Point Judith and into a safe harbor at Stonington, Connecticut.[3]

Silas Talbot was a hero once more. The Rhode Island General Assembly voted him a silver sword and the Continental Congress rewarded him with a promotion to Lieutenant Colonel. Rank and a sword were not his only rewards. After accounts had been settled, Talbot's share from the sale of *Pigot* and her equipment amounted to better than 500 pounds.[4]

Encouraged by such success, Talbot decided to take on bigger prey. Late in the fall of 1778 HMS *Renown*, a vessel of 50 guns and an old adversary from the fireship days, was sent to take up a station off Rhode Island. Her presence lured Talbot and his friends into a scheme to take her as they had taken *Pigot*. *Renown*, however, was no mere schooner. With her armament and a crew of more than 400 men she would not be easy prey. Just getting a boarding party over her high gunwales posed a challenge to Talbot and his crew.

Driven by cupidity and the desire for revenge Talbot concocted a complex plan. With the help of his Providence friends he managed to charter an old 400-ton merchantman. On her top deck he rigged a platform high enough so that a boarding party could charge across to *Renown*'s deck. Surprise, of course, was vital. If they should be discovered it would take only one British broadside to blow Talbot and his crew all over Narragansett Bay. Talbot reassured his nervous men that the plan could work if for no other reason than that the crew aboard *Renown* were poorly disciplined and inattentive. This he knew, he told them, from reports of escaped prisoners.

The most ridiculous adventures are often conjured out of the most fragile intelligence. Reports from escaped prisoners of the British should have been received carefully and with skepticism. Talbot was far too credulous. That he could conceive of taking a vessel of such manpower and firepower in this harum-scarum fashion, particularly after the British were on alert from the *Pigot* embarrassment, is a measure of his impetuous character. Fortunately, before he could get his scheme underway, the temperature fell, ice formed and his vessel was imprisoned. Mother Nature had saved him from probable disaster. A few weeks later the Admiralty saved Rhode Island. *Renown* was ordered to another station.[5]

In the spring of 1779 news arrived that General Sullivan was leaving Rhode Island to take command of an expedition against the Iroquois in upstate New York. His replacement was General Horatio Gates, the celebrated victor of Saratoga.[6] Talbot may have hoped for action, but he was soon disappointed. It was not Washington's intention to assign anything more than a small holding force to Rhode Island. Indeed, the Commander-in-Chief was pleased to have the British holed up in Newport. Several thousand British troops who might otherwise be on the march against Washington's forces elsewhere were occupied in garrison duty.

With military affairs at a standstill in Rhode Island, Talbot had little to do. He was bored. Anxious for employment, his ears perked up when he heard rumors of a scheme thought up by Sullivan. Shortly before he left, Sullivan had hired the sloop *Sally* from Clarke and Nightingale, local merchants who were acting on behalf of the sloop's owner, Nicholas Lowe of New York. It was Sullivan's intention to use *Sally* and *Pigot* (*Hawke* had apparently been returned to her owners) to cruise the coast. A few days of experience with *Pigot*, the vessel that Silas Talbot had captured the previous fall, showed her to be a sailing slug and not suited for much of anything. *Sally*, on the other hand, showed promise. Sullivan renamed her *Argo*, and in one of his last acts as commander in Rhode Island turned her over to Talbot. With no other offers beckoning, Lieutenant Colonel Talbot accepted command.[7]

After a few weeks for fitting-out, *Argo* was ready for sea by the middle of May. Acting as the new Rhode Island commander, Gates ordered Talbot to sail towards Buzzards Bay and into Dartmouth where he expected the Colonel would find other American vessels. After joining up with them Talbot was expected to sail into Vineyard Sound and clear the area of "Plunderers."[8] These "Plunderers," as Gates referred to them, were Tory privateers from New York City and Newport who made their living tormenting trade in

Narragansett Bay and on Long Island Sound. Talbot went to Dartmouth, and from there commenced cruising the coast. *Argo* was an ideal little warship, fast and well-armed. With a crew of sixty men and twelve guns she was more than a match for the Tory gnats, and news of her appearance sent the enemy scurrying for safety.

Having cleared the coast, Talbot asked permission to sail off soundings. Gates was hesitant. What good would it do to have *Argo* sailing beyond the region bounded by Cape Cod and Long Island? Talbot saw profit in it. In both the *Pigot* and the *Argo* adventures he had been able to smite the enemy and make money too. He had been so successful in local waters he had worked himself out of a job. Offshore, however, were greater opportunities. Beyond soundings he could hope to find not small Tory privateers but rich merchantmen bound home to England from the West Indies. Talbot persuaded the General to allow *Argo* to go hunting offshore.[9]

Operating out of Boston and New London, Talbot made two voyages during the summer of 1779. On the first he captured six enemy vessels, including the privateer *Lively* of 12 guns and two letter-of-marque brigs bound to England from the West Indies. On his second voyage in August Talbot had the great good fortune to meet with the privateer *King George* out of Newport. She was commanded by the notorious Stanton Hazard, a Tory whose obstruction of Rhode Island trade had been particularly obnoxious. Hazard's fearsome reputation was apparently folklore, for on closing with *King George*, and with fewer men and guns, *Argo* managed to deliver a crippling broadside. Talbot brought his vessel alongside, grappled and boarded. In minutes *King George* was his. No men were killed on either vessel. Talbot carried his prize into New London and received acclaim that echoed all the way to Philadelphia.[10]

Talbot's stay in New London was brief. Within a few days he was to seaward of Long Island again. Early one morning *Argo*'s lookout spotted a large vessel to windward. Through the morning the two vessels closed until within speaking distance, at which point each discovered the other was an enemy. *Argo* was soon exchanging broadsides with the privateer *Dragon*, 14 guns and 80 men, out of New York. For several hours the two slugged it out. With the lucky exception of the Captain himself every man on *Argo*'s quarterdeck was either killed or wounded. Finally *Dragon*'s mainmast went over the side. Wallowing helplessly, the British privateer had no choice but to strike. Talbot's triumph, however, was brief. *Argo* had taken several shots in her hull and water was rising in her hold. The pumps could not keep up and Argo was settling deeper. Talbot had to both secure *Dragon* and save his own vessel—and quickly. He did both. His carpenter took men below to plug the holes from the inside while at the same time a crew climbed over the side to nail sailcloth over the gaping holes outside to slow the rush of water.

Barely had Talbot put his prize crew aboard *Dragon* and plugged the holes when another enemy privateer hove into view. She turned out to be the brig *Hannah*, 14 guns. Again *Argo* sailed to action, but before Talbot could claim her as his own the Philadelphia privateer *Macaroni* joined the fray. Together *Argo* and *Macaroni* made short work of *Hannah*. Talbot escorted both prizes into New Bedford. *Argo* was in desperate condition. According to one account, "She was so much shivered in her hull and rigging by the shot which had pierced her in the last two engagements that all who beheld her were astonished that a vessel of her diminutive size could suffer so much and yet get safely to port."

Nevertheless, *Argo* was repaired in New Bedford and quickly put back to sea. She headed down Buzzards Bay, gave a wide berth to Montauk Point and sailed for Sandy Hook where she intended to lie in wait for New York trade. Off Long Island Talbot fell in with the *Saratoga* out of Providence, commanded by a Captain Munroe. The two captains concocted a scheme to ensare the enemy. *Argo*, the smaller of the two, would close with Sandy Hook to entice attack. *Saratoga* would stay at a distance and then pounce. The first part of the plan worked well. The New York privateer *Dublin* took the bait and sortied against *Argo*. For two hours *Argo* took the worst of the battle and waited for *Saratoga* to come to the rescue. She did not.[11]

> The Saratoga *was steered with a long wooden tiller on common occasions, but in time of action the wooden tiller was unshipped and put out of the way, and she was then steered with an iron one that was shipped into the rudder head from the cabin. In the hurry at preparing for battle, this iron tiller had been shoved into the opening of the rudder case, but had not entered its mortise in the rudder head at all, and the* Saratoga *went away with the wind at a smart rate, to the surprise of Captain Talbot and the still greater surprise of Captain Munroe, who repeatedly called to the helmsmen:*
> *"Hard a weather, hard up there!"*
> *"It is hard up, sir."*

"You lie, you blackguard! She goes away lasking. Hard a weather, I say again."

"It is hard a weather, indeed, sir," was the only reply the helmsman could make.

Captain Munroe was astonished, and could not conceive "what the devil was the matter with his vessel." He took in the after sails and made all the headsail in his power. "All" would not do, and away she went. He was in the utmost vexation lest Captain Talbot should think him actually running away. At last one of his under officers suggested that possibly the iron tiller had not entered the rudder head, which on examination was found to be the case. The blunder was soon corrected, and the Saratoga was made to stand toward the enemy: and that some satisfaction might be made for his long absence Captain Munroe determined, as soon as he got up, to give them a whole broadside at once. He did so, and the Dublin *immediately struck her colors.*

Through the remainder of the summer and into the autumn of 1779 Talbot made several more voyages in *Argo*, each yielding success and profit. She was a fortunate vessel. At a time when other American cruisers were being rounded up by His Majesty's squadrons, *Argo* managed to thrive. Her speed, crew size and armament gave advantage, but none of that would have mattered if she had not been well-commanded. Talbot was a good seaman and a bold commander, and in that season of 1779 he managed to capture eleven merchantmen and five armed vessels. None of Talbot's captures were more trouble than the infamous *Betsey*.[12]

On 29 August *Argo* set out on a cruise that took her along the New Jersey shore. On 6 September at position 39° 4′ north and 71° 24′ west *Argo* sighted and pursued an unknown vessel. *Argo* overtook the vessel, and Talbot and his crew found her to be the 200-ton letter-of-marque *Betsey* out of Montserrat bound to New York with a cargo of rum.[13] *Betsey* surrendered to *Argo*. Of *Betsey*'s 14-man crew Talbot removed 11 to *Argo*. He then put a prize master and 11 of his own seamen on board *Betsey* and ordered her to New London in company with *Argo*. Almost as soon as the battle was over *Argo*'s lookout spotted three brigantines on the horizon making straight for them. Suspecting that the three sail might be British, Talbot decided to run for it. The captured *Betsey* proved to be a poor sailer and within a few hours she was overtaken by the strangers. *Argo* stood off some distance to leeward while

Talbot and his men watched the proceedings. After securing their prize two of the brigantines set a course for *Argo*, forcing Talbot to make a hasty departure. The third brigantine stayed in company with *Betsey*. Talbot managed to elude his pursuers and in a few days he was safely at Dartmouth, lamenting in dispatches to Gates that he had lost a prize so rich as *Betsey*.

A few weeks after returning to Dartmouth Talbot was pleased to learn that the British were evacuating Newport. General Clinton had decided to consolidate his forces and focus on a southern campaign. There was no value in maintaining a garrison at Newport. Once the British were gone Talbot brought *Argo* around to Newport, and shortly after his arrival he met an American seaman who had just been released from a British prison in New York. This man told a tale that shocked Talbot. He had been in prison with another seaman who had been captured while a member of a prize crew on *Betsey*. *Betsey*, he said, had been taken from Talbot not by enemy vessels but by three Americans. While the seaman could not remember the names of the three vessels he did recall that they hailed from Philadelphia.

Talbot was furious. He had been cheated. The men who took *Betsey* from him surely knew that their seizure was illegal, if not cowardly. Another vexing twist to the story was that *Betsey* had been shortly recaptured by the British, leaving the three thieves with nothing to show for their perfidy. Talbot wrote to Henry Marchant, one of the Rhode Island delegates in Congress, asking him to lay the matter before that body. He wanted recompense from those who had stolen and then lost his prize. He told Marchant that he was prepared to pursue this case until he received justice.[14]

Talbot engaged counsel and undertook to find the culprits. The three brigantines turned out to be *Achilles*, *Patty* and *Hibernia*, all of Philadelphia. Talbot pursued them and discovered how long and how expensive a legal battle could be. When finally cornered in a Pennsylvania court the owners argued that Talbot had not given his prize master a written commission, and therefore the prize was not valid. This legal chicanery did not hold and the court decided in favor of Talbot to the amount of nearly £13,000. Unfortunately, appeal was piled upon vexatious appeal until it took six years for Talbot to collect his money. How much was left after the lawyers were paid is not known.

Betsey notwithstanding, the cruising season of 1779 was a great success. Other prizes were captured, and with half the proceeds coming to him and his crew, the other half going to the Providence owners, Talbot was doing well. It was precisely his success, however, that distressed him. He longed to further the success he had already had as an army officer. As a Lieutenant Colonel he deserved a field command. Washington and others, however, had made it clear that this was impossible. The American army had a surfeit of officers. Having reconciled himself to not commanding a battalion, Talbot began to wonder why he should not have a captaincy in the Continental Navy. His record afloat was surely as distinguished as his history in Washington's army.

Talbot lobbied Gates to help him get a naval command. He even wrote to his friend and political ally Henry Marchant to ask his intervention and advice. When Marchant began to make the rounds on Talbot's behalf he generally found that his irrepressible and ambitious constituent had already visited or written nearly everyone he was now waiting upon. Marchant's visits availed little. Congress had no battalions to give Talbot, nor did they have any ships. Talbot felt slighted and threatened to resign. Marchant entreated Talbot not to leave the service and told him to listen to Gates, "a father to the brave," who also asked Talbot to remain. His threat to leave did have some effect. Promises were made to Talbot to persuade him to stay in the service. There was, he was told, a fine copper-bottomed brig in Boston that the Marine Committee had ordered purchased for him. Alas, the intention may have been good but the Committee was not as decisive as privateering interests in Boston who outbid the Congress for this fine fast vessel.[15]

As a consolation to Talbot, and a ploy to keep him on duty, on 17 September Congress commissioned him a Captain in the Continental Navy. It was an incongruous appointment, for while Congress exalted him with the rank of Captain, the highest rank in its navy, it left him in command of his old sloop *Argo*. Whatever solace the new rank may have provided disappeared in late 1779 when Nicholas Lowe, *Argo*'s original owner, demanded the return of the vessel. Captain Talbot was on the beach.

For the time being Silas Talbot was content to retire to his home on Weybosset Street. The house was a bit noisier and more confused these days. In August a new son had arrived, named Theodore Foster for his father's friend and business partner. Anna and the children occupied his time, and so did his investments. Thanks to the sale of his prizes Talbot had been able to take advantage of opportunities in the Providence real-estate market. He had made several property purchases and even put some cash into trading ventures.[16]

In addition to Silas and Anna, and his sons Cyrus, George and

Theodore, plus one or two servants, another person moved into the house. For most of February Robert Gibson, a young man with seagoing ambitions, boarded at the Talbots. He was there to learn the "Art of Navigation" from Captain Talbot. The experience was not cheap. For his services Talbot collected £30 in tuition and more than £67 for board.[17]

As the spring of 1780 drew near the Captain's prospects for a naval command looked bleak. By 1780 the history of the Continental Navy had been, in the words of John Adams, one of its strongest supporters, "enough to bring tears to my eyes." Congressional enthusiasm for the navy, fed by a desire to protect trade and award lucrative contracts, far exceeded the resources available. What had been a great year for Silas Talbot, 1779, had been a particularly bad one for the navy. In July the Continental Navy had participated in an attack on a British concentration in Penobscot Bay, Maine. In all of American naval history, only Pearl Harbor ranks as a greater disaster. Ill-planned, ill-executed, and characterized by what can only be called cowardice, the adventure cost the Americans their entire squadron. Not even the glorious, but strategically unimportant, victory of John Paul Jones off Flamborough Head in September of the same year could ease the shame of Penobscot Bay.

As if to underscore their naval incompetence, late in 1779 Congress dispatched four vessels, nearly all that was left of the Continental Navy, to Charleston, South Carolina. They were ordered to defend the city against an anticipated enemy attack. It was a sad mission for vessels equipped and intended to sail gallantly against the enemy. Now they were condemned to end their careers as floating forts—ideal targets for British guns. When the attack came in the spring three were captured and one was scuttled.

Discouraged by events, Talbot took his best alternative and went to see Providence's most enterprising and richest citizen—John Brown. It was time to go a-privateering again. Brown was ready to invest in any enterprise with promise, especially a privateering venture commanded by the able Captain Talbot. With others he secured a commission from the State of Rhode Island for *Argo*. Apparently Brown and his associates had found a way to quiet Nicholas Lowe's claim to the sloop. Naturally Talbot would be in command.[18]

Despite his appointment, Talbot did not sail with *Argo*. Brown and company found a better opportunity with the ship *General Washington*. Larger and better-armed than *Argo*—19 guns versus 12, and a crew of 120 as against 60—*General Washington* promised a much better return. Talbot agreed and quickly shifted to the larger ship.[19]

The cruise went awry. For several weeks Talbot sailed off and on without a single sighting. The British were not foolish. London merchants had lost enough vessels in these waters to instruct their captains to give the coast a wide berth. At the same time the Royal Navy had decided to sweep through in hopes of bagging some Americans. Early on a fresh October morning Talbot watched in horror as the rising sun revealed a British squadron all around him. In the darkness *General Washington* had sailed smack into a trap. As Talbot made all sail to escape, two of the squadron's 74s came up to chase. A line squall forced one of the pursuers to take in sail and give up the chase; but the other, HMS *Culloden*, persisted and by nightfall she overtook *General Washington*. Resistance was futile and Talbot surrendered without a fight. He and his crew were removed from their ship and carried as prisoners aboard *Culloden* into New York.[20]

Silas Talbot had become a prisoner of war—and to his coming distress he had become one of the Royal Navy's prisoners of war. To a remarkable degree the American Revolution was a genteel affair, at least by the standards of twentieth-century warfare. Atrocities were rare; fighting to the last man was considered silly; and non-combatants were generally unmolested. A most notable exception to this warfare by gentlemen was the treatment of naval prisoners of war.[21] For the British, American prisoners of war were an embarrassment. Since Britain refused to recognize American independence, the King's government could not legally detain American rebels as prisoners of war. War could only be waged against another sovereign nation. Not until six months after Yorktown did Parliament finally enact a law that authorized "rebel prisoners" to be legally held as prisoners of war. In the early days of the conflict British authorities simply took rebel Americans prisoner while recognizing that the prisoners were fellow citizens. Indeed, on some occasions in the West Indies prisoners were actually released by local magistrates when confronted with a writ of *habeas corpus*. Parliament closed these legal loopholes with statutes passed in December of 1776 and March of 1777. These allowed British magistrates to imprison Americans on probable cause and hold them at the pleasure of the King.

In eighteenth-century warfare prisoners were normally a minor problem. No belligerent wanted to expend resources watching over them. What happened most often was that after a relatively short confinement prisoners were exchanged or ransomed via a formal arrangement known as a cartel; but because Britain refused to recognize or deal with the American Congress no formal cartel could be arranged. Legal impediments notwithstanding, reason dictated that there had to be some sort of exchange, and in February 1776 Lord George Germain, the Secretary of State for the American colonies, and one of the principal architects of British policy, told General Sir William Howe that he must find a "means of effecting [prisoner] exchange without the King's Dignity [and] Honor being committed or His Majesty's Name used in any Negotiation." In America a system of informal exchange was worked out between field commanders, and with some notable exceptions the exchange of captured soldiers was carried out reasonably well during the war. This was not the case for sailors like Silas Talbot and his crew. Once captured, American seamen could despair of exchange and could expect little except rotting in jail. The principal reason for this, aside from the usual complications of politics and bureaucracy, was that Americans had very little to exchange. Precious few British seamen fell into American hands, and although Washington did have numbers of British soldiers under guard, he was generally not willing to trade them for sailors. He preferred to use them to get back soldiers for his own army.

Upon arrival at New York Talbot and his men were dumped into the bowels of a prison hulk anchored in Wallabout Bay. Because of the shortage of space to confine American seamen ashore, in the fall of 1776 the British began to moor decrepit vessels in the harbor as floating jails. As the number of prisoners grew, more ships were added, and in April 1778 the most infamous member of this death fleet, *Jersey*, a former sixty-four-gun ship built in 1736—was towed to her mooring. Hundreds, perhaps thousands, of Americans perished aboard this rotting hulk whose stench rose so strong that she could only be approached from windward. Each day began with the command "Rebels, turn out your dead." Talbot lived to describe the horror of being confined in *Jersey*'s hold:[22]

> *All her port holes were closed....There were about 1100 prisoners on board. There were no berths or seats to lie down on. Many were almost without cloathes. The dysentery fever, phrenzy and despair prevailed among them, and filled the place with disgust and horror. The scantiness of the allowance, the bad quality of the provisions, the brutality of the guards, and the sick pining for comforts they could not obtain, altogether*

furnished continually one of the greatest scenes of human distress and misery ever beheld. It was now the middle of October, the weather was cool and clear with frosty nights, so that the number of deaths per day was reduced to an average of ten, and the number was considered by the survivors a small one when compared with the terrible mortality that had prevailed for three months before. The human bones and skulls, yet bleaches on the shore of Long Island.

Talbot's imprisonment aboard *Jersey* was brief. In December Admiral Lord George Rodney ordered 71 American naval officers aboard *Jersey* to be carried to England for confinement in a more regular prison. Rodney's motives were clear. He once said that the commander in North America would only be successful when he hated the Americans in principle. He told Germain that "the sword must cut deep." Rodney followed his own advice and took as his special mission making life miserable for rebel seamen. Talbot, because of his fame, was singled out for attention. The Admiral took satisfaction in sending men 3000 miles from home to a place and fate about which they could only speculate with trepidation.

Talbot and the others were locked into the hold of HMS *Yarmouth* for a long, cold, miserable winter crossing. Adding to the terror of the voyage were the threats passed by the guards that the Americans were being taken to England for hanging. Admiral Rodney's misanthropic notions were not government policy, and there would be no hangings; but many of the prisoners must have believed that their future was the noose. As soon as *Yarmouth* was secure at her Plymouth dock the prisoners were trudged off to nearby Mill Prison to join several hundred other American and French prisoners.

Although hardly pleasant, Mill turned out to be an improvement over the misery of the hulks. For many like Talbot the worst punishment was living under a crushing pall of gloom and boredom. There was simply nothing to do. Leaving sailors to their own devices meant the usual amount of gambling, brawling and improvising games. Sometimes the more talented and industrious turned to carving wood, scribing bone with scrimshaw or making model ships. Talbot and his fellow prisoners were allowed to buy books and stationery and write letters, and frequently, although forbidden, newspapers would circulate inside the walls. Rations at Mill, while not exciting, were adequate. Health care, albeit primitive, was usually provided. Enlisted prisoners were assigned space in open barracks while officers were, at their own request, segregated in separate quarters.

Those with money at Mill found ways to make life easier for them-selves. With cash, better food was available, warmer clothes might be acquired and living in general could be made far more tolerable. Indeed their British keepers were delighted to be of any help they could, for a fee, so they encouraged the prisoners to seek outside funding. Talbot took the message and set about scouting for support.

Learning that the American Commissioners in Paris might be good prospects, Talbot wrote in June 1781 seeking help from John Adams. Adams responded and sent Talbot £10 from his own "pockets." He also told Talbot that "Mr. F [ranklin] at Passy is the only one in Europe who has power to offer you relief." Talbot, according to Adams, should write to him but under no cir-cumstances was he to mention Adams' name. Adams and Franklin were, as usual, feuding. Talbot never forgot Adams' generosity. Captain Talbot also received help from an old Providence acquaintance, Elkanah Watson, who was in England on business.[23]

In November 1781, after more than a year in confinement, Silas Talbot was released as part of a general prisoner exchange. He made his way across the channel to Cherbourg, traveled to Paris and met with Franklin. On Franklin's advice Talbot went to Nantes, where in February he managed to find passage on a vessel bound to Providence and commanded by a Captain Folger, probably one of Benjamin Franklin's Nantucket relations.

The voyage was a tonic to Talbot. Pushed westward by the southern trade winds, Folger's vessel made good progress toward America. For the first time in more than a year Talbot had a chance to think and dream about the future without the odor of prison in his nostrils. Soon he would be home with his family and friends. But fifteen days out calamity struck. A sail was sighted to windward bearing down menacingly. The stranger was the British privateer *Jupiter* out of Bristol, England. She overhauled Folger and signaled him to heave to. There was no mistaking her intention. Folger, his crew and all the passen-gers were placed aboard one of *Jupiter*'s other prizes and ordered to New York.

Facing further confinement, Talbot must have been in despair. Fortunately for him, enthusiasm for the war had waned by early 1782. The New York garrison was still reeling from Cornwallis' inglorious defeat the previous October, and rumors were abroad that peace was in the offing. Sensing that the end was near, the British commanders in the city had little heart for imprisoning a brave officer who had already been confined for so long. As soon as he was landed in New York the officials bade him farewell. Talbot found a local wood boat to take him up the Sound to Stony Brook on Long Island. From there he walked to a tavern just below Huntington kept by an innkeeper named Munroe who helped him find passage across the Sound to Fairfield, Connecticut. From there he took passage on a small coaster to New London and then home to Providence.

It was a sad homecoming. Talbot did not know that in April 1781 Anna had died.[24] Although they had lost their mother the boys were coping well. Grandfather and grandmother Richmond had hired Solomon Bradford to tutor Cyrus and George Washington, and by all accounts they were good students. Theodore, of course, was too young for school, but he was cared for by the Richmonds and others in the town. Never inclined to wallow in sentimentality or grief, Talbot quickly took charge of his sons, his property and his business. As he sorted through the pile of papers and documents that had accumulated on his desk during a two-year absence he discovered that while he was gone Congress had done him ill.

Like most armies, the Continental Army had too many officers. Congress had never been shy when it came to handing out commissions. Under the pressures of war this surplus of officers was neither a problem nor much of a thought in the minds of the delegates, but now as peace approached and the army grew smaller the problem loomed large. During Talbot's confinement Congress had been debating what to do with so many officers. Even worse than the numbers was the alarming discovery that many of these men were still on the rolls and collecting pay. Not only were these idle officers a current drain, but if they remained on the rolls through the end of the war they would be entitled to half pay for life. On 31 December 1781 Congress dealt with officers who were "without employ." The solution was harsh. All officers who were not on active duty as of the next day, 1 January 1782, were considered to be retired and their pay ended as of that date. Since Talbot was without a billet he was among the suddenly retired.[25]

To be denied his pay in a way he viewed as indecent and peremptory was galling to Talbot. It was all the more so because the discussion and decision had taken place while he was a prisoner and unable to protest. This was only part of Talbot's grievance. His September 1779 commission as a Captain in the Continental Navy had never been delivered to him and he had never received any pay as an officer in the naval service. The only effect of the commission seems to have been that its issuance caused his army pay to cease so that, since September of 1779, he had received no compensation from either the army or the navy. Full of righteous anger he wrote to anyone he thought might help. His best hope was Washington. He wrote to the Commander-in-Chief to remind him that he had visited with him in February 1780 to ask for leave so that he might take a command in the navy. Talbot's goal was simple. If he could get Washington to verify that he gave Talbot verbal leave to join the navy on a temporary basis he might then be able to make a case that he was entitled to be kept in the service and to receive his army pay.

Washington gave Talbot short shrift. The Commander-in-Chief was being pestered nearly to death by swarms of officers asking for similar help. Washington replied bluntly that he had no recollection of such a conversation and that Talbot's case was weakened by the fact that when he did leave the army he went to sea not as a Captain in the Continental Navy but as a privateer. He was implying, of course, that Talbot had been well compensated from prizes and ought not now be seeking additional pay. Talbot, however, refused to back down.

To advance his case Talbot traveled to Philadelphia to lobby in person. He spent several weeks in the city during the early summer of 1782 visiting congressmen, bureaucrats and even Robert Morris, the Superintendent of Finances and by all odds the single most influential person in the government. Talbot, of course, was only one of dozens, perhaps hundreds, of former officers who were pleading such cases. Now that the war was nearly over Congress was trying desperately to make sense of their accounts. Although his naval commission made his situation somewhat different, for the most part all to whom he spoke had heard it before. And also not heard it. An impecunious Congress was turning a convenient deaf ear. Under the circumstances Talbot seems, for the time at least, to have given up hope for back pay. He did pursue his rights to be recompensed for certain bills long overdue. Morris was sympathetic and told him that he would lay Talbot's accounts before the treasurer, but he also noted that Congress was broke and the whole issue of payment was moot until the states paid the Congress sums now far in arrears. Disgruntled and disappointed, Talbot returned to Providence.

Talbot's lobbying had not been entirely in vain. He might be a prematurely retired Lieutenant Colonel but he was still in the active ranks as a Continental Navy officer, although he was not drawing pay. In private Morris had told him that he would do everything he could to find him a command. Given that Morris, in addition to his other duties, was now also in charge of the Continental Navy this was not an idle promise. The difficulty was that the navy had almost no ships, and with the war virtually over the likelihood of any new vessels coming into service was remote.

Nevertheless, there was one ironic possibility. Since her capture in the fall of 1780 Talbot's old command, *General Washington*, renamed *General Monk*, had been used by the enemy to block American shipping off the Delaware Capes. Her successes so alarmed the Philadelphia merchants that in March 1782 they bought and fitted out their own well-armed vessel, *Hyder Ali*, to seek and destroy *Monk*. Under the command of Joshua Barney, a young Captain from Maryland, *Hyder Ali* tracked down her prey. On 8 April 1782, at the entrance to Delaware Bay, *Hyder Ali* engaged *General Monk*, and after a rollicking fight lasting just over 30 minutes the British vessel hauled down her flag. Back in Philadelphia the state authorities ordered the name *General Monk* scraped off the transom to be replaced with *General Washington*. Since she was a better sailer than *Hyder Ali*, Barney took her for his own command. In August of 1782, when Morris needed a fast and well-armed vessel to carry specie to France, he bought *General Washington* from Pennsylvania.

Since she was now a Continental vessel, and since he was in charge of the navy, Morris intended to give command of *General Washington* to Talbot. It seemed only fair to give back to Talbot what had been his before. Joshua Barney, however, did not agree. Whether she was Continental or Pennsylvanian, *General Washington* was his to command and he would not give her up. Barney kept his ship. Talbot stayed on the beach.[26]

For the Continental Navy the fall of 1783 was a time for reckoning. While the peace negotiators in Paris put the final touches on a treaty to end the war, courts martial were convening in Philadelphia and Boston to dispense justice to certain officers of the navy. As one of the few naval officers available, Talbot was summoned to sit on these courts. The officers were charged with a variety of offenses, none of them severe (e.g., showing disrespect for a senior officer, ungentlemanly behavior). It was all curiously irrelevant. Since officers could not be confined or flogged, the most severe punishment was dismissal from the service. What service? The war was over and the ships were gone. This was all part of a mentality that Herman Melville would refer to as "forms, measured forms." It was pitiful business, but it was easy duty and it paid. Over the next few weeks seven courts convened to try eight officers. Six were found guilty of the charges levied and dismissed from the service. Two were acquitted. Having finished this moot business Talbot returned to Providence.[27]

Notes

1 Lafayette to Talbot, 8 September 1778. Talbot Papers, RIHS.; Henry T. Tuckerman, *Silas Talbot: A Commodore in the Navy of the United States* (New York: J. C. Riker, 1850), 52-54.

2 Agreement Between Nicholas Cooke and Silas Talbot, Sloop *Hawke*, 23 October 1778. B1 F3 STP.

3 Silas Talbot to General John Sullivan, 29 October 1778. PCC, M247, r 103, i78, vol. 22:605; Tuckerman, *Silas Talbot*, 52-61.

4 Accounts for *Hawke*. B1 F4 STP; JCC 12:1132; Henry Laurens to Silas Talbot, 17 November 1778, Papers of Henry Knox, MHS; and John R. Bartlett, ed., *Records of the Colony of Rhode Island and Providence Plantations in New England,* 10 vols. (Providence: A. Crawford Greene, 1862), 8:491.

5 Tuckerman, *Silas Talbot*, 65-66.

6 Gates had first been offered the command against the Iroquois. He declined and went to Rhode Island while Sullivan took his place in New York. Christopher Ward, *The War of the Revolution*, 2 vols., (New York: The Macmillan Company, 1952), 2:638.

7 Talbot's time as commander of *Argo* may be followed in the correspondence between him and Gates preserved in the Talbot Papers, RIHS. Similar material may be found in the Gates Papers at the NYHS.

8 Gates to Talbot, B1 F6 STP. In 1787 this area was set off from the town of Dartmouth to form New Bedford.

9 Instructions to Silas Talbot, December 1779. Talbot Papers, RIHS.

10 Testimony of Horatio Gates, 17 July 1783. Talbot Papers, RIHS; Samuel B. Webb to Jeremiah Wadsworth, 15 August 1779, W. C. Ford, ed., *Correspondence and Journals of Samuel B. Webb*, 3 vols. (New York: Wickersham Press, 1893), 3:356; Edgar Stanton Maclay, *A History of American Privateers* (New York: D. Appleton and Company, 1899), 91-112; and William James Morgan, *Captains to the Northward: New England Captains in the Continental Navy* (Barre, Vermont: Barre *Gazette*, 1959), 179.

11 Quoted in Maclay, *A History of American Privateers*, 107-8.

12 *Betsey's* long legal career may be followed in *The Resolution of the High Court of Errors and Appeals for the State of Pennsylvania in the case of Silas Talbot, Quitam, etc. Against the Commanders and Owners of the Brigs Achilles, Patty, and Hibernia*, 14 January 1785 (Philadelphia: T. Bradford, 1785); and *Judgments in the Admiralty of Pennsylvania in Four Suits Brought As For Maritime Hypothecations. Also the Case of Silas Talbot Against the Brigs Achilles, Patty and Hibernia And of the Owners of the Hibernia Against Their Captain John Angus. With an Appendix Containing the Testimony Exhibited in the Admiralty In Those Cases.* The Hon. Francis Hopkinson, Judge (Philadelphia: T. Dobson, 1789).

13 A letter-of-marque vessel was one whose

primary purpose was the carrying of cargo and passengers but which, if the situation permitted, was allowed to seize enemy vessels. This is in contrast to a privateer, a vessel commissioned to seek out enemy vessels. To what degree this fine legal distinction was important is unclear.

14 Talbot to Marchant, 11 November 1779. PCC, M247, r44, i3, 193.

15 JCC 15:1075; Henry Marchant to Horatio Gates, 27 September 1779, Edmund C. Burnett, ed., *Letters of the Members of the Continental Congress,* 8 vols. (Washington: Carnegie Institution, l921-36), 4:448-49; Navy Board of the Eastern Department to Marine Committee, 29 September 1779. PCC, M247, i37,145; and Marine Committee to Navy Board of the Eastern Department, 12 October 1779, PCC, M332.

16 Talbot Genealogy, typescript, NEHGS.

17 Bill, ll March 1780, B1 F8 STP.

18 Privateering Commission, 14 April 1780. Talbot Papers, RIHS.

19 Bond for the ship *General Washington.* PCC M247, i203, vol. 6:48.

20 Maclay, *History of American Privateers,* 111.

21 For a general description of the treatment of American naval prisoners in the Revolution see William M. Fowler, Jr.

Rebels Under Sail: The American Navy in the Revolution (New York: Charles Scribner's Sons, 1976), 256-6l.

22 Quoted in Danske Dandridge, *American Prisoners of the Revolution* (Charlottesville, Virginia: Michie Company, 1911), 252.

23 Silas Talbot to John Adams, 5 June 1781, Adams Papers, Letters Received, reel 355, MHS; John Adams to Silas Talbot, 5 June 1781, Adams Papers; and Silas Talbot to Elkanah Watson, 9 August 1781, Winslow Watson, ed., *Men and Times of the Revolution: Or Memoirs of Elkanah Watson ...* (New York: Dana and Company, l856), 137.

24 Providence *Gazette,* 28 November 1781.

25 JCC 21:1186-87. The issue of pay and pensions would bedevil the Continental and the Federal Congress for many years to come.

26 Robert Morris to Talbot, 3 September 1782, John Catazariti, ed., *The Papers of Robert Morris,* 7 vols., (Pittsburgh: University of Pittsburgh Press), 6:318; Ralph D. Paine, Joshua Barney, *A Forgotten Hero of Blue Water* (New York: Century, l924).

27 See PCC, M247 i149 i137 v. 2 for information regarding courts; Stephen T. Powers, *The Decline and Extinction of American Naval Power* (Ph.D. Dissertation, University of Notre Dame, 1965), 208-12.

JOHNSON HALL, WITH its two flanking stonehouses, was built in 1765 for Sir William Johnson as the seat of his holdings in the Mohawk River valley. At his death in 1774 it passed to his son, Sir John Johnson, a Tory who fled to Canada during the American Revolution. Confiscated by the State of New York when the war was over, it was bought by James Caldwell, an Albany merchant, then by Robert and Eleanor Johnson, and in 1786 by Silas Talbot.

(Courtesy of the New York State Historic Trust)

Chapter Four

Silas Talbot, Landed Gentleman

While the Revolution did not yield all that Silas Talbot might have wanted, it had defined and altered his life in ways that he could hardly have imagined. He was a hero, a soldier wounded at Mud Island, an officer who had fought bravely with Greene, Lafayette and Sullivan. He had been a privateersman and naval officer so successful at the game that when captured by the Royal Navy he was given special and cruel treatment. He had been a prisoner of war in New York and in Europe. He had been to England and France. He had corresponded with Adams and met with Franklin. He was a man with a reputation—a good one.

As his reputation had grown, so had his purse. For Silas Talbot the war had been profitable. Privateering had brought handsome returns he had invested wisely in Providence land, houses and wharves. And the war had sent him from the tiny world of Rhode Island out into a world of merchants, politicians, diplomats, generals and admirals. He had been to Boston, Paris and Philadelphia. He had met and been befriended by Adams and Franklin. He had conferred with Washington. He had talked as an equal with the men in the Congress and had sat as an officer in judgment of his peers. Providence could never contain him now. We see the new Silas Talbot in the portrait he commissioned from the well-known Philadelphia painter Robert Edge Pine. The painting, completed by Ralph Earle, shows a Lieutenant Colonel of the Continental Army in a tailored uniform of the sort that Talbot probably never even saw during the war. After the war, however, display was vitally important for Talbot and others establishing themselves in the new order. Talbot was also clear in his instructions to the painter that he be shown wearing the medal of the Society of the Cincinnati, an hereditary organization open only to officers who had served in the Continental Army. It was an unmistakable symbol of status in the new nation.[1]

Founded in May 1783 by General Henry Knox and other high-ranking officers of the Revolution, the Society had as its mission "to perpetuate as well the remembrance of this vast event, as the mutual friendships formed." These officers pledged "in the most solemn manner [to] associate, constitute and combine themselves into one Society of Friends, to endure so long as they shall endure, or any of their eldest male posterity." Although he had not been one of the founders, George Washington was persuaded by Knox to assume the presidency of the Society.

Nothing in post-revolutionary America so unnerved people as the Society of the Cincinnati. Its critics saw it as an elite military society with pretentions to an hereditary aristocracy. Franklin and both Adamses railed against the Society as inimical to the republican spirit of the Revolution. Talbot was anxious to join. To be listed in the company of George Washington, Henry Knox and Alexander Hamilton was a great social uplift. To be a member of the Society was to be among the best people, and that was precisely where Silas Talbot wished to be. His portrait shows us his ambition in the new world forming.

Talbot was quick to get back to business in the postwar world. In the fall of 1783 he bought the sloop *Peggy*, engaged Ezekiel Durphy as her master and sent her off on a voyage to North Carolina. *Peggy* and Durphy were to become frequent visitors to the Carolinas and Virginia. These southern ventures shipped out foodstuffs from Rhode Island's South County and Blackstone Valley, and brought back tobacco and rice for domestic consumption as well as for export.

This Virginia connection was enhanced about 1785 when Talbot's brother-in-law, Ebenezer Richmond, moved to Leesburg, Virginia, to set up a medical practice. From his vantage point in Virginia, Richmond kept Talbot informed of local land values, crops and land sales. What he heard from Virginia encouraged him to speculate. With Richmond as his agent and partner Talbot bought up discounted Virginia state notes, hoping to grab a profit as the Old Dominion paid off its debt.

Talbot saw opportunity in the south. Everywhere it seemed demand was growing for land, and the south had an endless supply. Richmond's letters from Leesburg told him this, and so did *Peggy*'s successful voyages in the tobacco trade. Rising demand for southern crops meant that more land had to be cleared and planted. This demanded more slaves, and so Silas Talbot bought a half interest in the slaver *Industry*, Captain Benjamin Hicks. Cyprian Sterry, a merchant of Providence, owned the other half. Rhode Island, and Newport in particular, had long been a center of this trade. Talbot, like most of his contemporaries, tolerated and indeed supported slavery as simply necessary. It was also profitable. By late 1785 *Industry* was off the Cormantyne coast buying slaves. She took nearly two hundred Africans on board and then managed to lose nearly half of them enroute home. Rarely philosophical or reflective about anything, Silas Talbot seems not to have concerned himself with the moral implications of the business, but this one voyage was his only venture in the African trade.[2]

Talbot's burst into trade grew directly out of his wartime experience. Through the endless and tiresome prize proceedings in Congress and court, as well as his incessant lobbying for rank and pay, Talbot had made contact with a variety of well-connected gentlemen and businessmen, lawyers and scalawags, all drawn into the wartime "sink" of Philadelphia. These gentlemen introduced him to new business possibilities, and they also introduced him to new social circles, not the most elite perhaps but far above what a former stonemason and sailor might have aspired to.

Postwar life was busy for Talbot, and it was fulfilling. Frequently he was off to Boston to sit once more on a court-martial board. The sessions were brief, the pay was good, Boston was pleasant and it gave Talbot an opportunity to be with his daughter Betsey. By all accounts she had grown into a lovely young lady. It is not altogether clear where she lived during the war years. She may have lived with the family on Weybosset Street or she may have remained with her uncle. Nonetheless, after Anna's death, and perhaps because of it, she seems to have drawn closer to her father. He doted upon her and brought her with him to Boston where she could find the latest finery which her father willingly bought for her.[3]

The boys, too, were doing well. On 7 April 1783, Talbot wrote across a page in his daybook, "George W. Talbot began to write." George was then seven, a bit old it would seem to be just beginning his letters. Both he and his older brother were being tutored in Providence by Nathan Dabell. In the spring of 1785, however, Cyrus, was sent off to Plainfield Academy in Plainfield, Connecticut, a small town located on the road between Providence and Hartford. Talbot was determined that his sons would have the education he never got.[4]

Although Talbot had every reason to be pleased with his success and what promised to be the success of his children, he was soon troubled by the economic unease of the new nation. Like all Americans, Rhode Islanders expected that peace would mean prosperity. They were disappointed. In the years immediately after the war the American Confederation suffered from the torment of adjusting to a new world outside the bounds of empire. Restrictions on credit, a surplus of paper money and a hostile international environment spelled trouble for America and for Rhode Island in particular. Heavily dependent on trade, and with very little hinterland to produce products for export, Rhode Islanders found themselves especially vunerable in the new economic order. During the heady days of the war these Rhode Islanders, Talbot included, had been quick to take on heavily inflated debt. As long as prices remained equally inflated one balanced the other. After the war prices collapsed while the debt obligations remained fixed at levels that suddenly seemed exorbitant.[5]

Talbot was caught in this trap. On paper he held considerable wealth, most of it in property and accounts receivable from his service during the war. Alas, the value of the former was falling while the latter promised to be a long time coming. Talbot had assets but little cash. He could, and often did, dun his debtors, but their situation was no different from his, and more often than not the return mail brought excuses for non-payment rather than payment.

On the other side of the ledger Talbot was a debtor himself. During the war it had not been uncommon for captains of privateering vessels to agree to act as their crew's agent for the purpose of selling prize goods and then distributing the proceeds among the men. It was equally common for a captain to actually buy a crewman's share at discount and then sell it for his own benefit. Sailors are impatient fellows, and a few shillings today were of greater moment than the promise of pounds tomorrow. As a commander Talbot was agent for his crews and often bought their shares. His crews, however, were not universally satisfied with the outcome, particularly those who sailed with him in the *Argo*.

Argo's accounts were confused. Crewmen claimed their captain had cheated them and taken their prize money. Talbot denied it, but lacking sufficient evidence he had difficulty proving his accusers wrong. Litigation followed, and this drew Lieutenant Colonel and Captain Talbot into a public brawl over the value of the prizes and the worth of his character.[6]

In the guerrilla war called politics in Rhode Island Silas Talbot was a natural target. Out of the state's economic woes two parties had emerged with dramatically different prescriptions for curing the state's malaise. One faction, the country party, sympathetic to debtors and inflationists, advocated issuing paper money. By increasing the volume of money in circulation they hoped to be able to discharge their obligations with a devalued currency. Their opponents, the mercantile creditor set, saw ruin in the notion of seeking economic salvation through the printing press. Although his roots were in rural poverty, Talbot was now a landowner, shipowner, merchant and creditor. He disdained those who advocated paper money. This position earned him powerful enemies, and in the *Argo* mess they found ammunition to fire at him. To discredit Talbot was to disgrace all those who held his views. With some clever work by his enemies Silas Talbot was made to appear a liar and exploiter of the poor.

Talbot and his friends never had a chance. There were too few of them and their politics were opposed by a vocal popular majority. So strong and united was the country party that nothing could stand in the way of its program of paper money and inflation. Creditors feared not only for their property but for their liberties as well, since there seemed to be no way to check the power of a faction not merely vocal but militant.

Talbot saw no way out. If he remained in Providence he was likely to be devoured by these wolves. If he fled their jurisdiction he might at least find personal peace and make it more difficult for his pursuers to find and torment him. But where to go? It was a question to be answered quickly, for if Talbot did not leave Rhode Island soon he stood to lose a great deal at the hands of enemies who controlled the state. One night, early in January 1786, Silas Talbot, quietly and unannounced, rode out of Providence. He left, he told his friends, "in consequence of a vile and wicked persecution."[7]

Talbot fled to Philadelphia where he had a number of friends and a great deal of unfinished business with the Congress. In March of the previous year Congress had seen fit to reverse itself and allow those officers who retired under the resolve of 31 December 1781 to receive commutation or half pay. Silas Talbot was among those made newly eligible. He was anxious to collect that debt as well as others still due from his service on court-martial boards. As soon as he arrived in the city he wasted no time in making the rounds.

For the time being Talbot knew he could not return to Providence. As his friend and Providence business partner Benjamin Bourne put it, the place was in "tumult." But even if the storm abated Talbot was unlikely to go home. Rhode Island was a little world that offered him no further opportunity. The longer he stayed in Philadelphia the more he came to realize that his future lay elsewhere. The question was where.

One possible answer was the west. Through his friend Bourne, Talbot had taken an interest in lands offered by the Ohio Company, and in the spring of 1786 he actually traveled to Ohio and Kentucky to see the lands for himself. He returned to Philadelphia with mixed emotions. Moving west had attractions for many but not for Silas Talbot. His children, all of whom he had left behind in Rhode Island, were young. To bring them west would mean delivering them to a howling wilderness away from proper social circles and the chance for a good education. Having come so far himself Talbot was determined to have his children advance ahead of him. There was also the matter of making a living. Although Talbot on occasion could fantasize, like many Americans of his time, about the virtues and rewards of working the land, the fact of the matter was that he knew nothing about farming. He had, in fact, left Dighton to escape rural poverty. The west offered a much vaster scale of agricultural opportunity than the Taunton River valley; nonetheless, it was not the kind of opportunity that attracted him. He instructed Bourne to sell his interest. Unfortunately, his orders to Bourne proved easier to give than to execute. Demand for western lands was falling.

In Philadelphia in the spring of 1786 Talbot caught up with news from Providence. None of it was good. As usual, the state was in economic and political turmoil, but that was of less concern to him than news of his children. Before he made his midnight ride out of town he had placed Elizabeth, George and Theodore in the care of Benoni Pearce. Cyrus was still at Plainfield Academy. In exchange for watching the three children, as well as managing some general business matters for the absent Talbot, Pearce had free board and room in the Talbot home. Apparently, Pearce found the arrangement unsatisfactory and with virtually no notice packed up and left. Fortunately for the children, Talbot's good friend and slave-trading partner

Cyprian Sterry came forward and placed the boys with their uncle William Richmond in Providence.[8]

Elizabeth, however, did not go with the boys. Talbot found her a more genteel, bookish and cultured environment at the home of Reverend Enos Hitchcock and his wife Achsah. Hitchcock had graduated from Harvard with the class of 1767 and had served with distinction as a chaplain during the war. He was with General Gates in 1777 and had been among those the General invited to witness Burgoyne's surrender. In 1783 he accepted a call to be minister to the First Church of Providence. Hitchcock and his wife had no children of their own. In Elizabeth, whom they came to love and admire, they found a daughter.[9]

For the time being Talbot was content with arrangements for Betsey. He sent her money, paid her expenses and was pleased at the letters she and her surrogate parents sent. They were full of newsy observations about relatives and neighbors. Elizabeth described her love of music, clothes and other feminine fancies. Mrs. Hitchcock was always lavish in her praise for Betsey. She thought, however, that this young girl belonged with her father. The Reverend praised her, too, but he had his concerns as well.

> *Eliza is fond enough of books, but needs directing to the*
> *choice of suitable ones—the trash of plays and novels, for*
> *which there is such a rage among young people, corrupts*
> *the taste, enlarges the imagination and prevents useful*
> *improvement. A well assorted collection from the best*
> *of poetry, of history and pieces moral and entertaining might*
> *afford food for the mind of a sentimentalist.*

The Reverend Hitchcock's concern for Betsey extended to other matters as well. He told Talbot that she must be protected from young men with good futures but no morals.[10]

As for his sons, particularly Cyrus and George Washington, Talbot was less at ease. Cyrus, according to Hitchcock, would "make a better farmer, mechanic or seaman than scholar." George, he reported "will make any thing to which he is trained." Theodore was yet too young to show promise in any direction. In casting about for their future Talbot had an intriguing idea. He thought his two oldest sons ought to become naval officers. Since the United States had no navy, this presented something of a problem. But there might be berths for his sons in the French Navy. To accomplish his mission he had to go to New York.

Talbot arrived in New York in late September 1786 and took up lodgings at the City Tavern. He had come to meet with John Jay, Congress's Secretary of Foreign Affairs. He and Jay were acquainted from the days of Mill Prison when Jay was the American representative at Madrid. Talbot had written to him, as he had written to so many others, seeking aid, and Jay had been generous in his response. Talbot was hopeful that he could turn to this New Yorker again, this time for help with his sons. Jay was agreeable, and shortly after meeting Talbot he wrote to the French chargé d'affaires, Louis Otto, asking that Cyrus and George Washington be appointed to the French Navy.

Otto saw no harm in the request. Granting it would please Jay, a person he was anxious to court, and it would serve the ends of enhancing the cordial relations between the two nations. He dutifully wrote to his superiors endorsing the request. When it reached the desk of the Minister of Marine at Versailles, Marquis de Castries, he too welcomed the idea and agreed to suspend the normal ordinances so that the two young men might be appointed as volunteers of the third class, roughly equivalent to midshipmen. He did this, he wrote, "on account of a particular regard for the friendly power whose subjects they are" and as a gesture of appreciation for Talbot's services in the war. It took some time to make the arrangements, but by the spring of 1787 Cyrus and George were on their way to France.[11]

Relieved that for the moment his sons and daughter were settled, Talbot took some time to look to his personal life. A widower for more than five years, he longed for the company of a woman. As was his wont he desired a wife to love, but it would not be inconvenient if she could bring him property and position as well. He returned to Philadelphia with someone in mind.

During his visit to Philadelphia in 1783, Talbot had been introduced to Rebecca Morris, the unmarried daughter of the prominent Quaker merchant Morris Morris. Her sister Sarah was married to Thomas Mifflin, a wealthy Philadelphian who had served in the Continental Army, became a Major General and served for a time as Quartermaster General. Mifflin was a calculating and clever man whose advancement owed as much to his political savvy as to talent. Talbot met him at a time when Mifflin was President of the Continental Congress, a position from which he could be of great help to a Lieutenant Colonel lobbying for additional pay and emoluments.

Mifflin was famous for his lavish lifestyle. He kept a grand home on the Schuylkill just outside Philadelphia and he loved to play host at his country house, the elegant "Angelica" in Reading. It seems likely that Talbot first met Rebecca at one of her brother-in-law's entertainments. Back in Philadelphia three years later Talbot renewed the acquaintance. Rebecca, or "Becky" as she preferred to be called, welcomed the attention of this handsome hero of the Revolution.

On the morning of 28 February 1787 Talbot sent a note to General Mifflin:[12]

> *It is with diffidence that I take up my pen to*
> *address you on a subject in which my future happiness*
> *depends. It is three years since I was highly honor'd*
> *with an Introduction to your Amiable Sister. At the*
> *interview I was sensibly delighted with her amiable*
> *Manners as well as the beauty of her mind - as the*
> *acquaintance has become more particular the impression,*
> *first made, has become more difficult to Erase, and*
> *I have reason to hope that my advances to Her would not*
> *be disagreeable should it meet your approbation. I am*
> *convinced of your kind attachment to her future*
> *happiness, as well as, her warmest gratitude to you as a*
> *brother and protector and altho my affections are fixed on*
> *the firm basis of mature deliberation yet I would not attempt*
> *a completion of my wishes without your approbation and*
> *that of your family.*

Mifflin told Talbot's messenger to wait. Within minutes he was on his way back to Talbot with an invitation from the General to join the family at lunch that afternoon. Mifflin promised Talbot that "We shall after Dinner have an opportunity of speaking without reserve or Interruption on the very interesting Subject of your letter this morning." Mifflin and Talbot did talk after dinner.[13]

Being a very practical man Mifflin undoubtedly quizzed the Colonel on his ability to care for his sister-in-law. Talbot had a good deal to offer. He would have told Mifflin that he had some small investments in trade, including the sloop *Peggy* and his ongoing Virginia investments. He owned real estate in Providence, and although his enemies were active against him there was no chance they could seize his Rhode Island property. He would also have noted his land speculations in the Ohio country and his intention to invest in eastern Kentucky where, as a result of his recent trip, he was negotiating to purchase nine large tracts of land from Gilbert Ismay. Most importantly, he and Mifflin would have discussed the Colonel's most recent and most significant acquisition—the former estate of Sir William Johnson in the Mohawk River valley of upstate New York.[14]

Born into a landed Anglo-Irish family in County Meath, Ireland, William Johnson came to the colonies in 1737 at the invitation of his uncle, Admiral Sir Peter Warren. Warren had invested heavily in frontier land in the Mohawk valley and was anxious to settle plantations in the region on the model used by the English in Ireland. Young, able, ambitious, and experienced in the English plantation system, at the age of 22 William Johnson was the perfect choice to manage his uncle's scheme. By 1738 Johnson had set himself up at a place near where the Schoharie River joins the Mohawk not far from Albany.

He was an extraordinary man. With his uncle's backing he established a trading post that did business with German Palatines and Iroquois. The Germans had been recruited by Warren and other speculators to settle and farm the valley. Johnson developed a close relationship with them. From his neighbor Alex Phillips he took on an indentured servant, Catherine Weisenberg, for £5. He and Catherine had several children, and while their baptisms are recorded the marriage is not. William Johnson always had a cavalier attitude about the institution of marriage.

Johnson's other customers, the Iroquois, were the most important and most feared Native American group in the Colonies. From their strategic location in the Mohawk valley they were able to dominate the fur trade and expertly play off the British in Albany against the French in Canada. William Johnson had a high regard for them, learned to speak their language, and by dealing fairly with this proud, powerful people earned their respect, so much so that within a few years he became the principal link between the Iroquois confederacy and the British authorities.

As Johnson's wealth and power grew he bought more land. Recognizing that south-sloping farmland had advantages over a northern exposure he moved his home across the Mohawk River and built Fort Johnson in present-day Amsterdam, New York. Here he lived the life of a feudal lord. He had his own fort, numerous retainers, tenants on the land and a number of offspring both white and half-Indian.

At the outbreak of the French and Indian War, many of the northern Indians allied themselves with the French. The Iroquois, thanks to Johnson's influence, remained with the British. In April 1755 General Edward Braddock directed Johnson to take charge of Indian affairs along the northern frontier. Shortly after, Johnson was commissioned a Major General and ordered to lead an attack against the French at Crown Point on Lake Champlain. Johnson failed to capture the fort but did manage to blunt a French invasion at Lake George, thus saving New York and New England from attack. His victory earned him a baronetcy from the King and the official title of Superintendent of Indian Affairs.

At the end of the war in 1763 Sir William Johnson was at the height of his power. He owned several hundred thousand acres of land. He was busy encouraging new settlers from Scotland and Ireland to take up farming in the valley, and on his own estate he was busy experimenting with new crops. Now that the war was over and the countryside was secure Johnson began to build a home more suited to his stature. In 1765 he commissioned Samuel Fuller, an engineer and architect, to prepare plans for the place he would name Johnson Hall. For his baronial home Johnson selected a hilltop site just west of Fort Johnson and about five miles north of the river.

It was a large, impressive residence with outbuildings, built in the Georgian style. Visitors entering the main door at the west end were ushered into a huge hall. It was here that Sir William greeted and hosted representatives from the Six Nations of the Iroquois confederacy, allies of the Crown. To each side of the main hall were smaller rooms for dining and socializing. The grand staircase sweeping up from the hall led to the family's private quarters on the upper floor. Outside the house and flanking it on the south and north sides were two stone blockhouses, places of refuge in case of attack.[15]

Sir William's home was the scene of a great gathering of chiefs in July of 1774. To the south on the Virginia frontier trouble had broken out. A series of incidents, including land-grabbing and murder, had stirred the Shawnee to attack local settlements. Fearful that the violence might move north, Johnson summoned the Iroquois chiefs to his home for a conference. While he was enjoining them to keep the peace Johnson suffered a stroke and died within a few days.

Sir John Johnson, Sir William's son by Catherine Weisenberg, inherited the title and lands. Within a year of moving into Johnson Hall the American Revolution erupted. Although he initially promised that he would remain neutral, Sir John fled to Canada and became one of the war's most famous and feared Tory leaders. Under his command Tories and Mohawks raided through the Schoharie and Mohawk valleys terrorizing the countryside. For his part in the war the state of New York confiscated the Johnson lands.

Although the Johnson holdings were broken up into several hundred parcels, (altogether the family had controlled more than 100,000 acres before the Revolution), approximately 700 acres remained attached to the great house in Johnstown. This was the property Talbot purchased for £2000 in July 1786. With this estate Silas Talbot was now a country gentleman in the style of General Mifflin himself. It was to Johnson Hall—which, despite a long succession of owners, has always been and continues to be known as Johnson Hall after its original owner—that Talbot offered to bring Becky should she and her brother-in-law consent to the marriage.[16]

Becky had much to offer to the union. Morris and Mifflin were among Philadelphia's best names. With Becky as his wife Talbot would be close to some of the young republic's most influential families. She also brought property and money. The family owned considerable real estate in Philadelphia and her personal estate of fine silver and furniture would go a long way to filling the vast empty spaces in Johnson Hall.

Mifflin might have hoped for a more advantageous marriage, both socially and financially, but Becky was 32 years old and there were few prospects on the horizon. He gave his consent, Becky concurred and the couple married in the spring of 1787. One problem did arise. Becky was a Quaker while Talbot was a Presbyterian. Because she married outside of the meeting Becky was dismissed. It was an action that seemed to distress neither her nor her brother-in-law.[17]

A few days after their marriage the Talbots were in New York City making preparations to send their furniture and other goods up the Hudson to Albany and thence overland to Johnson Hall. Talbot had already made arrangements for Cyrus and George, who were still waiting for passage to France, and young Theodore to come to New York to join him and his new wife. He also sent for Elizabeth. Early in June, after nearly a year and a half of separation, the family was reunited in their new home in the Mohawk valley.

For Becky it must have been a bittersweet time. Johnson Hall had all the appearances of Tintern Abbey, a hollow reminder of glories past. The house stood but had been ransacked during the war and the barns and blockhouses were crumbling. Talbot was confident that he could rebuild the structure, reinvigorate the lands and bring the estate back to its former glory. Becky was not so sure.

The family reunion was all too brief. In July it was time for Cyrus and George to leave on their journey to France. They bade farewell and made their way overland to Albany where they boarded a Hudson River sloop to take them down to New York where they met the packet for Le Havre. With the two oldest boys gone, the remaining Talbots settled into life at Johnson Hall.

The Mohawk River rises about 20 miles north of Rome, New York, and then runs approximately 150 miles south and east to join the Hudson just above Albany. It carves a lovely course through undulating hills and black-soil countryside. Unfortunately, this river that serves an agricultural paradise had little to offer as a means of transportation. The Mohawk River valley's transportation problems were solved by the Erie Canal system in the 1820s, but in Silas Talbot's time the river's shoals and rapids were no advantage to farmers and shippers. Travel down the valley was most often overland by wagon and in the winter by sleigh. Nonetheless, before the Erie Canal the Mohawk valley was the chief route between the Hudson River valley and the newly opened western lands. In the late 1780s, as more lands were made available in western New York, the road through the valley was busy with people driving their wagons on to what they hoped would be a better future in territory that was as much a frontier as Tennessee and Kentucky.

Talbot himself often entertained guests bound west. Elkanah Watson, his old friend from Providence, came to visit one summer. He was scouting new lands for investors back east. He and Talbot had a good deal to talk about. They reminisced about the past but most of their time focused on the future. These were years of great movement of families out of New England and into the new western lands. Talbot was among the first to make such a move and now his counsel was sought by others. Even the conservative Enos Hitchcock, who had no intention of leaving Providence, caught the fever and asked Talbot to suggest some "speculations." Some who could not afford to purchase land asked if they might come and work at Johnson Hall. He obliged, and on several occasions he counted among his hired hands men from Rhode Island.[18]

For those who had romantic notions about life in the wilds of New

York State, a visit with the Colonel must have been a sobering experience. Johnson Hall was a working farm and Talbot did a good deal of the work. Not since the days when he had been a deckhand on a coaster or a mason in Providence had he worked as hard. His old skills with stone and mortar came in handy for repairing walls and foundations. To help him out he had five hired men, two women and three of his own slaves in addition to a few tenants. Everyone, even young Theodore, pitched in. They planted wheat, rebuilt a small grist mill, and began orchards.[19]

The winter of 1787-88 passed without difficulty, although the new couple soon discovered that even an ordinary winter at Johnson Hall was far more severe than anything they had known before. As the snow drifted up around the northern sides of the house and barns Becky and Silas understood Sir William's wisdom in building his home on an east-west axis. In the unbelievable cold, at least there was morning and afternoon sunlight poking through the great windows in the front and back of the house. They would also have appreciated the diary entries kept by Sir William's brother Warren when he came to visit the Mohawk valley in the winter of 1760-61:[20]

> *It freezes so hard January the 11th, 1761, that Strong Punch in 20 minutes is covered with a Scum of Ice, and Ink on a Table is frozen before the fire, the wind being generally at N. West.*

> *There is about a foot of Snow on the ground all the Winter, back in the woods - about four feet; February generally is the Month of great Snow. To know whether Ice be Strong Enough to bear you, let fall an axe on it. And if it does not get to the Water you may safely venture on it.*

> *January the 13th, 1761.*
> *Weather so Excessive Cold that Madeira at 50 pounds English Pipe bottles in a room where a good fire is kept, is quite frozen; Lemon juice in large Bottles, 3 parts String frozen, Jamaica Rum alsoe quite frozen in a Room with fire in it and the Strongest Rum left out over Night is quite frozen in the Morning.*

> *January the 18th, 1761.*
> *The Snow 28 Inches deep, it is generally very dry.*

January the 23rd, 1761.
Extreme Cold and a very hard frost. If one walks two Miles in European Shoes and gloves, he is frostbitten.

January the 24th, 1761.
The Weather soe cold that handling Brass or Iron leaves Blisters on the Fingers; and in Bed people are cold even with 10 Blankets.

February the 24th, 1761.
Frost and very cold Weather, but Clear. Noe medium in this Climate, the Summers always Excessive hot, and the winters as Cold; the Latter End of September and the Month of October is the most Agreeable Time, being somewhat Temperate.

Spring announced better weather and promising crops to the Talbots. The news from Albany and New York City was encouraging as well. Demand for flour was high. The wheat market was rising. Talbot was in an optimistic mood when in May he received a letter from an old Rhode Island friend, Theodore Foster, for whom he had named his son.[21]

Foster was preparing a history of the Revolution and needed information from Talbot. The Colonel was more than happy to reply. He took the time to write a lengthy letter detailing his adventures during the Revolution and then went on to share a few observations about his life in the new republic. It was, he wrote, a welcome change to be at last settled with his family. Although Cyrus and George were away they had written to him and he was happy to report that both were well and enjoying service with the French. Becky, Betsey and Theodore were with him, he wrote, and concluded that "no man can be more domesticated than myself."

If Talbot had a problem, it was, he reported to Foster, that he worked too hard. Whatever illusions he entertained about being lord of the manor evaporated at Johnson Hall along with his own sweat. The house was large, the acreage vast, and the labor supply small. Everyone had to work. Talbot was exhausted but, as he told Foster, there could be no rest "as there is such a demand for service to put the farm in good condition."

After reciting his wartime exploits and his current situation to Foster, Talbot could not resist sharing some of his bitterness and disappointment. He had little love for the Congress.

> *No officer in the service of the United States served his country more with all his heart, with all his mind and strength, and notwithstanding I am graced in the annals of Congress in more special instances than any other officer in the American army, and my body remains loaded with lead received in action, yet, since peace has taken place not a single compliment has been paid me of an easy appointment under congress; how soon mortals forget their friends.*

That Talbot should be critical of Congress is hardly surprising. In this unhappiness he was joined by many former Continental officers who felt betrayed by an ungrateful nation and a niggardly Congress. Soldiers after war have always expected more than politicians have been willing or able to give. Talbot was no exception, and for him there was deeper bitterness. Colonel Silas Talbot, hero of the Revolution, had not merely been neglected by Congress, he had been unceremoniously driven from his Rhode Island home by radical elements let loose by the Revolution he had helped win. Even in his new home Talbot saw signs of unrest. During the winter of 1786-87 there came alarming news of disorder not far to the east of Johnson Hall. Pressed by debts and threatened by foreclosures, farmers in western Massachusetts were marching behind the leadership of Daniel Shays, a former Captain in the Continental Army, to close local courts to prevent legal action from being taken against them. This ragtag "army" demanded relief from debt and taxes. Having fought the Revolution to throw off repression, or so they thought, they now believed the government in Boston to be as insensitive to their needs as King George had been.

While the rebellion in Massachusetts was only a tremor, many of those in power perceived it as an earthquake in the making. If Shays and others like him were allowed to go unchecked, what could prevent them from overturning the new order, or at the least throwing it into chaos?

Silas Talbot, landed gentleman, had such fears, and he warmly endorsed the action of Governor James Bowdoin of Massachusetts when His Excellency raised the militia and sent Shays and his army of farmers scurrying. Nevertheless, he was still concerned. In Vermont, for example, he knew of the continuing unrest over land titles, and there were rumors of violence in New Hampshire as well. From his own unhappy experience in Rhode Island Talbot knew what might happen when the "lower orders" took control. Despite his poor beginnings, or perhaps because of them, Talbot had grown to have little faith in "the people." Along with many of his colleagues from the Revolution, he began to doubt that the states by themselves were capable of keeping good order. Their solution to the threat of chaos was a stronger central government, one less subject to popular pressure. Just such a solution was underway in Philadelphia during the summer of 1787 as delegates from 12 states met to discuss, and then draft, a constitution for the nation.

Talbot followed the proceedings in Philadelphia with great interest. Although the delegates were pledged to secrecy, word of their debates inevitably leaked out. Finally in early September Talbot and the rest of America read the results of the Philadelphia Convention. Talbot liked what he read.

What happened in Philadelphia set the stage for 13 dramas to be acted out in each of the states as their citizens debated the momentous issue of ratification. New York's approval of the Constitution was vital. There could be no federal union without it. Talbot watched with growing concern during the spring and summer of 1788 as the New York ratifying convention prepared to convene in Poughkeepsie.[22]

Debate over the Constitution in New York was furious. On one side were the Anti-Federalists led by Governor George Clinton. For nearly a decade Clinton had been the preeminent influence in New York, and his opposition to the Constitution boded ill. Clinton's opposition was in degree, not in kind. He and his followers did not necessarily oppose strengthening the central government, but they felt the current proposal went too far in surrendering the rights of the states and people and not far enough in protecting those rights. On the other side the Federalists, ably led by John Jay and Alexander Hamilton, argued in favor of ratification and dismissed the notion that the Constitution was a threat to liberty. Indeed, in their eyes, without the Constitution there would be no order, and liberty could only exist with order.

Talbot was a firm Federalist. Nonetheless, he needed to be careful. Johnstown and the surrounding Montgomery County countryside were decidedly Anti-Federalist territory. Farmers in the Mohawk valley were afraid of the Constitution and suspicious of those who supported it. They found much to worry about in the fact that the strongest advocates of ratification were among the greatest landowners, and their interests were not those of the smaller proprieters. The two groups were natural political enemies. As a landholder Talbot fell into a sort of middle ground. Although he owned a good deal of property it was not to be compared to the holdings of families such as the Livingstons and Schuylers. Furthermore, most of the great landowning families were old New York stock. Talbot was a newcomer and had none of their influence or prestige. Talbot's plan was to discreetly support ratification while at the same time tempering his vigor so as not to alienate his neighbors.

Straddling the fence did not prove to be easy. In March 1788 Talbot was a guest at the home of John Duncan in Albany. Also present was Robert Yates. He along with Alexander Hamiliton and Robert Lansing had represented New York at the Constitutional Convention. Yates had returned to New York before the final vote and was now lobbying against ratification. The discussion that evening was warm and focused on the question of whether or not the state convention could ratify the Constitution with conditions—conditions, of course, that the Antis hoped would weaken the document. According to rumors circulated about this meeting, apparently by Duncan himself, Talbot, perhaps after too much punch, proclaimed that "unless the people would receive [the Constitution] as it now stood it should be crammed down their throats," and that the power of the Society of the Cincinnati would help in the effort. Talbot may have held these views but it seems unlikely that he would have shared them with two such well-known Anti-Federalists as Yates and Duncan.[23]

By the time Talbot visited Albany again in June ratification was on everyone's mind. The New York convention had just gathered on the 17th in Poughkeepsie, and the whole town was buzzing with news, including the rumor about Talbot and his Constitutional opinions. The Colonel rushed to deny that he ever spoke such words. He was careful not to deny that these were his sentiments, only that these were not his words. Events in Poughkeepsie were meanwhile moving toward a reasonably amicable solution. Although they began the session in the minority the Federalists were emerging with a slight edge. They were helped by the fact that during the debates New Hampshire and Virginia both ratified. The new Federal Union was thus a near certainty, and New Yorkers understood the need to be aboard. On 26 July, by a narrow margin, 30 to 27, the convention supported ratification. They voted "in full confidence" that the other states would approve the amendments recommended by New York. It was not a conditional ratification, but it was certainly the next best thing.

Talbot's delight at New York's ratification was made even sweeter by news of ongoing bizarre behavior in the politics of Rhode Island. The radicals were still in power and were determined to keep Rhode Island out of the Union. "The ruling party," according to Enos Hitchcock, "are as usual ignorant stubborn & wicked to a most astonishing degree." The split was principally between the towns and the countryside. According to Talbot's informant, the crisis had grown to such an extent that the citizens of Providence, Newport and Bristol were contemplating a petition to the new federal government to take them under its protection. It took until May of 1790 for Rhode Island to ratify, and in the meantime politics in the tiny state remained hot and confused. Talbot was pleased to watch from a distance.[24]

There was other news from Providence as well. It had been nearly a year since Cyrus and George had left for France. The last Talbot knew of his boys was a letter they had sent in December reporting that they had landed safely at Brest and everything was going well. Early in the summer more news arrived. Cyrus wrote from Port-au-Prince, Hispaniola, to tell his father that the stay in Brest had been brief. They had been assigned to the 32-gun frigate *Fine* which sailed with the squadron on 4 January bound for Hispaniola. After a long and difficult voyage they arrived at Cap François on 25 March and then at Port-au-Prince on 7 April. The place, according to Cyrus, was dreadful. Nearly everyone was sick and many had died. If all went well his ship would remain on station until July and then sail north either to New York or Boston. The letter ended on a pitiful and reproachful note. Cyrus told his father "I write you this letter with tears in my eyes. What makes me most sorrowful is that I have not had one word from America since I have been in France." Cyrus also reported that neither had they received any money.[25]

Talbot knew nothing of his sons' problems until he received this letter from Port-au-Prince. Shortly afterwards more news arrived from Enos Hitchcock in Providence, telling him that his sons had been at his home for dinner. *Fine* had put in at Boston and the captain had given the boys a four-day leave. Talbot was unaware of their arrival until well after they had left. It was not a happy time for either father or sons. The boys complained to Hitchcock and their Uncle William Richmond that they had no money and that their father had never written to them. They also feared they were losing their language and fretted that if war came between France and he United States they would not know what to do.[26] Adding to their adolescent woes were conditions aboard ship. Rather mysteriously Cyrus referred to having been put "in the prison for Disobidunc." He also complained that the future looked bleak. "We are volunteers that can never Come more than a Ceckond left Tenant Cant never come to be Capt. of a frigate."[27]

Talbot offered no excuse for not writing—he had none to give—but in the matter of money he felt he had been used badly. He had sent funds. Through a friend in New York City he had forwarded several hundred dollars to an agent in France. Obviously it had not arrived. Talbot wrote first to Jay who then wrote to the American minister in Paris, Thomas Jefferson. Jefferson agreed to do what he could to supply the boys with cash, even if it meant paying out of his own pocket. For the time being at least Cyrus and George were supported through the largesse of some sympathetic French officials.

The boys' problems, however, did not end. Late in 1788 *Fine* anchored at Brest. The boys were put ashore to await assignment. It was, of course, the "worst of times." With a revolution in progress the French Navy had more to be concerned with than the fate of two young Americans. For the next year and a half Cyrus and George lived at Brest pretending to be gentlemen officers awaiting a new posting. Why they bothered to remain is something of a mystery. Finally in May of 1790 they received their discharges from the French Navy and took passage home.

By the time Cyrus and George were reunited with the family at Johnstown their father had taken steps to insure their future. George was thoroughly unfit to be a seaman. He had, however, shown some interest in business. Through John Blanchard, a New York City merchant, Talbot made arrangements for George to begin a three-year apprenticeship with Blanchard's firm. For Cyrus, on the other hand, who seemed to like the sea, and disliked anything that might keep him confined, his father found a berth on a vessel bound for St. Petersburg, Russia.

Talbot had also come to an important decision about his own career. Being lord of the land was one thing; working it was quite another. He had found farming neither profitable nor interesting. He was equally tired, and perhaps his Philadelphia-born wife was even more so, of living in the backwoods of the Mohawk valley. Frontier life did not suit her, and she may well have blamed the rough conditions at Johnson Hall for the death of her infant daughter Sally. Born in March, Sally struggled through the spring and summer and died in October. Early in the spring of 1791 Becky was pregnant again. In December Henry was born. She was determined that he would not be reared in the wilderness.[28]

Even before Henry's birth Talbot had begun to shift his investments away from Johnstown. In March 1789 he leased most of his land to Nathaniel Thompson and Joseph Bentley, keeping for himself only the manor house and barns. He took the lease money, along with some cash raised from the sale of property in Rhode Island, and invested in public securities. He bought obligations being offered by the new federal government. They were rising in value, a sure sign the new government was expected to succeed. Not only did Talbot invest his capital in the new government, he also decided that it might be just the place to find a new career. He wrote to his old Commander-in-Chief, now President Washington, as well as to his friend Henry Knox, the recently appointed Secretary of War, and argued that as a veteran of the Revolution and a staunch supporter of the federal government he deserved a post. Collector of Customs for New York perhaps?

Notes

1 Receipt dated 21 October 1785, B1 F14 STP. The painting presents a problem. Talbot was not elected to the Society of the Cincinnati until later. It seems likely that the medal was painted on the portrait at a later time.

2 Cyprian Sterry to Talbot, 25 August 1785, B1 F14 STP; Benjamin Hicks to Talbot, 19 January 1786, B1 F15 STP, and Murray, Mumford and Bowen to Talbot, 6 September 1786, B1 F17 STP.

3 Since the Talbot papers show no entries for any payments to anyone for Betsey's care it seems likely that she in fact lived with the family.

4 Receipted bill from Nathan Dabell, 1 November 1784, B1 F14 STP, and Cyrus Talbot to Talbot, 14 April 1785, B1 F13 STP.

5 For an analysis of Rhode Island's condition after the Revolution see Irwin H. Polishook, *Rhode Island and the Union* (Evanston, Illinois: Northwestern University Press, 1969) and William M. Fowler, Jr., *William Ellery: A Rhode Island Politico and Lord of Admiralty* (Metuchen, New Jersey: Scarecrow, 1973), 140-63.

6 Talbot's difficulties are well documented in the STP.

7 Clarke and Nightingale to Talbot, 13 February 1786, B1 F15 STP; Talbot to Christopher Champlin, 21 July 1786, Wetmore Collection, MHS.

8 Cyprian Sterry to Talbot, 19 June 1786, B1 F15 STP.

9 "Enos Hitchcock" in *Sibley's Harvard Graduates*, vol. 16, edited by Clifford K. Shipton (Cambridge: Harvard University Press, 1972), 16:475-84.

10 Enos Hitchcock to Talbot, 23 October 1786, B1 F17 STP.

11 Receipted bill for City Tavern, 9 October 1786 - 1 November 1786, B1 F17 STP; Otto to Jay, 3 November 1786, PCC, M40, 2:483.

12 Talbot to Mifflin, 28 February 1787, B2 F17 STP.

13 Mifflin to Talbot, 28 February 1787, B2 F17 STP.

14 In June 1787 Talbot purchased nine tracts of land in Nelson County, Kentucky, from Gilbert Ismay. Nelson County Kentucky Deed Book 1:96, Bardstown, Kentucky.

15 James Thomas Flexner, *Mohawk Baronet: Sir William Johnson of New York* (New York: Harper and Brothers, 1959) is the best biography of Sir William Johnson. See also Katherine M. Strobesk, "Sir William Johnson's Legacy," *Mohawk Valley Happenings* (Amsterdam: Montgomery County Historical Society, 1990), 20-21.

16 Talbot's deed for Johnson Hall is in B1 F15 STP.

17 *Encyclopedia of American Quaker Genealogy*, William Wade Hinshaw and Thomas Worth Marshall, compilers (Baltimore: Genealogical Publishing Company, 1991), 2:663.

18 Winslow Watson, ed., *Men and Times of the Revolution; Or Memoirs of Elkanah Watson Including Journals of Travel in Europe and America From 1777 to 1842*

(New York: Dana and Company, 1856), 268; for a general description of the Mohawk valley during this time see David M. Ellis, *Landlords and Farmers in the Hudson-Mohawk Region, 1790-1850* (Ithaca, New York: Cornell University Press, 1946), and *History of Montgomery and Fulton Counties, New York* (New York: F. W. Beers, 1878); Ephraim Bowen to Talbot, 29 September 1786, B1 F17 STP; Agreement between Talbot and Stephen Walker, 17 April 1787, B2 F2 STP; and Enos Hitchcock to Talbot, 2 July 1787, B2 F2 STP.

19 United States Census 1790, New York, Montgomery County, Caughnawaga Township.

20 Quoted in Strobeck, "Winter Along the Mohawk," *Mohawk Valley Happenings*, 51.

21 Talbot to Foster, 26 May 1788, Talbot Papers, RIHS.

22 For a complete discussion of ratification in New York see Linda Grant De Pauw, *The Eleventh Pillar: New York and the Federal Constitution* (Ithaca, New York: Cornell University Press, 1966) and Alfred Young, *The Democratic Republicans of New York* (Chapel Hill: University of North Carolina Press, 1967).

23 Talbot to Duncan, 29 June 1788, B2 F5 STP.

24 Hitchcock to Talbot, 29 April 1789, B2 F7 STP.

25 Cyrus Talbot to Talbot, 22 April 1788, B2 F4 STP; Talbot to Robert Morris, fall 1788, B2 F6 STP.

26 Cyrus Talbot to Talbot, 16 June 1788 B2 F5 STP; same 12 September 1788, B2 F6 STP.

27 Cyrus Talbot to Talbot, 12 September 1788, B2 F6 STP.

28 Carl Boyer, *Brown Families of Bristol County* (Newhall, California: C. Boyer, 1981), 138; Talbot to Knox, 31 January 1790, Knox Papers, MHS.

*S*ILAS TALBOT SPENT *the winter of
1792 in New York City as a state
legislator meeting and deliberating
with his colleagues at Federal Hall,
shown here at Wall and Broad Streets
in 1797. He returned to New York in
the summer of 1793 as a Captain in
the revitalized U.S. Navy, in general
charge of the construction of a new
frigate in the Theodore Cheeseman
shipyard between Pike and Rutgers
Streets on the East River.*

(The New York Public Library)

Chapter Five

Silas Talbot, Office Seeker

Talbot was anxious to shed the burdens of managing Johnson Hall, chief among them the fact that he had to live there. On the other hand, he was not eager to surrender the position and honor of being lord of the manor. Having become, at least in his own eyes, accomplished and polished, Talbot wanted more. Unfortunately "more" did not include a Customs post, for Washington declined to appoint him Collector at New York. Since no other "important appointments" seemed to be coming his way Talbot took a new tack. Another route to status in the new republic was elected office. By skillfully exploiting his fame as a war hero and his influence as a major landholder, Talbot won election in the fall of 1791 to be a representative from Montgomery County to the New York Assembly.[1]

The fact that the Assembly sat in New York City and met only during the winter months could not have been lost on either Becky or Silas. Here was a chance to do public duty and avoid the ordeal of winter in the Mohawk valley. Talbot brought Becky, one-year-old Henry, Elizabeth and Theodore to the city. Cyrus had left Johnson Hall and was on his way to Russia. George was already learning business in New York. All the family were pleased to be in the city.

Talbot's political debut came at a moment when politics in New York centered on Governor George Clinton.[2] Although Clinton is associated with the Jeffersonian Republicans, he defies careful definition. He was by no means a wild leveler. He held the rights of property owners to be sacred. He was, for example, quick to condemn the uprising led by Daniel Shays as "horrid and unnatural." Nor was he necessarily enraptured by Jefferson's romantic vision of an agrarian America. He saw the need for manufactures and supported some measures to encourage them. Clinton, however, was an anti-Federalist who feared the Constitution, and even after its adoption he remained suspicious of a strong and vigorous central government. Hand in hand with this view of limited government went a belief in low taxes.

Talbot and his constituents were certainly not opposed to low taxes; nevertheless, their expectations of what the state should be doing for them would cost money. As farmers they wanted roads and navigable waterways built and improved at the expense of the state. After all, their livelihoods depended upon convenient access to markets. Contention over this issue was complicated by an even more bitter fight over the distribution of the land itself. Under Clinton's leadership much of the New York land confiscated from the Tories had been sold in huge plots under arrangements very favorable to the buyers. Some of these deals, involving hundreds of thousands of acres, had a faint odor of corruption about them. During the summer of 1791 Talbot's old friend Elkanah Watson had written a two-part article attributed only to "A Northern Centinel" in which he roundly condemned the land sales. His critique was widely reprinted.[3]

When the Assembly convened in early January there were plans concocted by Talbot and others to use the land scandals to embarrass and weaken the governor. They planned to offer resolutions condemning the sales. At first the suggestion was put forward to have Philip Schuyler lead the attack. Wealthy, influential and widely connected (Alexander Hamilton was his son-in-law), Schuyler thought it best to remain in the background. As a huge landowner himself he was probably guilty of some of the same charges as those being aimed at Clinton and his associates. Someone blameless had to be found to lead the attack.[4]

Whether he volunteered or was solicited is uncertain. What is certain is that Talbot got the job. At that point in the session Talbot had been faithful in attendance and had spent his time on committees dealing with improving roads and rivers, matters close to the interests of his constituents. On 9 April he rose to move a series of 16 resolutions. The substance of the resolutions asserted that it had been the original intent of the legislature to insure a fair distribution of land and, although "fair" may not have been well defined, what the Clintonians had done was a far cry from any reasonable definition of the word. According to Talbot "extravagantly large tracts" had been sold to wealthy speculators, monopolizing land in a way that made purchase impossible for people of modest circumstances. Talbot spoke with passion, conviction and self-interest.[5]

The irony of Talbot's argument was not lost on the listeners. There sat Schuyler, one of the greatest landowners in the state, carefully listening to Talbot's argument. In the developing politics of the state and the new republic, Talbot and his allies were Federalists, men whose political inclinations were hardly democratic or egalitarian. In this instance they were up against the Clintonians, a faction normally identified with the democratic ideals of the Jeffersonian Republicans. It was a strange moment for both. The two sides found themselves at odds over an issue that, for the sake of consistency, each should have been arguing from the other side.

Consistency is not necessarily a virtue in politics, and in the debates of 9 and 10 April 1792, neither side seemed particularly concerned about it. In fact, one of Talbot's resolutions proposed the maximum sale to be 25,000 acres, an entire township. That was hardly a small plot of land. In reality, since both sides enjoyed support from large speculators, the point of these resolutions was less to reform the system and more to embarrass Clinton. In that Talbot and his party failed. On 10 April, by a vote of 35 to 20, a resolution was moved and adopted that praised the work of the government. Talbot's resolutions were dead.[6]

Although the cause was lost there were some rewards for Silas Talbot. Having led the fight, he had established some valuable friendships, Schuyler's among them, and he had shown himself to be a reliable fellow. That may well have been his chief goal, for even as he was arguing in the New York legislature he had already set his eyes on a higher prize—a seat in the United States Congress. To achieve that goal he would need the help of his friends.

Among his friends no one was more important to Talbot than his new son-in-law George Metcalfe. He and Betsey had married on 5 March 1791 in the Presbyterian Church at Johnstown. Born in 1764 in Middlesex, England, Metcalfe landed in America in 1781, probably at New York City, then under occupation by British forces. Following the peace he remained in New York, studied law, and finally settled in Albany where he met the Talbots. Metcalfe handled a variety of legal and business matters for Talbot, and kept him informed about local affairs during his frequent absences. Late in 1791, shortly before he left to attend a session of the General Assembly, Talbot asked Metcalfe to inquire around about his chances of being elected to Congress. In particular Talbot instructed Metcalfe to visit with his most likely opponent, Judge William Cooper of Cooperstown.[7]

Cooper and Talbot were much alike. Nearly the same age (Talbot was only three years older), they both came from poor rural families. Neither had much in the way of formal education, and both were artisans. Cooper was a wheelwright. Ambition drove both men along like paths. Cooper married well (Elizabeth Fenimore), moved into town (Burlington, New Jersey) and bought property. Unlike Talbot, however, Cooper did not serve in the Revolution. After the war he engaged in land speculation, and along with some partners bought extensive property in Otsego County, New York, which had been seized from Tory estates. In 1787 Cooper moved to those lands and founded Cooperstown at the southern tip of Lake Otsego. Like Talbot, Cooper counted himself a Federalist.[8]

Electioneering in the early republic, particularly along the frontier, was rough, rowdy and corrupt. Cooper and Talbot both knew how to play this ungentlemanly game, and the battle between them for New York's northern congressional seat was tumultuous. One of Cooper's constituents, James Moore, described the sort of intimidation that was an accepted part of the process. He said that when he came to the polling place Judge Cooper was already there. According to Moore, as he came forward to complete his ballot Cooper pressed an already completed ballot into Moore's hand. To Cooper's dismay Moore refused to cast it and insisted that he make his own choice. Cooper, who was not accustomed to such impertinence, grabbed the ballot back, denounced Moore as a "fool" and then stomped away in a funk.[9]

Late January 1793 was set as the election time, and so the campaign heated up during the cold months of December and January. For the Federalists the prospects were alarming, for they were, ironically, cursed with two strong candidates, Talbot and Cooper. By splitting the Federalist vote they could well fell each other, leaving their enemy Sheriff John Winn standing.

Cooper's strength was an extensive network of friends and business associates linked via land speculation. The "Judge" could be ruthless when necessary, ready to do almost anything to insure the right election results. In this election he faced a formidable challenge, for he was up against an adversary with one of the most powerful political weapons any candidate can possess—an outstanding war record. With the aid of a liberal budget for food and drink, Talbot's supporters gathered crowds at nearly every public house in the district and there recited their candidate's brave deeds. General Horatio Gates, the victor of Saratoga whose reputation was high in those parts, had written a glorious testimonial to Talbot's exploits that the Colonel had used years before to extract his pension from the Congress. That document was recalled to duty and circulated throughout the district.

In addition to his reputation as a war hero Talbot enjoyed another advantage, this one based on demographics. He was, like his neighbors, a New Englander resettled in the west. In the period following the Revolution hundreds of land-hungry New Englanders, many from Connecticut and Rhode Island, had settled in the valley of the Mohawk. Talbot was a politician with whom his neighbors felt an identity. Talbot was also close to the Dutch families of the region. Here he owed a great debt to the support of Jeremiah Van Rensselaer, whose name alone gave credibility to Talbot's candidacy.[10]

The Clintonians were not without plans for the election. Talbot and Cooper were bound to split much of the vote. If the Clintonians could unite behind a single candidate they might well carry the election. That indeed was Metcalfe's own prediction when late in December he estimated that Sheriff Winn, the Clintonian candidate, would take the seat despite the fact that more Federalist votes—that is, votes for both Cooper and Talbot—would be cast than votes for Winn.[11]

Since the political issues were murky, as were party affiliations themselves (even the use of the word "party" might be questioned), serious debate among the candidates was virtually nonexistent. Not missing, however, was political slander. Winn, for example, circulated a rumor that Talbot was preparing to leave New York and take up residence in Philadelphia. Another rumor also flew around that Rebecca Talbot was a "Negro wench."[12]

On election day sleighs were sent into the countryside to bring supporters to the polls. At the voting places men gathered to encourage their neighbors to cast the right vote and to insure a "fair"—that is, favorable—count for their own candidate. Talbot's district was enormous. It covered a large portion of central New York State, encompassing the counties of Montgomery, Otsego, Tioga, Herkimer and Ontario. At the several polling places in each county voters presented themselves to a board of inspectors to cast ballots. The boards, composed of the local township assessor, supervisor and clerk, accepted the ballot and deposited it in a sealed box. Ballots were not standardized. Voters were provided ballots with the name of their candidate either written or printed on it. The law required that the ballot be "folded or rolled up and tied, or otherwise closed," to conceal the writing. Since ballots were not standardized, however, the very shape or color of the paper might tell observers for whom the vote was being cast. It was not unknown for inspectors to challenge a voter if it appeared that his vote was not the desired shape or color. At Cooperstown, where Judge Cooper ruled, voters were not allowed to enter the building where the inspectors sat. Instead, they were required to pass their ballots through an open window to the inspectors inside. This procedure, admittedly unusual, seems not to have been unique. Reports of fraud abounded throughout the district. Indeed, even by the loose standards of New York politics, the election was particularly venal.[13]

Voting at the local polls took place over a period of five days, after which the boxes were sealed and sent on to the legislature for a final count. In the final tally Talbot received 1209 votes, Cooper 961, and Winn 838. The vote did produce some oddities. In Otsego County, for example, Cooper's home county, Talbot got 14 votes to Cooper's 790. In Montgomery, Talbot's seat of strength, Cooper received 15 votes to 694 for Talbot. It is an open question whether these figures reflect an extraordinary degree of loyalty to favorite sons or some imaginative vote counting.[14]

Talbot could take little comfort from his victory. Metcalfe told him bluntly that in his opinion the election was a fluke. Already the Clintonians were rallying, and with their man in the Governor's office they had the unbeatable advantage of patronage to carry them forward. Talbot had won, according to Metcalfe, because of his record as a war hero and because the Clintonians were caught napping. In the next election, according to his son-in-law's somber assessment, his luck would not hold.[15]

Metcalfe's blunt assessment set Talbot to thinking. If being a congressman from upstate New York meant living in upstate New York—and what else could it mean?—then he was tired of it and would never have any desire to seek reelection. Clearly, the single most critical item on Talbot's congressional agenda was getting a job in the new government. Congress was the perfect spot from which to go hunting.

Meanwhile, on 28 February 1793 the Joint Committee of the Senate and Assembly of New York informed Silas Talbot that he had been elected from the congressional district composed of the counties of Montgomery, Otsego, Tioga, Herkimer and Ontario. Official news of his election was delivered to Talbot in New York City where he was sitting in the sixteenth session of the Assembly. This body adjourned on 12 March, and a few days later Talbot boarded a sloop bound up to Albany and thence overland to Johnstown.[16]

Affairs at Johnson Hall were in a mess. Winn's rumor that Talbot had plans to leave Johnstown were not without foundation. Talbot arrived home to the disturbing news that some of his speculations, particularly in western lands, had soured. He needed cash. His most valuable and marketable asset was the land around Johnson Hall. The lease arrangement with Thompson and Bentley was due to expire. But renewing these leases would not answer Talbot's cash needs, so in January 1792 he quietly sold most of the land, keeping the Hall for himself and his family, to Obadiah Bowen, the son of his old Providence friend and business partner, Jabez Bowen. It is unlikely that Bowen had an agricultural interest in the land. He was speculating, and apparently doing so without much capital. Shortly after taking out a mortgage with Silas Talbot, Bowen announced he could not pay.[17]

Bowen's predicament put Talbot in a tough position. He needed the money, but dunning the impecunious Bowen was clearly not the answer. Bowen had no money. Talbot offered a solution. He asked Bowen to give him power of attorney to sell or lease the farm on his behalf. Bowen agreed, and within a few days Talbot had arranged a fourteen-month lease with a neighbor, Nathan Miles.[18]

Obadiah Bowen's problems did not end here. In the summer of 1792 he went to Europe to straighten out his foreign accounts. Enroute a fierce summer storm wrecked the ship and Obadiah perished. His father, full of grief, asked Talbot if under the circumstances he would take the mortgage back. Bowen told him that his son's accounts were hopelessly muddled and that there were so many claims on the estate that fulfilling the terms of this mortgage was impossible. Talbot was not swayed. He refused to take back the mortgage, and indicated that he was ready to move in court against the estate. Only at Bowen's pleading, and in callous recognition that there was precious little in the estate to take in any case, did Talbot back off. In the meantime, however, Bowen agreed to advertise the estate in Providence while Talbot sought a buyer in Albany and New York City. In the meantime Talbot had to be content to collect rent from Nathan Miles.[19]

On 2 December 1793, the first session of the Third Congress convened at Congress Hall in Philadelphia. Becky had come down with her husband

and they were living with her sister Susan until they could find appropriate accommodations of their own. She was delighted to be back home and wasted little time greeting old friends and moving into the social whirl of the city. As for her husband, although he always enjoyed good society, for the time being he was preoccupied with matters of state.

No one doubted that Silas Talbot was a good Federalist. Indeed, he hardly ever wandered from the course set by leaders of the party such as Alexander Hamilton and Fisher Ames. In matters of foreign affairs, despite his former admiration for the French, he was now decidedly anti-French and pro-British. The violent and radical turn of events in Paris frightened him as it did conservatives everywhere. On 21 January the revolutionary government executed Louis XVI and his queen. A few days later republican France declared war against Britain, Holland and Spain. Reverberations from these acts swept across the Atlantic. Within America and within the Congress, Talbot saw pro-French forces at work which he believed were determined to rekindle the return of war between the fledgling American republic and Great Britain. Such an event, in his judgment, would "plunge this Country into all the Horrors of a war to assist France an event that could not fail to involve this infant country in difficulties incomprehensible and perhaps end in the loss of our freedom and independence." Talbot was not alone in his concerns, and three days after Congress convened Washington laid a message before them concerning the war in Europe.[20]

The outbreak of a major European war had grave consequences for the United States. From the moment the news arrived in the spring until Congress convened in December, the administration spent time and energy trying to remain neutral in an extremely polarized world.[21] It was not easy. Washington proclaimed neutrality, but mere words were thin armor in the face of determined belligerents. The new French minister to the United States, Edmond Charles Genet, heightened tension with a series of very provocative acts, including arming French ships in American ports, meddling in domestic politics and signing up soldiers for filibustering expeditions against neighboring Spanish and British territory.

Exasperated with the French, Washington fared little better with the British. As soon as the war had begun the French government threw open its previously closed West Indies trade to all comers, and American ship owners rushed to pick up their share of the lucrative business. Flying a neutral flag, Americans were doing for the French what Britain's navy had made it impossible for the French to do for themselves. This subterfuge had a short life. Through a series of Orders in Council (June and November 1793, January 1794) the British plugged this loophole by unilaterally invoking the Rule of 1756, which stated that trade illegal in peace may not be made legal in war. Armed with this declaration, the Royal Navy quickly swept up Americans carrying French goods, confiscating vessels and cargoes.

While Talbot and his colleagues struggled to cope with bad news from the West Indies and Europe, more woes arrived from North Africa. For centuries the Moslem states of Morocco, Algiers, Tunis and Tripoli had sent ships into the Mediterranean and out into the neighboring Atlantic to prey on merchant shipping. These Barbary States, a name taken from the Berber tribes that inhabited part of their territory, were ostensibly vassals of the Sultan of Turkey. In fact, however, they operated independently. They viewed the western Mediterranean as their private preserve, and those wishing to sail it had to either fight or negotiate and pay. The latter was the preferred remedy; most of the European powers found it cheaper to talk and pay tribute than to go to the trouble and expense of sending naval squadrons.

Although the Barbary corsairs had attacked American ships after the Revolution, their depredations had been curtailed by the Portuguese. Portugal had been at war with Algiers, and as part of her strategy the Portuguese Navy had sealed the Straits of Gibraltar and kept the corsairs out of the Atlantic. Thanks to the efforts of the British, in the fall of 1793 Algiers and Portugal concluded a truce. The Portuguese lifted their blockade and once again the Algerine corsairs prowled the Atlantic trade routes. Within a span of a few weeks, eleven American vessels were taken. More than one hundred seamen were prisoners, and marine insurance rates that had been running at 10 percent shot up to 30.

David Humphreys, the American agent who had been trying to negotiate with the Algerines, reported to President Washington that "a naval force has now (to a certain degree), become indispensable."[22] Washington was receptive, and so were the Federalist members of the Third Congress. Alexander White, a former Federalist congressman from Virginia, summed up his party's expectations when he wrote to his old friend James Madison that the mood created by news of war and piracy from abroad would make it easier to create a strong defense. In these threatening times the citizenry would be far more willing to support "regulations and burdens to which they would not submit until the danger became imminent."[23]

White was prescient. The first session of the Third Congress enacted a host of military and naval measures designed to defend the new republic. They authorized arsenals and magazines as well as fortifications to protect harbors. The regular army was expanded and state militia were brought under closer regulation. Talbot supported all these measures enthusiastically.

If confined to the land, however, this martial spirit would do nothing to address the dangers posed by the Barbary pirates. On 2 January 1794, after secretly debating the Barbary menace, the House voted up three resolutions. The first resolution increased appropriations for diplomatic expenses. This was a gesture of peace; but, lest there be any misunderstanding about the mood of the nation, the next two resolutions were more warlike. The House resolved to build a naval force adequate to protect American commerce from the North African menace and to appoint a committee to examine the "ways and means" to accomplish the task. At last, Talbot thought, the nation was bound on the right course. It was a course he understood, and one that might bring a new role for a former officer.

The news that Congress might establish a new navy spread quickly. Job-seekers were alerted, and in little more than a week Talbot got his first letter from a former shipmate seeking a commission in the yet-to-be-established federal navy. The inquiry came from Hoysteed Hacker, a Rhode Islander and former officer in the Continental Navy. Talbot saved Hacker's letter, but if a new navy were launched, and if billets became available, Talbot was determined to look first to his own career, and only secondarily to his friends'.[24]

Debate over the creation of a navy engrossed the Congress from the middle of January through the first half of March in 1794. Support for the navy was strongest in the north and along the coast, areas where maritime commerce played an important economic role. From a geographic perspective Talbot's fierce support might seem to place him at odds with his inland constituency. On the other hand, the wheat farmers of the Mohawk valley were aware that the price of their crop depended upon a strong overseas market that could best be reached across peaceful and protected sea routes.

A few days into the debate Talbot and his wife were invited to dine with the President. Although neither party has left a record of the dinner-table conversation, there can be little doubt that talk of a new navy was part of it. Under the Constitution, Article II Section 2, it was the President, as Commander-in-Chief, who appointed naval and military officers. Perhaps Washington inquired if Congressman Talbot might be interested in taking on a post in the new navy. If the President asked such a question we can be certain of Talbot's response.

After some narrow escapes, the final bill authorizing the purchase or construction of six frigates passed the House by a vote of 50 to 39 and became law on 27 March. Passage, however, had come only after some compromise. In its preamble, for example, the bill stated, "Whereas, the depredations committed by the Algerine corsairs on the commerce of the United States, render it necessary that a naval force should be provided for its protection..." This was a clear indication that Congress had in mind only a temporary force. Even more indicative of the will of the body was section 9, tacked on at the very end: "if a peace shall take place between the United States and the Regency of Algiers, that no farther proceedings be had under this act."

In one important respect the law was vague, for it did not specify how the President was to fashion his fleet. He was authorized "to provide, by purchase or otherwise," four 44-gun frigates and two 36-gun frigates. The quickest way to "provide" such vessels was to buy them outright, as had been done so often in the Revolution. Although Washington was charged with this decision, the man with the real responsibility was Henry Knox, Secretary of War. Knox was not a navy man, his principal experience afloat having occurred on that memorable evening when he led Washington's artillery across the Delaware River to attack the Hessians at Trenton. Nevertheless, for some time he had been in consultation with experts in these matters, including former Captain in the Continental Navy John Barry and the well-known Philadelphia shipbuilder Joshua Humphreys. Their advice, added to his own concerns, created, in Knox's words, "an anxious solicitude that this second commencement of a navy for the United States should be worthy of the national character. That the vessels should combine such qualities of strength, durability, swiftness of sailing, and force, as to render them equal, if not superior, to any frigates belonging to any of the European powers." The Revolutionary experience had shown that first-class warships were built, not bought or converted from lubberly merchant vessels. After the decision to build, there remained vexing questions. Who would design them? Where would they be built? Who would build them?[25]

For the first question the answer was obvious: Joshua Humphreys, by common consent America's best and most experienced designer. Because of a delay in appropriations, Humphreys' actual appointment as naval constructor did not come until late in June. While Humphreys is ordinarily given credit for the design of the new frigates, another designer also played a role: Josiah Fox. Fox was an English Quaker who arrived in America in 1793. In April 1794, when Fox was about to return home, Knox summoned him and asked him to stay to help with the new ships. Fox agreed, but since the billet for constructor had already been filled by Humphreys, and there was no post for an assistant, he was given the rather common title of clerk in the War Department. Within a year he was promoted to the rank of assistant naval constructor and sent off to Norfolk to supervise the construction of a 44-gun frigate. The credit for the design of the frigates ought to be shared between these two men, but in what proportion will always remain clouded.[26]

The debate over where to build these vessels excited the twin forces of patriotism and cupidity all along the coast. Both the British example and the Revolutionary experience showed that major shipbuilding benefited from concentration. Building vessels in as few locations as possible simplified control and eased logistics; however, not since the days when the Continental Congress launched its first shipbuilding program had spoils on such a grand scale been available. Politics and economics mitigated against good naval policy. As a result, Knox decided to build the six frigates at six different locations: forty-fours at Boston, New York, Philadelphia and Norfolk; thirty-sixes at Baltimore and Portsmouth, New Hampshire. So that he might better control the enterprise, the secretary also determined that the building would not be done by private contract but by agents employed by his department to supervise construction. Since the government owned no yards, the building would be contracted to private builders, but only under the careful scrutiny of the agent, who would secure supplies, disburse wages, and provide general supervision. For this the agent was paid a commission of 2½ percent. In addition, at each building location Knox engaged a superintendent, a naval constructor and a clerk of the yard. The superintendent had general charge of the project, and the constructor was responsible for day-to-day work in the yard and maintaining the vessel's specifications. The clerk was involved with the daily maintenance of records and accounting for public property. There must have been a fair amount of overlap and perhaps even conflict among these men—but that suited Knox, for in this way they provided a check on one another.

Without question the most sensitive issue was who would command. The President and Secretary did not lack for candidates. Men such as Talbot's friend Hacker had already begun their lobbying campaigns. And so had Congressman Silas Talbot. Quite aside from his war record Talbot had some other advantages over his rivals for command. He was a sitting Congressman, a faithful Federalist and a friend to both Knox and Washington. Never happy as either a farmer or legislator, Talbot saw at last a chance to return to the scene of his glory days, on the quarterdeck of a warship.

Talbot's lobbying efforts paid off. Early in June Washington made his decision, and at his instruction on 5 June Knox wrote to the lucky six men that "The President of the United States, by and with the advice and consent of the Senate, has appointed you to be a Captain." In order of seniority they were: John Barry, Samuel Nicholson, Silas Talbot, Joshua Barney, Richard Dale and Thomas Truxtun.[27]

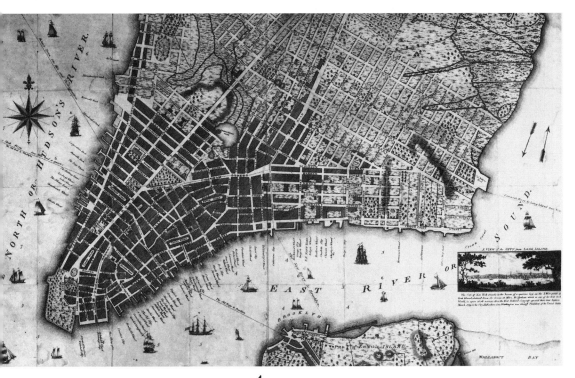

*A*BOVE ARE THE *narrow streets and waterfront of New York in 1796. At that time the shipyards were on the East River at approximately the center of this image.*

(*The New York Public Library*)

All of the captains had served in the Revolution, as either officers in the Continental Navy or as privateersmen; fitness for command played no role. No one disputed "Gallant" John Barry's position at the top of the list. At 50 he was a bit ancient for the strenuous business at hand; nevertheless, this Philadelphian had distinguished himself in the Revolution and no one dared gainsay him. Samuel Nicholson's rank was accepted as well, despite the fact that his wartime record was thoroughly undistinguished. Washington and Knox might well have grimaced at appointing such a well-known mediocrity, but political realities left no choice. Nicholson stood at the head of a powerful political clan of Marylanders.

While the first two rankings provoked no open dissent, Talbot's appointment as number three did cause some grumbling. No one questioned Talbot's heroic exploits in the Revolution; what they did point out was that he performed them as either an army officer or a privateersman. To be sure, he held a commission as a Captain in the Continental Navy that was dated 19 September 1779, but he had never sailed in command of a Continental vessel. Furthermore, whenever he had asked for recognition either with a pension or land grants after the war was over, he had always sought the benefit in recognition of his rank and service as Lieutenant Colonel, not Captain.

Not surprisingly, the man who felt most aggrieved at Talbot's third ranking was the Captain who ranked fourth—Joshua Barney. Barney had been commissioned a Lieutenant in the Continental Navy, and although he had technically never risen above that rank he had, in fact, commanded the Continental ship *General Washington*, as Talbot had good reason to recall, and was referred to in that capacity as Captain. Accordingly, he informed Knox that he and not Talbot deserved to be number three. A small matter, perhaps, but not to naval officers who all subscribed to John Paul Jones's dictum that "Rank opens the door to glory." When Knox refused to alter the rankings Barney refused the commission and went off in a huff to serve in the French Navy. To replace him, Knox added James Sever as number six, a man described as having "not much experience ... but he is supposed to possess all the requisites to form a very good Officer." Fifth on the original list (now fourth as each moved up to replace Barney) was Richard Dale, who had served on board *Bonhomme Richard* during her famous battle with *Serapis*. The last man on the list was Thomas Truxtun, a well-known privateersman of the Revolution who hailed from Long Island.

Talbot was overjoyed. He was even more pleased when informed that his command would be the forty-four building at New York. He wasted no time. On 9 June, the same day that the first session of the Third Congress adjourned, he officially accepted the appointment and on the 13th he resigned his seat in the House and made plans to return to New York. Becky scurried about seeing to the movement of furniture and other belongings, to say nothing of getting her sons Henry and Theodore organized (Cyrus and George were in New York and pretty much on their own). Before he left Philadelphia Captain Talbot visited a bookstore. It had been more than a decade since he had been to sea and he needed some refreshing. He came home with copies of *Falconer's Marine Dictionary, The Shipbuilder's Assistant, Naval Tactics, Moore's Navigation,* and *The Seaman's Assistant.*[28]

Notes

1   Edgar A. Werner, *Civil List and Constitutional History of the Colony and State of New York* (Albany: Weed, Parsons & Co., 1888), 368.

2   For a full discussion of New York politics during this era see Alfred F. Young, *The Democratic Republicans of New York* (Chapel Hill: University of North Carolina Press, 1967).

3   Albany *Register*, 27 June 1791.

4   Young, *Democratic Republicans*, 295. For a discussion of the land speculation see Thomas C. Cochran, *New York in the Confederation: An Economic Study* (Philadelphia: University of Pennsylvania Press, 1932), 105, and E. Wilder Spaulding, *New York in the Critical Period, 1783-1789* (Port Washington, New York: Ira J. Friedman, 1963, repr.), 54-55.

5   *Journal of the House of Assembly of the State of New York, Fourteenth Session* (New York: Printed by Francis Childs and John Swaine, 1792), 9 April, 1792, 199.

6   *Journal*, 203.

7   George Metcalfe to Silas Talbot, B2 F15 STP; the most incisive analysis of election practices in upstate New York may be found in an essay scheduled to be published in the *Journal of American History*, Alan Taylor, "'The Art of Hook and Snivey': Political Culture in Upstate New York During the 1790s."

8   Ralph Birdsall, *The Story of Cooperstown* (Cooperstown, New York: The Arthur H. Crist Company, 1917).

9   *Journal of the House*, Sixteenth Session, 193.

10 David Paul Davenport, "The Yankee Settlement of New York, 1783-1820," *Genealogical Journal* 17 (1988/89): 65.

11 George Metcalfe to Silas Talbot, 26 December 1792, B2 F15 STP.

12 Henry Cook to Silas Talbot, 30 March 1793, B3 F2 STP.

13 I am indebted to Alan Taylor's soon-to-be-published article for this description of the polling place. Metcalfe to Silas Talbot, 27 January 1793, B3 F1 STP.

14 Young, *The Democratic Republicans*, 592.

15 Metcalfe to Talbot, 2 February 1793, B3 F1 STP. Metcalfe's assessment proved to be inaccurate; in subsequent elections Federalists continued to carry this seat.

16 David Rye et al. Joint Committee of Senate and Assembly of New York to Silas Talbot, 28 February 1793, B3 F1 STP. *Journal of the House*, Sixteenth Session.

17 Deed 3 January 1792, B1 F13 STP; Obadiah Bowen to Silas Talbot, 22 May 1792, B2 F14 STP; and Silas Talbot to Jabez Bowen, 22 December 1793, B3 F2 STP.

18 Obadiah Bowen to Silas Talbot, 13 March 1793, B3 F2 STP.

19 Jabez Bowen to Silas Talbot, 12 November 1793, B3 F2 STP; ST to Jabez Bowen, 22 December 1793, B3 F2, STP; Silas Talbot to Jabez Bowen, 20 February 1794, B3 F3 STP; Jabez Bowen to Silas Talbot, 17 March 1794, B3 F3 STP.

20 Draft of a letter written by Silas Talbot on back of letter received from Elkanah

Watson dated 29 January 1794, B3 F3 STP.

21 The following sections rely heavily upon my previous work, *Jack Tars and Commodores: The American Navy, 1783-1815* (Boston: Houghton Mifflin, 1984), 15-33.

22 Quoted in Marshall Smelser, *Congress Founds the Navy* (South Bend, Indiana: University of Notre Dame Press, 1959), 51.

23 Quoted in Smelser, *Congress Founds the Navy*, 59.

24 Hoysteed Hacker to Silas Talbot, 11 January 1794, B3 F3 STP.

25 *American State Papers, Documents, Legislative and Executive of the Congress of the United States: Naval Affairs* (Washington: Gales and Seaton, 1832-61), 1:6.

26 William M. Fowler, Jr., "America's Super Frigates," *Mariner's Mirror*, 59 (1973), 49-56.

27 Henry Knox to Silas Talbot, 5 June 1794, B3 F4 STP.

28 Talbot's resignation produced a minor storm in New York politics. As governor Clinton had the authority to appoint a successor for Talbot; however, he delayed acting and for nearly a year the people of Talbot's district went without a representative in Congress; receipted bill dated 12 June 1794, B3 F4 STP.

*S*HOWN HERE IS *the building of the 36-gun frigate at Philadelphia, a project that proceeded with more material and better luck than Silas Talbot's frigate at New York. The original plan called for four 44-gun frigates and two 36-gun frigates. By 1801 three 44s and five 36s had been launched. Both* Philadelphia, *shown here, and* New York *were 36s.*

(Courtesy of the Free Library of Philadelphia)

Chapter Six

Sojourn in the West Indies

As the Talbots rode north across New Jersey, the new Captain had much to occupy his mind. Quite aside from his new responsibilities in the navy Talbot was deeply concerned about his oldest son. Of all his children Cyrus was most like his father, a rough-and-ready seaman, a man not much suited for or interested in schooling but always eager for adventure. Talbot knew his son well, and he had arranged for him to ship as a foremast hand on a voyage from New York to St. Petersburg, Russia. It was an experience Cyrus would never forget.[1]

The fo'c'sle world is a singular place. Formed by the ship's hull into a triangular shape, stacked with bunks, littered with sea chests and inhabited by Neptune's orphans, it can be for the uninitiated a perfect bedlam. Cyrus bunked with his mates and shared their mess, but he never made it into their society. Like Melville's Redburn, he was the son of a gentleman. He was better, he thought, than those around him. Although forced to live in their world Cyrus was not inclined to share their company. When the ship arrived in port Cyrus refused to go ashore with his shipmates. As they left the ship to frolic in the town and come back with their pockets empty, they accused him of being "two fond of /his/ money." Ignorant of his own arrogance, he despised these men and wrote whining letters home complaining of mistreatment. Despite his unwinning ways with the crew Cyrus showed himself to be a capable seaman and impressed the vessel's owners and officers.

Competence had resulted in promotion such that Mr. Barrett, the owner for whom Cyrus had been sailing, offered him command of a 260-ton ship. Cyrus was ecstatic.[2]

Alas, his hopes were to be dashed back in New York after the St. Petersburg voyage. Having offered the young man command Barrett came about and withdrew the offer in a manner so abrupt as to be humiliating. Young Talbot was devastated. Barrett, when pressed by Cyrus to explain, apparently told him that he was unqualified for command and then, adding insult to injury, offered him a berth as mate in the same vessel. "Deranged," Talbot flew from the ship and that night ended up in the apartment of a friend, a Mr. Mitchell. The next morning Mitchell wrote a hasty and worried letter to Silas Talbot. He told him that he had kept Cyrus[3]

> *in my apartment all night and rendered him every assistance that could possibly be afforded. He slept tolerably well the latter part of the night and this morning seemed more composed. He went to his vessel and committed some irregularities not common which has proved to every one that he is not himself. He returned to my quarters and appears worse than ever. He cries and laughs alternately, rails against his relatives in a most bitter manner. God knows what may be in the wind....*

Suicide was in the wind. The attempt failed and a Doctor was called. As was common, he prescribed bleeding, but Cyrus would have none of it. Mitchell thought a trip into the countryside might be helpful.[4] Silas Talbot, who was still in Philadelphia during this episode, was naturally distraught. His anguish grew to anger when Mitchell told him that Barrett had dismissed Cyrus out of a wicked desire for vengeance on his father. According to Mitchell, Barrett was a Tory scoundrel who fired Cyrus, son of a hero of the Revolution, so that he might give command of the ship to a "friend of George the Third."[5]

Within a few days the father was in New York City with his son. For the next year Cyrus fades from the scene. It is likely that Talbot, who still had some time before beginning work on his frigate, brought his son with him up to Johnson Hall to join the rest of his family and friends. Wherever he went, Cyrus was back in New York the following spring. Recovered from his breakdown, he borrowed £2000 from his father and invested the money in a trading voyage to France. He sailed as Captain.[6]

Almost as soon as the Talbots alighted at Johnson Hall they were joined there by an unhappy Jabez Bowen. Having failed either to sell the estate from Providence or persuade Talbot to take back the mortgage, Bowen was there to plead with Talbot in person. Bowen's situation was desperate. On all sides he was being dunned by his son's creditors. He desperately needed to be rid of the Johnson Hall mortgage. Would Talbot please take back the mortgage? The answer was no. Furthermore, he told Bowen that he was tired of being importuned. His own financial situation was such that he could not take back the mortgage. He needed cash.

Another solution apparently suggested itself in the course of this refusal. Perhaps, he told Bowen, there was a way out. Abraham Morehouse of Alexandria, Virginia, had shown some modest interest in the estate. Talbot thought he might be persuaded to make an offer but not to Bowen. Morehouse was Talbot's friend and would only buy the estate from Talbot. Bowen was perplexed. If there were a buyer he wanted the sale and the profit. Talbot was insistent. He would only take back the mortgage if Morehouse agreed in advance to buy from him. Bowen was angry. He suspected some kind of double game. What was to prevent the Colonel from taking the mortgage and then selling the farm at a profit, leaving Bowen to sputter? Whatever his emotions told him about such a deal, his best option might be to let Talbot have the mortgage, make the sale and just be done with it. Talbot knew that his chum was in a corner and he was prepared to take full advantage. Bowen left Johnson Hall having grudgingly given the nod to Talbot's scheme.[7]

Summer life at Johnson Hall was leisurely and pleasant. With the exception of George, who was down in the city, Talbot had all his children with him, including Betsey. Her husband George had so endeared himself to his father-in-law by his successful management of the congressional campaign that Talbot was now depending upon him more and more to manage all his upstate business affairs. Indeed, with the farm leased and Metcalfe handling most of the day-to-day affairs, Silas Talbot was bored. He had some small diversion when the township asked him to oversee some road and bridge construction, and he welcomed a request from Alexander Hamilton's able assistant Tench Coxe to provide information about local iron founding. But family, roads and inquiries notwithstanding, Silas Talbot was anxious to get on with the business of building a frigate.[8]

No one in the new American government, least of all Henry Knox, had ever undertaken shipbuilding on the scale now proposed. Had these vessels been conventional frigates the task would have been trying; however, by the naval standards of the time these were "super frigates." Intended to be bigger and more powerful than any other vessels of their class, they were an eighteenth-century precursor of the famous pocket battleships of the Second World War. Building ships of this magnitude would have challenged any naval establishment.

From the outset Washington and Knox decided that the construction of these ships would be undertaken with public supervision. Agents responsible to the Secretary would oversee construction. Chief among these, of course, were the Captains themselves, who were designated as superintendents with overall responsibility for moving these projects along. They were charged to send weekly written reports to the Secretary detailing progress on their vessel. To assist them the Secretary appointed two additional supervisors. The naval constructor was the boss of the yard. He employed the men and saw that the work was accomplished in accordance with the specifications sent by the Secretary. The third person appointed was the agent. While most of the major contracting for supplies was handled by the Secretary's office, each yard did have some responsibility and discretion for local procurement. This was the task of the agent. There was also a clerk appointed to keep records.

The superintendent (Captain) was in overall command. However, since both the naval constructor and local agent owed their appointments to the Secretary, each enjoyed a special relationship with him and never hesitated to communicate directly with his office on a variety of topics. As a practical matter then, at each building site there were three men who served as checks upon one another. For the work to proceed successfully it was vital that the superintendent, constructor and agent be willing partners.

Talbot was lucky. The agent and constructor assigned to the New York frigate were men of ability, integrity and conviviality. The agent was John Blagge, a respectable New York merchant, reliable Federalist and Alexander Hamilton's friend. The constructor was Foreman Cheeseman. His father Theodore was a highly regarded shipbuilder, and the son showed every sign of following in his footsteps.[9]

Appointing captains, agents and constructors took most of the summer of 1794, but by early August Knox was ready to get building. On 8 August he ordered Talbot to "immediately repair to the City of New York for the purpose of superintending the construction of the Ship to be built at that place and to concert everything with the Agent Mr. John Blagge." Having spent the summer waiting for this order, Talbot was ready to go. Within a few days he was enroute down river.[10]

Since it was August Talbot decided to go alone leaving Becky and the children to finish the summer in the more comfortable surroundings of Johnson Hall. New York City had a well-deserved reputation for being a miserable summer habitation. The heat and humidity were discomforts, but worse was the threat of yellow fever. New York was no stranger to the disease, and the summer of 1794 saw a virulent visitation.

Talbot took rooms at Anne Banecker's on Pearl Street. Once settled, he made straight for the Cheeseman yard between Pike and Rutgers Streets. At the yard he met Cheeseman and Blagge. These men, all three prominent New York Federalists, were known to each other, and so the preliminaries were undoubtedly brief. They understood their duties and were ready to get underway. Talbot hired Daniel Tingley to be his clerk and ordered a storehouse to be erected in the yard in preparation for the arrival of large quantities of timber.

Not everything went well. First there was the problem of finding good workmen. With the Royal Navy having driven the King's enemies from the seas the demand for neutral carriers was skyrocketing. Cargoes which had once filled the holds of Spanish and French ships were now being stowed and carried in American bottoms. Shipyards and owners in New York and elsewhere were paying good wages to men who could build and sail ships. Talbot was drawing from the same well and having difficulty.

Workmen were not the only resource he found in short supply. He needed timber, and he especially needed live oak. In ordinary circumstances, the average lifespan for a wooden ship was between ten and twelve years. Constant exposure to wind and water, drying and wetting, caused rot, and even in well-maintained ships wooden spars and hulls would eventually suffer fatal damage. Such deterioration was impossible to prevent and could only be delayed by good maintenance and the use of superior materials. Humphreys and a few of the new captains made their choice of materials clear. The frigates ought to be built "of the most durable wood in the world"—live oak.[11]

Live oak (*Quercus virginiana*) is a semi-evergreen found along the American coast from Virginia to Texas. It grows to a fairly large size—forty to seventy feet high and upwards of twenty feet in girth—and like the white oak, another shipbuilding tree, it divides into large branches that often take on tortured shapes. These limbs, with their curious curves, are made to order for the ribs, knees and other frame pieces of wooden ships. The most attractive attribute of this wood is its extraordinary hardness and durability. Its advocates predicted confidently that if live oak were used it "would be a great saving to the United States, as we are well satisfied (accidents excepted) that they (the frigates) will be perfectly sound a half century hence, and it is very possible they may continue for a much longer period."[12] Drawbacks to live oak were the considerable distances between the trees and the yards, and the difficulty of harvesting them. Stands of live oak were hundreds of miles from the shipyards and in locations where cutting was anything but pleasant. Getting to them in the swamps where they grew was arduous and dangerous. Snakes, alligators and disease were the live oak's close neighbors. Once at the site workmen found their tools inadequate and quickly dulled by the tough wood. To complicate matters further Knox decided that to save bulk, and therefore shipment costs, the timbers would be rough-hewn to desired shapes at the point of cutting. In the southern coastal regions where the trees grew, the only men available were unskilled farm laborers, most of them black slaves. Skilled workmen had to be sent south from the yards.

Early in June, Coxe ordered John T. Morgan, a master builder from Boston, to take charge in Charleston and Savannah. A few days later Coxe wrote to Jedediah Huntington, Collector of Customs at New London, and ordered him to hire 60 skilled cutters to assist Morgan in felling and hewing the live oak. Coxe thought the best men for the job could be found on the coasts of Connecticut and Rhode Island as well as in New Bedford and Dighton. Coxe's specific mention of Dighton may have been a recommendation from Talbot.

For Morgan and his men the work was misery. On 30 August he wrote to Humphreys, "I have not seen 10 fair days since I left you.... The whole country is almost under water and if the rains continue it will be impossible almost to get the timber for where the live Oak grows is all low Land and Swampy in a dry time, but there never was so much rain known in this Country."[13] Months later, December 1794, when Morgan was finally able to ship timber, the situation for him and his men had only grown worse. On 18 December he wrote to Captain John Barry:[14]

Comodor Sir in your Leter from Savanah you promised me that you would
see that I should Com from heair But I now begin to think that I shall be
planted hearir the feveuorer has fel in to all my Lims and I can not walk
you will see by the Leters to Mr. Cox What a State the Bisness is in all the
fin oxen that you Brought is dead Save 4 - and have not been abel to
haul a Long stick this month till with in a fue days past for god Sack
dont send more.

Morgan was obviously not a very literate man; his letter to Joshua
Humphreys must have been written, or re-written, by a more skillful pen.

In accepting the advice of Humphreys and others to build "superior
frigates," Knox demonstrated the unnerving tendency of bureaucrats to listen to experts, whose advice is never disinterested. By insisting that live oak
be used Knox introduced problems that caused construction to be stretched
out for years. At the same time the costs were more than doubled. No one,
then or now, debates the sturdiness of live oak; nonetheless, these frigates
could certainly have been built faster and cheaper had more available materials been used.

Talbot quickly came to understand the problems visited upon him by
the Secretary's policies. Week after week in his reports to Knox he announced
that the timber had not yet arrived. It had been his hope, as well as
Cheeseman's, that by the first of the year the keel and frames would be in
place. But with each passing day, and no timber, achieving that goal grew
more unlikely.

In November Becky joined her husband and they moved into a rent-
ed house on Pearl Street not far from the yard. Little Harry was the only one
who came with her. Theodore was in Schnectady studying with John Taylor,
who was preparing him for entrance into college at Princeton. Before marrying Becky, Talbot had never thought much about sending his children to college. Cyrus, of course, was not interested in school work, and George, while
a bit more intellectually talented, had never been encouraged toward education beyond the academy level. Experience via a good apprenticeship was
the path his father had chosen for him. He would likely have pushed
Theodore and Henry in the same direction had Becky not changed his
mind.[15]

Rebecca Morris Talbot understood that, quite aside from any other
merits a college education might confer, the social benefits were consider-

able. Talbot came from nothing. She did not. She had every intention of maintaining her status and that of her children. Talbot, whose own social ambitions were unquenchable, needed little persuasion from his wife that the two younger sons ought to go to college.

With Becky and little Harry with him at Pearl Street, Silas Talbot had agreeable company, but the days dragged along. Without timber there was little to do in the yard. He went down there each day, surveyed the work, what little there was, checked the records and prepared his reports for Knox. Not until December did the first shipment of live oak go north from Georgia, and that went to the yard in Philadelphia. In January, frustrated and anxious over the lack of progress, Talbot reported to Knox that although he had been able to lay a keel it sat on the ways in four separate pieces held together loosely by clamps since the iron drift bolts had yet to arrive. Through the winter the story remained the same—no timber. Having gone to great difficulty recruiting men Talbot now found himself in the embarrassing situation of being forced to let them go.[16]

It was a glum winter for the Captain. Becky was ill and missed Philadelphia. She had few friends in New York, and the city's social circles were notoriously snobbish. As for her husband it seemed to him that his frigate would never be launched and that he would never get to command at sea.

On the private side Talbot was still bedeviled by the financial mess left behind by the unlucky Obadiah Bowen. In January, however, the mortgage problem began to be solved. Alexander Morehouse had taken the bait. He and his wife were interested in purchasing Johnson Hall, but only on the condition, according to Talbot, that it be from Talbot and from no one else. Talbot wrote to Bowen reminding him of their summer conversation on this matter. Bowen's memory needed no jogging. While not entirely pleased at being excluded from the deal, to say nothing of the profit, he was relieved to be throwing off this albatross. With no commentary or complaint he returned the deed to Talbot with the full understanding that Talbot would sell to Morehouse. On 29 January Talbot took back the deed and paid Bowen a symbolic ten shillings. One month later Morehouse purchased the property from Talbot for £5000. At long last Talbot was rid of the house and farm, and at the same time he had gained a tidy profit.

The new year of 1795 brought a new Secretary of War, Timothy Pickering. In reviewing the lack of progress on the frigates he concluded that the whole business of building with live oak had been a mistake. No matter, the work had commenced and it was up to him to finish it. However, with complaints about shortages of materials and reports of skyrocketing costs flooding into his office, the new Secretary concluded that completing six frigates was out of the question. Pickering, on his own authority, decided that for the time being work would continue on only two frigates in the hope that they at least could be launched.[17]

Talbot's frigate was not among the blessed. Ironically, it made very little difference, for in the coming months none of the frigates advanced to any great degree. Dutifully each week Talbot made his report to the Secretary on a project now in greater uncertainty all the time. It was all depressingly predictable—materials not yet arrived, progress slow. A shipment of live oak arrived in the spring, and this brought some life to the Cheeseman yard. But summer brought a near halt to live-oak cutting in the pestilential swamps of the south, and once again shipments ceased.

Lack of material was not the only difficulty for Talbot and his frigate that summer. As had been so often the case before, yellow fever swept into New York with the warm weather. For a time Talbot tried to keep his crews at work, but the men were frightened, and finally Cheeseman ordered the yard closed early in September. When the yard reopened a few weeks later there was a whisper of hope, for word arrived of a large shipment of live oak coming from Georgia. Then disaster struck. Hit by a sudden gale, the schooner full of shipbuilding wood was wrecked on Cape Hatteras.[18]

On 12 December 1795, Secretary Pickering, on the orders of the President, forwarded a report to the Senate "of the progress in providing materials for the frigates, and in building them." Nowhere was the news good. None of the yards—Norfolk, Baltimore, Philadelphia, New York, Boston or Portsmouth—could provide much in the way of encouragement. Pickering's plan of concentration had proved futile; all the frigates were hopelessly behind schedule. At New York, however, the news was the worst. Talbot's frigate had made the least progress and was farthest from completion.[19]

In the fall Talbot went in person to Philadelphia and met with his counterparts John Barry and Thomas Truxtun. They discussed the problems of building and speculated a bit on the dimensions proposed for the masts and yards, although all had serious doubts that their ships would ever see such finishing touches. Had Talbot and his brother officers known what was underway in the Mediterranean, they would have been even more convinced that the vessels would never get their bottoms wet.

Although he brandished the trident by building frigates, Washington had not neglected more peaceful means to settle the nation's dispute with the North Africans. American diplomats had been hard at work in the Mediterranean world and their efforts were bearing fruit. In his annual message to the Congress on 8 December the President himself alluded to the promise of a "speedy peace," and the capital was filled with rumors of treaties at hand. Indeed, on the same day that Pickering was delivering his glum assessment on the status of the frigates, a truce with the United States was signed by "Hadge Ally Vikel, Charge des Affaires and agent for the Regency of Algiers and Tunis." Three months later Washington announced the good news to the Congress.[20]

Triumph on the diplomatic front was not good news for the navy. The ninth and last section of the Naval Act of 1794 provided that "if a peace shall take place between the United States and the Regency of Algiers, that no farther proceeding be had under this act." If taken literally (how else could it be interpreted?) construction work on the frigates should halt immediately.

The Federalists had no intention of abandoning their naval enterprise; nonetheless, they were sage enough to recognize political reality. The whole program, six frigates, could not be salvaged, and indeed strong suggestions were being made to abandon the construction completely. To prevent such a thing Washington on 15 March wrote the Senate and House to ask their advice. He warned them that a complete abandonment would derange the "whole system" and ill serve the public interest. Washington's ploy excited a good deal of debate, and after no small amount of political maneuvering a compromise was reached. Congress authorized the completion of three frigates, two forty-fours and one thirty-six. Which to complete was left to the judgment of the President and Secretary.[21]

Talbot knew that his frigate was doomed for the time being. He had been given a hint of that when he had written the Secretary to inform him that his clerk Daniel Tingley had died and to ask authorization to appoint a successor. With unwonted speed Talbot was told four days later that under the circumstances the Secretary preferred not to make any new appointments in New York. One month later the official word arrived. Blagge was instructed to close down the yard. Talbot was ordered to make a complete inventory of stores and if possible prepare to ship materials to the other yards at Philadelphia, Baltimore and Boston where construction was to continue. As for the Captain himself, the Secretary was vague. He was left a Captain without a ship, but a Captain nonetheless.[22]

Although Talbot kept his rank he did not keep his pay. Once his accounts were settled his salary stopped. For Silas Talbot this was no small matter. As usual he was land rich and cash poor. He frankly needed money even more since Theodore, having done well at school in Schnectady, was now enrolled at Princeton. Tuition was a financial burden, and so was Theodore's lifestyle. Always an indulgent father, Talbot had trouble saying no. To support his own style of urban living, as well as those of his children, Silas Talbot needed employment. And he needed something appropriate to a person of his rising station.[23]

In May, while Talbot was still closing out business at the shipyard, a worthy position sailed into view —Agent for Impressed Seamen. Impressment was a rough-and-ready form of selective service long practiced by the Royal Navy. In wartime the King's navy had a nearly insatiable hunger for men. Warships are huge consumers of manpower. In peacetime when a good portion of the fleet was laid up in ordinary, volunteers were sufficient to fill the crew list. In wartime, however, when large numbers of vessels were brought into service, the demand for men far exceeded the supply of volunteers. Such was the case after 1793 when England and France went to war.[24]

Even in peacetime, service in His Majesty's fleet did not offer many attractions. Harsh discipline, low pay, long periods away from home, and the ever-present spectre of death or injury from combat, disease or accident kept seamen away from the navy in droves. The same rotten conditions of service enticed those already on board to desert, a practice which in wartime reached near-epidemic proportions. The only way to keep the King's ships at sea was to maintain the ranks by the detested custom of impressment.

There was no quicker way to empty a waterfront tavern or brothel than the cry "press gang!" Nor was there anything to make a merchant sailor more nervous at sea than to have his vessel ordered to heave to and prepare to receive a press gang from one of His Majesty's warships. Had the British confined this practice to their own shores and ships it would have been bad enough, but the desperate need for men, and the well-known fact that many British deserters were serving aboard American merchantmen, caused officers of the Royal Navy to feel justified in stopping, searching and removing any men they considered to be British subjects. Even those who could produce naturalization papers were not safe. His Majesty's government held to the doctrine of indelible allegiance—that is, once an Englishman, always an Englishman.

No one is certain how many American seamen may have been impressed into British service in the 1790s; nonetheless, by early 1796 the fact that any American citizen had been so mistreated caused a rising public demand for action. Since the Congress had already partially aborted the navy, the use of force was out of the question. Diplomacy was the only answer.

In March a Committee of the House, on which Talbot's Rhode Island friend Benjamin Bourne served, brought in a bill "For the Relief and Protection of American Seamen." By the provisions of this act the President was to appoint two or more agents, one of whom was to reside in Great Britain and the other anywhere the President thought best (by common consent this was the West Indies). These agents were charged to inquire into any allegations of impressment of American citizens and were to secure their release by any legal means. Each agent was to receive a generous $15,000 per year for salary and expenses.[25]

In addition to appointing agents the act also sought to solve a nagging problem related to impressment. American seamen born on these shores had no means to prove their citizenship. Henceforth, seamen might present themselves to the local collector of customs, public notary or U.S. Consul in a foreign port, establish their citizenship and then receive a protection certificate. This document, signed by the appropriate authority, certified that the bearer (a physical description of the person was part of the certificate) was an American citizen. The hope was that a seaman threatened with impressment might simply produce this document to prove his citizenship and thereby escape service in the Royal Navy. In a cruel reversal of intent the act had a very unpleasant result because so few American seamen went to the trouble to obtain certificates. This failure to procure certificates proved a great convenience to British officers who took the position that if a man did not have a certificate he might be judged not to be an American citizen and thereby liable to seizure.[26] Even having a certificate was no solution, since so many counterfeits were in circulation. The mere possession of a protection certificate, according to the British, proved nothing since there was a good chance it was fake.

The law was enacted on 28 May 1796. On 3 June Timothy Pickering,

Secretary of State, to whom the agents reported, informed Silas Talbot that he had been nominated for the post of Agent for Impressed Seamen in the West Indies. Colonel John Trumbull of Connecticut was appointed to serve as agent in London. The very next day Pickering, who because of the sudden resignation of Edmund Randolph was simultaneously serving as Secretary of State and War, wrote to Talbot in his latter capacity to inform him that, as of 30 June, because he no longer had a ship, his pay as Captain would cease. Pickering's one-two blow pushed Talbot to a quick answer. Not wanting to miss a payday he readily accepted the post in the West Indies. Two days later he was having dinner with Pickering and the President as they described his new duties to him.[27]

The President and his dinner guests could not have been oblivious to the irony, and perhaps the appropriateness, of Talbot's new post. There was precious little difference between the treatment meted out to prisoners of war and the Royal Navy experience of impressed seamen except that prisoners would probably be flogged less often. Talbot knew first-hand what it was like to be at the tender mercies of the Royal Navy. This man who had earned his fame fighting the British was now called upon to negotiate with them about the conditions of men for whom he felt a special closeness. During the conversation both the President and the Secretary made it clear that they wanted Talbot on station as quickly as possible.

As Becky read her husband's instructions sadness welled up. The West Indies were an inhospitable place, full of war, disease and endless heat. It was no place for Harry, nor was it a place she wished to live. Furthermore, Talbot's instructions were precise. He was not to remain at any one place but rather to move about to as many islands as possible searching for seamen. Becky would stay in New York.[28]

As Talbot prepared for his assignment he sought advice. Having never been to the West Indies, he had no first-hand knowledge, and his greatest concern was health. This accounts for a document carefully preserved among his private papers. It was written by Dr. C. McCarthy, a physician expert in the West Indies. McCarthy's prescription gave the best advice that eighteenth-century medicine had to offer. It centered around the belief that the body's humors or fluids determined the patient's health and disposition. Keeping those humors in balance was the best guarantee for good health.[29] Here is Dr. McCarthy's counsel:

UNITED STATES OF AMERICA.

STATE OF NEW-YORK, *ss.*

BY this Public Instrument, be it known to all whom the same doth or may concern, That I, JOHN KEESE, a Public Notary in and for the State of New-York, by Letters Patent under the Great Seal of the said State, duly commissioned and sworn; and in and by the said Letters Patent invested " With full power and authority to ATTEST Deeds, Wills, Testaments, Codicils, Agreements and other Instruments in Writing, and to administer any Oath or Oaths, to any Person or Persons;" Do hereby certify That *Andrew Boteler Mariner* who hath subscribed these Presents, personally appeared before me, and being by my duly sworn according to Law, Deposed, That he is a Citizen of the United States of America *and born in the State of Maryland* *five* Feet *four and half* Inches high, and aged *twenty eight* Years And I do further certify, That the said *Andrew Boteler* being a Citizen of the United States of America, and liable to be called in the Service of his Country, is to be respected accordingly at all Times by Sea and Land.

WHEREOF an Attestation being required, I have granted this under my Notarial Firm and Seal.

DONE at the City of New-York, in the said State of New-York; the *eleventh* Day of *May* in the Year one thousand seven hundred and ninety- *Six*

QUOD ATTESTOR.

A PROTECTION CERTIFICATE issued 17 days before passage of the act that prescribed the use of such documents.

(Mary Anne Stets photo, Mystic Seaort Museum, MSM 92-4-14)

120

With respect to the Regimen, all that is necessary is to live plain & temperately. If he is of a robust or plethoric habit, his losing a Little Blood on approaching the warm Latitudes will be proper, and at the same time a cooling purge is to be taken. From this period great attention should be paid to the State of the bowels and [constipation] carefully avoided by occasional Laxatives; for this purpose Six grains of calomel & 40 grains of sulfur formed into common sized pills will answer, two or three to be taken when Necessary. In addition to the above I would recommend as the chief reliance, *small doses of mercury to be taken daily as an alteration [alterative], so as merely to touch the mouth upon Landing. The blue pill or small doses of Calomel will answer equally well. But Mercury in some shape or other should be persisted in so as to give evident proof that the system is to a certain Degree charged with it. When he arrives remove him to the Country as soon as possible, let him avoid getting wet or exposure to the sun as much as circumstances will admit.*

Despite nudging from Pickering, Talbot did not get away from New York until 28 July when he boarded a vessel bound for Barbados. With him he carried a letter of introduction from Sir Robert Liston, the British Minister to the United States. Liston was sympathetic to Talbot's mission and anxious to do all he could to resolve difficulties between the two nations. Liston's position did not necessarily reflect the sympathies of the British government. Although the Minister in London had no desire to antagonize the Americans unnecessarily, Britain was in the midst of a war with France. To win that war the navy needed to be manned. If that meant impressment, so be it. The men responsible for manning the fleet, officers of the Royal Navy, were rarely known for their toleration or tact. Talbot's task would be difficult.

After an unusually long and tedious passage Talbot arrived at Barbados on 2 September. He went immediately to visit the Royal Governor, G. P. Ricketts, who told him that he knew of no impressed Americans on the islands. He did admit that the previous spring some Americans were discovered aboard British warships, but said that he had been able to negotiate their release. The Governor, a rather amiable sort, went on to advise Talbot that he was in for a tough time. The Royal Governors, all civilians, were inclined to be reasonable on the impressment issue. Indeed, since American merchants and vessels supplied most of the food, livestock and building materials for their islands, they had a great incentive for maintaining cordial relations. Were it up to them, the Governor implied, no Americans would be impressed and those that were would be released. But it was not up to them. Whatever the Governors thought was irrelevant. Those who made decisions in matters of impressment were the men who wore the blue uniform of the King's navy.[30]

From Barbados Talbot sailed to Fort Royal Bay, Martinique. Here he met Rear Admiral of the Red Henry Hervey, Commander of His Majesty's naval forces on the Leeward Island Station. To his great pleasure Talbot found Hervey to be a person well disposed towards his mission. Talbot asked Hervey to instruct his officers to cease impressing Americans and release any they might now be holding. Talbot also asked permission to visit the ships in Hervey's command.[31]

Hervey's response was encouraging. He told Talbot that "the most positive orders will be given to the Captains and Commanders of the King's Ships and Vessels, not to Impress American Seamen and to pay due regard to the Protections with which they may be furnished." Hervey said nothing about allowing Talbot to visit his ships. When Talbot pressed the issue Hervey told him that it would be best in these matters if he communicated directly with his superior, Admiral Sir Hyde Parker. Talbot took the advice and wrote Parker, who happened also to be in Fort Royal.

Talbot only knew Parker by reputation, and most of what he knew was bad. Ironically, Talbot had known the Admiral's late father, also Admiral Sir Hyde Parker, for it was he who had threatened to hang American prisoners and had personally selected Talbot for transport to Mill Prison while in command at New York during the Revolution. Unfortunately for Silas Talbot, the younger Parker had inherited his father's disdain for Americans. The Admiral shot back a quick and curt reply. Parker told Talbot that if he wished any man released he must first identify the person with particulars and then present "incontestible proofs that the Individual is a Citizen of America— Upon which proof I shall determine how to act." Parker did not volunteer any suggestions as to his definition of "incontestible," although he implied that the "Protections" were not what he had in mind.[32]

On this discouraging note Talbot left Fort Royal and spent the next six weeks traveling among the Leeward islands. A pattern emerged. The civil authorities cooperated; the naval officers evaded. Finally near the end of November Talbot decided to sail to Kingston, Jamaica, the Royal Navy's principal base in the West Indies. Since it was wartime he would have preferred to sail on a neutral vessel. None was available so he booked passage on *Queen Charlotte*, an unarmed British merchantman.

As far as Parker was concerned Talbot was a piddling annoyance. Like most British officers he was convinced, and not without cause, that the American merchant marine was filled with subjects of the King, some of whom were deserters. These men were Royal Navy property, and Parker was determined to take them. As for the U.S. Congress's "Protections," he dismissed those documents with a sniff. Everyone, including Talbot, knew that counterfeit "Protections" were for sale in every port of the West Indies. Since these documents were worthless, and since those sailors without them had no possibility of proving they were Americans, it followed that any seaman who gave the slightest hint of being English was, by the Admiral's logic, probably English and subject to impressment.

Aside from arrogance, with which the Royal Navy was always well equipped, Parker's position on impressment was dictated by the demands of war. During his passage to Jamaica Talbot got some first-hand experience of how dangerous these waters could be. Only three days out of port, *Queen Charlotte* fell in with three French frigates and after a brief chase she was taken. Talbot was ordered aboard one of the frigates, but after establishing that he was an American the Captain ordered him back to his vessel and dispatched her as a prize to Curaçao. The next day *Queen Charlotte* was retaken by a British privateer. She reset her course for Kingston only to be captured once more. Another shift of course towards Curaçao was followed shortly thereafter by recapture again by another British vessel. This time *Queen Charlotte* made it under the Union Jack to the safety of Kingston harbor. It had taken Talbot three weeks and four captures and recaptures to arrive in Jamaica. During the trip he had been stripped of nearly all his clothes, been forced to lie on deck at night, and had contracted a fever. By the time he set foot on a pier at Kingston he was tired, angry and sick.[33]

Shortly after arriving Talbot secured an interview with Admiral Sir Richard Bligh, second in command to Parker. Like Parker's other subordinate, Admiral Hervey, and unlike the Commander-in-Chief himself, Bligh was pleasant and seemed to wish to cooperate. He agreed that Americans ought not to be impressed and those that had been ought to be released. But Talbot soon discovered that neither Hervey nor Bligh could deliver more than cooperative conversation.

Imperious independence was not a characteristic unique to Captains in the Royal Navy. Commanders of all vessels share this trait to some degree or another, but the King's officers managed to carry it to a degree only imagined by others. In matters of impressment they felt themselves justified in deciding who was or was not properly impressed. Even if they made a mistake they still got the men they needed. Furthermore, no matter what the dispatches from Hervey and Bligh said, everyone knew how the Commander-in-Chief felt. Who among them had ever been reprimanded for impressing an American?

Despite his cool reception, and the evasiveness of the Royal Navy Captains, Talbot went about his work. Once his presence was known he began to receive information about alleged impressed seamen, including letters from the men themselves. He did what he could with the naval authorities, and in several instances succeeded in securing some discharges.

While in Jamaica Talbot took time for some personal business. To add status to his station Talbot felt that he needed a personal servant. At Jamaica he found the price of slaves attractive so he purchased a young man, William Roberts, from Thomas and Ann Bennett. With Roberts to serve him Talbot was now properly outfitted as a gentleman.

Shortly after Talbot arrived in Jamaica, Admiral Parker, with a goodly portion of his command, sailed for St. Nicholas Mole on the island of Hispaniola. Ostensibly French, the island was torn by vicious civil strife. A slave rebellion led by Toussaint L'Ouverture had taken control of much of the countryside. The British, admittedly not much interested in supporting a slave rebellion, were nonetheless anxious to discomfort the French and perhaps add another island to the realm. By 1796 the British had secured positions on the western end of the island at the Mole, and at Jeremie and Port-au-Prince, from which they provided discreet support for Toussaint. Talbot soon sailed to Hispaniola himself.

Parker was annoyed when he discovered that Talbot had followed him to the Mole. He made it clear via his subordinates that under no circumstances would he permit a personal interview. He also made it known, and his Captains surely took the hint, that Talbot could expect very little cooperation from him. But Talbot persisted and over several weeks wrote a number of letters to the Admiral. No replies were ever forthcoming. Frustrated, angry and feeling the effects of a long unpleasant stay in the tropics, Talbot wrote a particularly pointed letter to Parker on 28 January. It had a threatening tone.

Talbot told Parker that more than a month had gone by since he first wrote the Admiral and provided him with a list of impressed men with proof of citizenship. Since that time several ships of the Admiral's fleet, with these impressed men aboard, had departed, taking these impressed men with them. Talbot accused the Admiral of abandoning all principles of law and justice. The Admiral had left him no choice but to seek "redress." This could, warned Talbot, lead to unpleasantness. It could, he wrote, "lead to the adoption of measures that are more or less unfriendly to the British Nation."[34]

Unlike previous communications, this letter did get a response—on the same day. Parker did not mince words. As far as he was concerned Talbot had never provided persuasive evidence that the men he listed were Americans and therefore he had no intention of discharging them. Nor would Sir Hyde be cowed by mention of "redress." To this implied threat he responded that he was "accountable" only to the King and his ministers "whatever may be the consequences." Two days after this exchange Talbot sailed for Kingston.[35]

Talbot realized it was hopeless to deal with the Royal Navy. Offers of sincere concern notwithstanding, Parker and his Captains had no intention of cooperating, and given the uncertainty of the evidence they could find ample sea room to avoid complying. Having lost the battle with Parker, Talbot was still not without a plan, and upon landing in Kingston he decided to try a different tack.

Talbot's plan was clever. He intended to use English law and civilian resentment toward naval officers to serve his ends. It seemed always to be the case in the British empire that civilian authorities and naval officers rarely got along. This was certainly the case with impressment. Wherever the press gang did its work, it left behind angry people who, since they could not take out their resentment on the navy, would often turn on the civilian authorities. For civil officers, charged with keeping the peace, press gangs were a never-ending annoyance, a threat to domestic tranquility and, in the West Indies, a threat to continued trade with the United States.

Having seen this on Barbados, where the local authorities directed by Governor Ricketts had been of considerable help in releasing men, Talbot decided to approach the civil authorities at Kingston. He found them similarly inclined, particularly with Parker still away at the Mole.

Talbot decided to play local authorities against the Royal Navy. He began to travel about the Kingston and Port Royal waterfronts securing infor-

125

mation about impressed seamen. After assembling his documents, instead of appealing to the Royal Navy he presented the evidence to the civil court. In most instances the judge found the material convincing enough to issue a writ of habeas corpus ordering the impressed man's release. Talbot then glee-fully served these writs on the Captains. Since the writs were issued by their own courts, and were thus clearly legal, the commanders had no choice but to release the named seamen. Between the middle of March and the middle of May in 1797 Talbot managed to obtain the freedom of 60 men through this device. This success ended after 8 May when Parker, by now informed of what had happened during his absence, sent orders that writs presented for impressed seamen were not to be honored.

Talbot's brief victory in the spring of 1797 did little to improve his spirits, and the news of Parker's counterattack put him into a funk. In just such a mood he wrote to Pickering:[36]

> The business I am intrusted with is perplexing beyond
> description, and requires all the fortitude & patience of
> which I am capable of exercising; to the unspeakable
> difficulty I have almost daily to encounter with his
> Majesty's Naval officers many of whom are not the most
> reasonable. I have great trouble with our seamen; their
> applications to me are incessant and I am employ'd
> Both by night and day. It seems as if nearly one half of our
> Seamen come out from America without Protections. When
> they arrive in these seas then their fears come on and those
> that escape being impressed before they land will not fail to
> apply to me for Protections immediately and my quarters are
> almost continually surrounded with them and if they are denied
> Protections for want of proof that same fear will urge them
> repeated applications until I am almost sickened with their
> importunity.

To escape the siege of seamen, and since there was little he could do for them in any case, Talbot decided to leave Kingston and take up residence on the north shore of the island at St. Ann's Bay where the summer weather was more tolerable. Talbot stayed for most of the summer at St. Ann's and returned to Kingston in the early fall.

During his absence not a great deal had happened. He was happy to advise Pickering that reports of new impressments were down. On the other hand some distressing news was circulating concerning activities of the French. While the British offended seamen by impressing them, at least they treated them with reasonable care—after all, they needed their manpower. The French, on the other hand, were not so inclined, and Talbot began to receive reports that Americans captured by French cruisers were being treated in a "cruel and inhuman manner." After their release Talbot witnessed them arriving at Kingston "Like Straggling Soldiers after a Battle and Defeat. Some of them when taken are striped naked, Drub'd and then put into a Small boat to make the Shore or perish in the Sea."[37]

Pickering may not have been surprised at this news of French outrages. After the United States concluded a treaty very favorable to their enemy Great Britain (Jay's Treaty), the French had begun pestering American trade, and in December they refused to receive Charles Cotesworth Pinckney as U.S. minister to France. The French appeared determined in the West Indies as well as in Paris to provoke the United States. By late 1797 these two former allies were on a collision course.

By late winter 1798 Talbot was anxious to come home. He missed Becky and Harry. As usual, Cyrus was in financial difficulty and Theodore, who had gone off to Princeton with such promise, was turning out, at least in his father's eyes, to be a wastrel whose high living at college was costing a small fortune.

With no reason to stay in the West Indies, and with every reason to want to be home, Talbot must have been delighted when on 17 July 1798 he received orders from Pickering to return to the United States. He was being recalled, Pickering told him, on the order of the President. Relations with France had deteriorated so badly that the navy was to be expanded and Talbot was to have command of a frigate. Captain Talbot wasted no time. Two days after opening Pickering's dispatch he was bound home.[38]

Notes

1   Cyrus Talbot to Silas Talbot, 23 June 1792, B2 F14 STP.

2   M. Mitchell to Silas Talbot, 19 May 1794, B3 F4 STP.

3   M. Mitchell to Silas Talbot, 19 May 1794, B3 F4 STP.

4   M. Mitchell to Silas Talbot, 20 May 1794, B3 F4 STP.

5   M. Mitchell to Silas Talbot, 20 May 1794, B3 F4 STP.

6   Cyrus Talbot bond to Silas Talbot, 2 June 1795, and Cyrus Talbot to Silas Talbot, 20 August 1795, B3 F15 STP.

7   Jabez Bowen to Silas Talbot, 17 March 1794, B3 F3 STP; Benjamin Bourne to Silas Talbot, 24 March 1795, B3 F7 STP; Silas Talbot to Benjamin Bourne, 30 March 1795, B3 F7 STP.

8   Silas Talbot to Montgomery County, New York, 3 August 1794, B3 F4 STP; Tench Coxe to Silas Talbot, 30 June 1794, B3 F4 STP.

9   John H. Morrison, *History of New York Ship Yards* (New York: Wm. F. Sametz, 1909), 21.

10 Henry Knox to Silas Talbot, 8 August 1794, B3 F4 STP.

11 For the best discussion of the use of live oak in shipbuilding see Virginia Steele Wood, *Live Oaking: Southern Timber for Tall Ships* (Boston: Northeastern University Press, 1981).

12 *American State Papers, Naval Affairs* (Washington: Gales and Seaton, 1834), 1:6.

13 John T. Morgan to Joshua Humphreys, 30 August 1794, quoted in Wood, *Live Oaking*, 27.

14 John T. Morgan to Captain John Barry, 29 December 1794, quoted in Wood, *Live Oaking*, 29.

15 John Taylor to Silas Talbot, 3 April 1795, B3 F7 STP.

16 Many of Talbot's reports to Knox, and later to Timothy Pickering, may be found in the STP. See also Timothy Pickering to Vice President of the United States, 12 December 1795, *DBW*, 1:122-25.

17 Pickering to Tench Francis, 29 June 1795, *DBW*, 1:103-4.

18 Wood, *Live Oaking*, 30.

19 Pickering to Vice President, 12 December 1795, *DBW*, 1:122-25.

20 Truce Concluded Between the United States of America and the Regency of Tunis, 8 November 1795, *DBW*, 1:121-22.

21 Washington to Congress, 15 March 1796, *DBW*, 1:139.

22 Silas Talbot to James McHenry, 18 March 1796, B4 F1 STP; Josiah Fox to Silas Talbot, 22 March 1796, B4 F1 STP.

23 "Theodore Talbot," Princeton University Archives, Princeton University; Theodore Talbot to Silas Talbot, 10 January 1796, Collection 151 STP; Theodore Talbot to Silas Talbot, 18 February 1796, Collection 151, STP; Theodore Talbot to Silas Talbot, 12 May 1796, Collection 151, STP.

24 For a discussion of the history and general conditions of impressment see James F. Zimmerman, *Impressment of American Seamen* (New York: Columbia

University Press, 1925).

25 *Annals* 4th Congress, 2nd session, 2919-21.

26 For a complete discussion of these "Protections" see Ira Dye, "Early American Merchant Seafarers," *Proceedings of the American Philosophical Society*, (1958) 120:331-60. For a description of the certificates see Douglas L. Stein, *American Maritime Documents, 1776-1860* (Mystic: Mystic Seaport Museum, 1992).

27 Pickering to Silas Talbot, 3 June 1796, B4 F2 STP; Pickering to Silas Talbot, 4 June 1796, B4 F2 STP; Pickering to John Trumbull, 9 June 1796, Pickering Papers, MHS; Pickering to Silas Talbot, 11 June 1796, B4 F2 STP.

28 Pickering's instruction dated 9 June 1796 may be found in Pickering Papers, MHS.

29 "Directions for Persons Coming to the West Indies," B4 F5 STP.

30 Lowell J. Ragatz, *The Fall of the Planter Class in the British Caribbean, 1763-1833* (New York: Octagon Books, 1963), 232-33, discusses the dependence of the islands on the United States for food stuffs.

31 Talbot's activities are chronicled in his correspondence, which may be found in STP B4, Folders 2-14. See also Roland Vinyard, "The Unhappy Sufferers: Impressment of American Seamen in the West Indies and the Efforts of Silas Talbot to Resist It." Typescript, G. W. Blunt White Library, Mystic Seaport Museum.

32 Admiral Sir Hyde Parker to Silas Talbot, 12 October 1796, B4 F4 STP.

33 Silas Talbot to Pickering, 22 December 1796, B4 F4 STP.

34 Silas Talbot to Parker, 28 January 1797, B4 F3 STP.

35 Parker to Silas Talbot, 3 March 1797, B4 F3 STP.

36 Silas Talbot to Pickering, 7 May 1797, B4 F10 STP.

37 Silas Talbot to Pickering, 12 December 1797, B4 F11 STP.

38 Pickering to Silas Talbot, 28 May 1798, Diplomatic and Consular Instructions of the Department of State, 1791-1801. RG 59, M28 4:298-299, roll 4.

*A*N ENGRAVING OF Constitution *that dates from 1813 shows her under full sail on a breezy day with whipped-cream clouds and an easy sea. Silas Talbot might have pictured her like this in his mind's eye when he was given command, in May 1799, of what was then the finest warship in the U.S Navy.*

(Courtesy Museum of Fine Arts, Boston)

Chapter Seven

Captain of
Constitution

Silas Talbot's homecoming was less than joyous. With the exception of Betsey, happily married and well settled in Albany, and Harry, who was too young to have a life of his own, the rest of his family seemed to be in their usual state of disarray. Becky had never much cared for New York, so she had spent a good deal of the last two years in Philadelphia and had taken Harry with her. The social life there pleased her and she enjoyed the company of her sister Sarah and their wide circle of friends. While Talbot was away she had moved from their modest home on Pearl Street to a larger house at 47 Vesey Street. When she was not visiting in Philadelphia Becky spent most of her time, and a good deal of her husband's money, buying furniture and redecorating the new house. Talbot returned to a home far more elegant and spacious than the one he had left two years before.[1]

Becky's Philadelphia sojourns, and affairs on Vesey Street, kept her, she said, very busy. So busy, in fact, that it supplied a convenient excuse to explain why she had not been able to keep in close touch with her three stepsons, all of whom for a good part of the previous two years were away themselves, and all of whom, in varying degrees, were in personal and financial trouble.

Theodore's situation was the worst. His natural mother Anna Richmond had died when he was less than two years old. He then spent the next eight years in a home without a mother with a father who was frequently absent, two older brothers who themselves were away for a good deal of time, and an older sister who managed the domestic affairs of the house-hold. Although Theodore's affluent childhood was vastly different from his father's poor beginnings, the two men were similar in at least one way. Silas and Theodore both grew up without the strong hand of a father. In Silas's case the constraints of poverty and work shaped his character. Theodore had no such influences. He was undisciplined and dissipated. That at least was the testimony of those who knew him, including his own brothers.[2]

The good news about Theodore was that, for the time being, he seemed to have reformed. After repeating several classes he was scheduled to graduate from Princeton in the fall with the class of 1798. George, Theodore's severest critic, could only remark that it was about time. As for Silas, he was relieved that an end to tuition bills was finally in sight. Nonetheless, he was still a bit uneasy. For all of his education Theodore seemed as much at sea as he had always been. With his father's encouragement, but with a noticeable lack of enthusiasm, Theodore made arrangements to return to New York to begin his job search.[3]

Cyrus, the seafarer and the son closest to his father, was having his own troubles. Having recovered from his breakdown, Cyrus made his way to London where he went aboard the ship *Nancy,* bound, he was told, for the East Indies. He stayed aboard her for eight months waiting for the promised voyage to begin. In fact the only place *Nancy* ever went in those months was a quick trip across the Bay of Biscay to the Spanish port of Bilbao. When Cyrus was finally convinced that *Nancy* was never destined for the Indies he left her and sailed for New York.

Despite his disappointments, Cyrus, like Melville's Ishmael, was drawn to the sea. As soon as he got back to New York he went at it again and bought a one-fourth share in a 124-ton ship bound for Dutch Curaçao with a cargo of flour. He shipped as master. As his father already knew, and the son would learn, trade in the West Indies was a risky business. Not far from Guadeloupe Talbot and his ship were taken by a French privateer and hauled into Basseterre. The price for release was one half the cargo, a ransom Talbot grudgingly paid. But before he cleared the harbor Cyrus himself was seized and brought before a local court. Someone on the island recognized him from his days in the French Navy and accused him of being a Royalist emigré. With the shadow of the guil-lotine looming, Talbot hastened to assure the court that while he indeed had worn the French King's uniform he was and remained an American citizen.[4] The court accepted his testimony and released him.

With a half-filled hold Cyrus Talbot sailed for Curaçao, and discovered that his hard luck was not over. Between Guadeloupe and Curaçao his ship went aground and was declared a total loss. He survived the wreck and made his way back to New York to lay the sad news before his father.

Cyrus's business affairs often took him to Boston. His route to and from Boston often included a detour through Dighton. Of all the New York Talbots Cyrus was the one who kept closest contact with the home-town relatives. His contacts were more intimate than anyone imagined. In March of 1798 Cyrus provided his father with some good news and perhaps a better explanation why the route between Boston and New York seemed always to pass through Dighton. Six weeks earlier, 20 January, he had married Alice Smith, the daughter of the Reverend John Smith, minister in Dighton. A bit taken aback at this unexpected news, but pleased nonetheless, Silas offered congratulations to his son and new daughter-in-law.[5]

The third member of this tormented trio of elder brothers, George, was in some ways the least likable of the boys. Sychophantic towards his father, he was always the first to reveal and revel in Theodore's peccadilloes and Cyrus's failures. Quick to condemn and scold others, there was an unbecoming shrillness to his character and demeanor. His rhetoric helped to mask some of his own problems, which, not surprisingly, mirrored the difficulties of his brothers, particularly those of unlucky Cyrus.

George had finished his apprenticeship with Blanchard, and in the spring of 1796 he was ready to go out on his own. He left for London in April, planning to join up with a vessel bound for the East Indies. The farthest he ever got was Havre de-Grâce, France, where his East Indian venture came to an abrupt and unexplained end. He decided to return to New York. Once home he shifted his attention to opportunities closer at hand and set out on a West Indian venture. Acting as an agent for his father's old friends, the Hervey brothers of Philadelphia, he sailed for Puerto Rico to buy the ship *Ellia* and her cargo. Like so many others he fell victim to marauding French privateers on the way. Thankfully his vessel was retaken, probably by an Englishman, but then in a reprise of his brother's experience George was wrecked on a lee shore. The Talbot boys were nothing if not resourceful. Somehow George managed to reach Puerto Rico, buy *Ellia* and load her with a cargo of salt. He brought cargo and ship home and made a tidy profit for himself and the Herveys.[6]

Silas and his two seafaring sons had experienced first-hand the torment being visited on American trade by the ongoing struggle between England and France. While the West Indies had never been anything like peaceable waters, in the current circumstances they had become exceptionally volatile and American trade was suffering.

For the Talbots the West Indies situation had a particular poignancy. They regarded the French as friends and allies. Silas remembered the heady days of the Revolution when the fleur-de-lis flew side by side with American battle colors. Indeed, his affection and regard for this nation had persuaded him to give over Cyrus and George to the care and instruction of their navy. When the Bastille fell, all Americans, including the Talbots, celebrated the arrival of the new republic and raised their voices in unison with their fellow republicans to chant the virtues of liberty, equality and fraternity. Alas, the sea of blood that flowed from the guillotine and the marching of French armies across Europe soon sobered these emotions.

Even in the early and optimistic days of the Revolution the leaders of the American republic had not allowed sentiment for the French to compromise the interests of the new nation. Washington and the Federalists understood the permanency of national interests and the frailty of alliances. They knew that rapprochement with Great Britain must be pursued. Yet inevitably as the United States grew closer to its old enemy she grew estranged from her former ally. The outbreak of war between these two superpowers in 1793 thrust the United States into an arena where opportunities were only matched by risks.[7]

The opportunities were those that always fall to a neutral carrier in time of war. Once the Royal Navy had virtually destroyed or bottled up the merchant vessels of her European enemies, those nations looked to neutral bottoms to carry commerce. Enterprising American shipowners soon made the United States the principal neutral carrier. This achievement bore within it the seeds of danger. International law notwithstanding, no warring power could sit idly by and watch a neutral carry an enemy's trade without interference.

Silas Talbot witnessed first-hand the ramifications of Europe at war. British impressment of Americans was a direct result of manpower demands put on the Royal Navy in the war against the French. Talbot had also seen how prone the British were to seize American merchantmen trading with France and her allies. Ironically, while the British repeatedly harassed American trade, American public opinion and government policy were inclined to a modicum of toleration for what amounted to kidnapping. One reason for this toleration was tradition. What the Royal Navy was doing in the 1790s was little different from what it had been doing in American waters long before the Revolution. In the American merchant and seafaring communities there was a long acquaintance with British impressment. A second and very practical reason is that while impressment was an outrage to seamen it did little to interfere with trade and profits. That their vessels should lose a few crew on a voyage was inconvenient but not critical for American merchants and shipowners, and in those cases where the British actually seized a vessel they were ordinarily careful to pay American owners for any losses.

The situation was otherwise with the French. Their privateers operated in a very loose fashion and were far less concerned with the niceties of international law and seafaring custom; nor did the French government feel obligated to compensate American owners for captured cargo. Furthermore, the new governments in France (they seemed to change frequently) left an impression of instability, insincerity and corruption. The nation that had once been an ally and later a sister republic, that stood in defense of liberty against the tyrannies of Europe, was now seen as no better than her despotic neighbors. The Talbots, because of their special association with France, felt more betrayed than most. George spoke for all when he shared his feelings with his father: "Sorry I am to see the friends of my youth & the Country you and I had fondly hoped, when I left it, would rise a Superb Spectacle to the world, of the influence of political liberty So far forget themselves, as to make Such unjust attempts on our rights."[8]

Betrayal was what the French saw as well—but from a different perspective. To the revolutionary governments in Paris the American-British rapprochement was evidence that their former friend was now the friend of their enemy. From that perception came a series of decrees culminating in February 1797 with an order that authorized the seizure of all neutral vessels destined to any of the Windward or Leeward Islands in America. By June more than 300 American vessels had been seized by French warships and privateers.[9]

In the summer of 1797 President John Adams, at great political risk, made a dramatic gesture to halt the drift toward war. He dispatched three commissioners to Paris to negotiate a settlement. To the embarrassment and anger of the President, the French showed no signs of willingness to talk. In fact, they treated the American envoys in such an insulting and humiliating fashion that two of the three stormed out of Paris in protest.[10]

Adams reported to Congress on the failure of the Paris discussions. In his message of 19 March 1798, he alluded to the distressing dispatches he had received from the commissioners. Congress demanded to see them. What they read sent members into a fury. The dispatches revealed that certain French agents, referred to only as X, Y and Z, had approached the American envoys and told them bluntly that only after a public apology from President Adams and the sweetener of a large bribe would negotiations proceed. Seeing in these letters an opportunity to whip up support for enlarging the army and navy to defend American rights, the Federalist majorities in the House and Senate voted to publish the documents.[11]

Public reaction was quick and furious. As one Federalist newspaper noted angrily, "To be lukewarm after reading the horrid scenes is to be criminal—and the man who does not warmly reprobate the conduct of the French must have a soul black enough to be *fit for treasons strategems and spoils*." The Federalists swept forward with their plans for arming America.[12]

On 17 April 1798 Congress enacted a law "to provide an additional armament for the further protection of the trade of the United States; and for other purposes." The law authorized the President to build, purchase, or hire "a number of vessels, not exceeding twelve, nor carrying more than twenty-two guns each to be armed, fitted out, and manned under his direction." For these purposes Congress appropriated $950,000. Three days after this expansion of the navy, which until this point had been administered as a part of the War Department, Congress created a Department of the Navy headed by a Secretary at full cabinet rank.[13]

To the post of Secretary, Adams appointed Benjamin Stoddert, a merchant who had held important jobs in the Continental Congress. He was well connected in business and politics and understood ships and shipping. He did not, however, have any seagoing experience. He was an administrator, not a seaman. Nonetheless, he accepted, and on 22 May Secretary of State Pickering forwarded his commission.

It took Stoddert nearly a month to wrap up his personal and business affairs. Not until 19 June did he take his oath. In the meantime, however, events moved rapidly. On the same day that Pickering ordered Talbot home, Congress instructed United States warships "to capture any French vessel found near the coast preying upon American commerce." In the weeks between then and Talbot's arrival at New York in early August the United States abrogated unilaterally all existing treaties with France while the Republic's fledgling navy took its first French prizes.

The government's vigorous action was a tonic to Talbot, but yet he was uneasy. Pickering's recall notice indicated that the President wanted him to command one of the ships being fitted for service. Did this mean he would return to the New York yard and his old job or was he to go to a new post? What Talbot dreaded most was being assigned to command a ship still building. He knew from experience the frustrations that went along with being a Captain/supervisor. He had been on the beach too long. He wanted a command at sea.

To discover more about Adams' and Stoddert's plans, Talbot rode to Trenton where the government had removed temporarily because of an outbreak of yellow fever in Philadelphia. He went both to present his accounts to his old boss Secretary of State Pickering and to meet his new boss Secretary of the Navy Stoddert. Talbot reminded Stoddert that he had already spent more than his share of time overseeing yard work on the New York frigate, and now he wanted to go to sea. Stoddert listened sympathetically but told Talbot that for the moment no other command was ready. He held out a promise that something might become available. In the meantime he asked Talbot to undertake a special mission.[14]

With a budget of $950,000 to spend on building and buying ships, Benjamin Stoddert was a popular figure among merchants with ships to sell. Standing at the head of this line of eager vendors was John Brown of Providence. Given the broad scope of his business activities, Brown was one of the best-known merchants in America, dealing in everything from cannon founding to the China trade. He was canny, aggressive, domineering and, according to some, a man who enjoyed sailing close to the wind. He had a ship for sale. Was Stoddert interested?[15]

Stoddert was interested but cautious. He needed to know more about the ship. He trusted neither Brown nor anyone else in Rhode Island to provide an objective opinion, and so he asked Silas Talbot to survey the vessel for purchase. Talbot agreed. He knew John Brown and he knew ships. After being home for less than a month he bade Becky goodbye and set out for Providence.

It was good to be in Providence again. Talbot had not been in town for more than a decade, and despite his untoward departure ten years earlier his friends welcomed him back as a distinguished son. Others embraced him as the agent of a government with money to spend. Whatever the cause Talbot was pleased at his reception and so was Stoddert. Indeed, the chief reason Stoddert had sent him was because he knew Talbot enjoyed a reputation in Rhode Island that would allow the Navy Department to stand on equal footing with the powerful and irascible John Brown.

Brown's vessel was *George Washington,* a ship built at Providence in 1793. According to Brown she was constructed of the best materials, "Cedar and live Oak, coppered, two suits of Sails, completely rigged, and fitted in all respects for a Ship of War." After his survey Talbot agreed with Brown's assessment and recommended that she be purchased. Stoddert was still wary, particularly when Brown tried to charge an exorbitant price for ballast. The Secretary was frank with Talbot. "Mr. Brown," he wrote is "a complete Master of the Art of bargain making. You must do the best you can with him, and let the public be Screwed as little as possible."[16]

Having acted as the agent in the purchase, Stoddert asked Talbot to remain in Providence and fit the vessel for sea. He was not, however, to command her. She was far too small a vessel for someone of Talbot's rank and seniority. If he remained, the Secretary promised him that he would be compensated at the rank of Captain even though at the moment he had no ship. Talbot agreed.

Talbot stayed with *George Washington* preparing her for sea. Since his duties in Providence promised to keep him away from New York for several weeks at least, Becky decided to return to Philadelphia. Late in September she took a side trip and drove up to Princeton to attend Theodore's graduation. Theodore had written to his father inviting him to attend, too, but duties in Providence prevented him from being there.

Like most college commencements it was a gay affair. The usual speeches were delivered, dinners hosted and toasts drunk. Theodore received his degree, collected his memories and bade farewell to his teachers and classmates. When the day was finished Becky headed back to Philadelphia while Theodore, complaining that he was exhausted from studying, took his father's money and went off with friends to spend a few weeks at the New Jersey shore. When that frivolity was over he traveled to Albany to visit his sister and brother-in-law. George Metcalfe was well connected in New York politics and could be helpful to him. Metcalfe, however, was as serious as Theodore was flighty. He seems to have had little advice for the young graduate, and by mid-November, his peregrinations over, Theodore was back in New York City. There, thanks to his father's influence, he joined the merchant firm of Richard Harrison.

In another move that disconcerted his father Theodore announced that he did not plan to live at home. He gave as his excuse that the house on Vesey Street was too small and he asked his father for money to board elsewhere. Suspecting that it was less the size of the home that concerned Theodore than the wish to be away from the scrutiny of his parents, Talbot must have wondered if his son would ever grow up. Nonetheless, the indulgent father sent the money.[17]

Brother George was in the city, too, in the summer of 1798. Since leaving Blanchard he had been struggling to make it on his own with indifferent results. However, the press of business was not so overwhelming that he could not spare time to keep his father informed of Theodore's every misstep. As an adjunct to supplying his father with all the family and local gossip, George also handled Talbot's business matters. Silas relied on George to carry some property to auction so that he could raise some much-needed cash. He told his son to go to the auction, bid up the price, and accept nothing but cash—"for who at this day can be trusted with perfect Saifty." George dutifully obeyed.[18]

While Theodore and George were doing business in New York, hardluck Cyrus was enduring another disaster at sea. Shortly after he learned of his father's recall to duty Cyrus applied for a lieutenancy in the navy. When no response was forthcoming from the new Navy Department he assumed his application was dead, and so early in September he signed on the ship *Henrietta* bound from the Chesapeake to Europe. Although *Henrietta's* cargo was tobacco and cocoa consigned to a Genoese merchant living in Cadiz, the ship's manifest listed it as American goods. Cyrus and his associates were likely involved in a subterfuge called the "broken voyage." Cargo, often Spanish or French, would be carried into an American port, entered at the local custom house, and then through a clever paper denaturalization reexported as American goods. It was a light disguise that fooled no one, but should the vessel be stopped by the Royal Navy the cargo could be claimed as belonging to a neutral. Three days out Cyrus and *Henrietta* got a chance to offer this explanation when they were brought to by HMS *Hind*. The Captain of his Majesty's ship was not persuaded and carried his prize into Halifax where he libeled her before an Admiralty court.[19]

While riding at anchor in Halifax harbor awaiting judgment, *Henrietta* was driven by a northeast gale into a neighboring vessel. She struck hard, bounced off, and then drove ashore. She lost half her cargo. When the court finally found in favor of Cyrus it was a decision that came too late to be of much help to him. With no way to ship his goods out he was forced to sell at a loss in a soft market. Small wonder that by the time he returned to New York in early November he told his father he would not go to sea again in the merchant service until the war in Europe was over.[20]

On 25 September Stoddert offered command of *George Washington* to Patrick Fletcher. He accepted, and by early November he was in Providence recruiting men. Talbot was pleased at the appointment, particularly since it marked the end of his duties in Rhode Island. Early in December Talbot bid farewell to *George Washington* as she left Providence and sailed down the bay, bound for her station in the West Indies.[21]

From Providence Talbot rode straight to Philadelphia. Becky was there with Harry, and so too was some important navy business. In June 1794, Washington had appointed six Captains for the six frigates and ranked them in the following order: John Barry (*United States* at Philadelphia), Samuel Nicholson (*Constitution* at Boston), Silas Talbot (*President* at New York), Richard Dale (*Chesapeake* at Norfolk), Thomas Truxtun (*Constellation* at Baltimore), and James Sever (*Congress* at Portsmouth). In the reductions of 1796, when construction on *President*, *Chesapeake* and *Congress* was suspended, their Captains were relieved from their duties—but in a manner that left their status unclear. Were they discharged or were they furloughed? The answer to this question would determine seniority. If the Captains were merely furloughed then their service, for purposes of reckoning seniority, would continue uninterrupted. On the other hand if they were discharged they were no longer in the service and would have to be reappointed with no seniority at all. At the time (1796) the issue seemed moot and no one, Talbot included, gave it much thought. With the naval expansion of 1798 the issue was no longer moot; now there were ships to command, glory to be sought, and seniority to be assigned.[22]

By October Stoddert sensed tremors of discontent from his Captains and began to realize that the issue of rank threatened to shake his infant service. He shared his concerns with President Adams. He told the President that no one disputed the rank of Barry and Nicholson. Both men had served in the Revolution, and in the reduction of 1796 both had been kept on duty. Their service was continuous and without dispute. That, however, was as far as agreement went. The arrangement of the next three in line—Talbot, Dale and Truxtun—was fraught with difficulty. The list of 1794 placed these men in the order of Talbot, Dale and Truxtun. In the reduction Dale and Talbot were left without commands while Truxtun continued with *Constellation*. Did that now mean that Truxtun ranked ahead of the other two? Talbot and Dale certainly did not think so. Truxtun held the opposite opinion.[23]

Ever the optimist, Benjamin Stoddert thought that if he got the three Captains together these issues could be ironed out. He planned the meeting for early December at Philadelphia. Talbot did not attend. He was busy wrapping up his business with *George Washington*; he was also confident that Stoddert would recognize his claim to rank above Truxtun, for not only did his rank date from 1794 but in addition he had served in the Continental Navy. Truxtun had not.

Shortly before Christmas, Stoddert, Dale and Truxtun met in Philadelphia at the Secretary's office on Walnut Street. Stoddert was a practical man. He knew that if Truxtun found himself inferior to either Dale or Talbot he would resign from the service. The Captain had left no doubt of this from the outset. Dale was more pliable. His most recent navy command was *Ganges*, a merchantman converted to a 26-gun ship. After a brief cruise in her, Dale had returned home and turned command over to Thomas Tingey. Dale assured Stoddert that he had no intention of taking another command as unworthy as *Ganges*. He wanted one of the new frigates. Stoddert hit upon a solution. He knew that Dale had been approached to take command of a merchantman bound for China. Such a berth promised rich rewards. If Dale took leave from the navy to command the voyage, perhaps by the time he returned to America, suggested the Secretary, a suitable frigate would be available. Dale agreed and Stoddert breathed more easily, now all that remained was to satisfy Talbot.[24]

Talbot had other concerns. He had not been in Philadelphia to participate in the Walnut Street negotiations. Instead he was consumed by family business and securing his pay and expenses for the two years, three months and thirteen days he had labored in the West Indies. With unwonted speed and largesse the Treasury Office settled his account to the tune of nearly $7000.[25]

Talbot's pleasure was short-lived, for what the government gave some of his family wished to take away. George Talbot, having had no recent successes in his mercantile career, had a plan to go into partnership with one Parker in Perth Amboy. As usual there were complications. Parker could not put up his share until his father's estate was settled. In the meantime George needed $5000. George and Parker believed that the war in Europe would soon be over (it ended 16 years later in 1815), and they wanted to be among the first to ship goods into what they were convinced would be a boom market. Brimming with confidence, George announced to his father that profits from this venture would move him forward into the best New York society, a place where he obviously wanted to be and where he thought he belonged.[26]

Talbot recognized hubris, although he called it "speculation," and chided his son first for engaging in such risky business and secondly for doing it with a partner. Parker was unreliable and the situation in Europe was far too unstable to even think about the export business. Talbot also took his son to task for associating wealth with worth. Character was more to be prized than cash. As far as he was concerned, George was better advised to put his money out at interest. Having thus advised his speculator son, Talbot, ever the indulgent father, then agreed to give George the money—but only on condition that he collect it from one of Talbot's debtors. After giving it some thought, and after his partner Parker seemed unable to come up with his share, George decided to forgo his adventure in foreign trade.[27]

Through the early months of 1799 Talbot and Becky stayed in Philadelphia and enjoyed themselves in the company of her friends and family. With the shipyard at New York virtually closed down for the winter there was little to draw Talbot north. What family business needed to be conducted was left in the hands of son George. Talbot took some of the time in Philadelphia to talk with Stoddert and others about the prospects of finishing the New York frigate and getting her to sea. Or might the Secretary have some other suitable command for him? The subject of seniority was not broached. Without a ship the issue was moot.

Nevertheless, the matter of rank was a problem to be solved. Stoddert knew he had a political time bomb on his hands. Despite his advanced years, it was all but certain that Barry would remain in command of *United States*. Nicholson, however, was not long for *Constitution*. His arrogance and incompetence were just too much. He had offended so many people so many times that the political liabilities of keeping him far outweighed any risks of removing him. Who would replace him? Here Stoddert's plan came into play. Dale was out of the way in the East Indies and Truxtun had *Constellation*. Talbot would take *Constitution*. One problem, however, needed attention. If Talbot went to sea, *Constitution* and *Constellation* would be cruising the same waters, and the matter of rank would become a problem again.

Stoddert always thought that Truxtun had the better claim to seniority. Not only did he believe that the reduction of 1796 broke Talbot's service, and hence his claim to seniority, but he also shared, quietly of course, Truxtun's unflattering opinion of Talbot as a naval officer. From his cabin aboard *Constellation* off Basseterre, Truxtun wrote a scathing letter to Stoddert suggesting that Talbot's appointment as Captain demonstrated that anyone could claim the rank. Referring to Talbot's career, Truxtun noted sarcastically that "A sailor will make a Soldier but a Soldier can never make a Sailor." As he told Stoddert, "I cannot bring myself to believe, that in the Line of a Sea Officer, particularly in an infant Navy, where every Officer looks up for Instructions, and Information, that he is a proper Person."[28]

Truxtun's broadside sent a shudder through the Navy Department, and Stoddert sought advice from Alexander Hamilton. The former Secretary of the Treasury was a friend of Talbot's, and Stoddert was sure that when he explained the situation to Hamilton he would intercede and convince Talbot to accept a ranking below Truxtun's. Instead, Hamilton sided with Talbot. Seeking other support, Stoddert turned next to his cabinet colleagues. There he found the Secretaries of State, War and Treasury standing with him while the Attorney General supported Hamilton and Talbot.[29]

Thus far in all the discussion the President had remained silent. As was his custom in the spring, Adams had returned home to Quincy. Prior to his leaving Philadelphia he and Stoddert had had little or no conversation on this issue. Stoddert was uneasy. He knew that because Adams had played a key role in the creation of the Continental Navy the President entertained a fondness for the men who had served in the Revolution. He may also have reflected on the fact that Talbot was a fellow New Englander and a faithful Federalist.

Stoddert was desperate. The madness over rank threatened all his plans for the upcoming campaign. Merchants in every port were demanding that the navy sweep the French off the coast and out of the Caribbean. Nicholson and *Constitution* were due home in Boston any day. She must have a new Captain and put back to sea as soon as possible.

In his own mind at least, Stoddert had decided that Talbot would command *Constitution* and that he would rank after Truxtun. Before he made that announcement, however, he tried to introduce the news gradually with the hope of making it more acceptable to Talbot. On 2 May he wrote a very friendly, and somewhat apologetic, note to Talbot telling him that soon either *United States* or *Constitution* would be his to command. He let Talbot know that in all likelihood he would rank beneath Truxtun. As an explanation for this decision he told Talbot that "accident and not design on the part of Government has made Captain Truxtun your Senior Officer." The next day the Secretary wrote again to Hamilton, enclosing a copy of his letter to Talbot, asking him to reconsider his opinion and encourage Talbot to accept this ranking. Hamilton refused. Talbot held firm, too, and told the Secretary that he would only accept command on condition that the President himself decide the issue of seniority.[30]

On 15 May the Secretary, without making any reference to rank, informed Talbot that Barry would remain with *United States* and that he was to take *Constitution*. Talbot agreed, but not before he announced that he would never serve under Truxtun and that he planned to take his case in person to the President, who happened to be at his home in nearby Quincy only a short distance from *Constitution*'s berth in Boston. Stoddert sputtered, but accepted that he had been outmaneuvered. He answered Talbot by assuring him that "Truxtun will not be sent on any service to meet with you." If the two Captains never served together how could seniority matter?[31]

Stoddert, the merchant and bureaucrat, was too rational to appreciate the depth of feeling commanders like Talbot and Truxtun had about status. Truxtun once referred to himself proudly as a "petty despot." No one disagreed. Eighteenth-century naval commanders were a special breed of men. In the Royal Navy, to which Americans looked for a model, a ship's captain was not simply above his men; he was on a different plane entirely. His cabin, always spacious even in the most cramped vessel, was aft in the special world of the quarterdeck. When he came on deck, the whole windward side was cleared for his promenade. He gave his orders crisply and expected, and usually received, instant obedience. In almost every respect his word was law, backed by hard discipline meted out to the slow and recalcitrant. Such men were not to be challenged at sea or ashore. For all of his considerable abilities Benjamin Stoddert was a landlubber administrator who could never comprehended the status games of his Captains. Rank was everything.

On 5 June Silas Talbot came aboard *Constitution*. In a brief ceremony he took command of the frigate from Samuel Nicholson. That same day he took the ship to an anchorage four miles out in the harbor at President's Roads. As soon as the frigate was secure he ordered his cutter to be put overboard. In the morning he planned to sail over to Quincy for a visit with the President.[32]

Adams was always partial to the navy, and in particular to its New England Captains. Both in person and in his correspondence he had made it clear to Stoddert and others that, should it come to choosing between Truxtun and Talbot, he would defend the Rhode Islander. Not surprisingly, in defense of his position he often cited Talbot's heroic service in the Revolution.[33]

As was the President's style, when Talbot arrived the pleasantries were brief. The two may have spent a few moments reminiscing about the Revolution and all that had happened since; but that was not the point of the meeting. Adams shared with Talbot his concerns for the new navy, especially the maddening delays in getting ships to sea. He was particularly distressed with Samuel Nicholson and his bungling command of *Constitution*. Adams wasted no words and he wanted Talbot to waste no time—*Constitution* must be made ready for sea as soon as possible. Affairs in the West Indies demanded the presence of a powerful American force to protect commerce.[34]

Undoubtedly as the conversation progressed the issue of rank arose. Adams reiterated the position of the Secretary—Talbot would never be required to serve with Truxtun. That, however, was not enough. Talbot made clear that he would be senior to Truxtun or he would not serve. The response of the President is not recorded; however, it seems certain that he said nothing to Talbot that would have given the Captain any reason to believe that he would not be senior to Truxtun. Talbot bade the President good day, returned to his cutter and sailed back to *Constitution*.

Stoddert and Adams were not communicating well. Their difference over Talbot was not the only point where their views diverged. Adams, as he had told Talbot, was insistent that *Constitution* return immediately to the West Indies. Stoddert had other ideas. His notion was to send *Constitution* and *United States* on a cruise across the top of Ireland and down into the English Channel. From there they would sail down the French coast and south to pick up a track that would bring them to the West Indies. It was a grand scheme that hinged on timing. Part of Stoddert's reasoning was to keep his ships out of harm's way during the summer hurricane season and then deliver them on station in the West Indies as early as possible in the fall. This meant sailing for Ireland no later than early July. Adams knew nothing of this plan and neither, apparently, did Talbot.[35]

Talbot laid on hard to get his ship ready. Stephen Higginson, the Navy Department's agent in Boston, did all that he could to help the Captain. Most perplexing was the problem of manning. Wages were high in the merchant service, and risks were fewer than they were in the navy. Talbot sent his officers, including his able First Lieutenant Isaac Hull, north as far as Portsmouth, New Hampshire, and south to Providence, Rhode Island, to recruit new hands.

Stoddert understood Talbot's problems and wisely refrained from bombarding him with the hectoring letters he so often sent to other Captains. Indeed, in one instance, as both a measure to assist in manning and a gesture to smooth relations with Talbot, the Secretary made an extraordinary offer. Would Captain Talbot care to have as his second in command his son Cyrus? After interrupted careers in both the French Navy and the American merchant marine, Cyrus had finally secured a commission as a Lieutenant in the United States Navy. Captain Talbot graciously suggested to the Secretary that such an appointment might be viewed by his crew, and the public, as inappropriate. The wisdom was obvious to all. Cyrus was excused from service aboard *Constitution* and was ordered instead to New York to command the brig *Richmond*.[36]

Stoddert was doing everything in his power to soften up Talbot for the blow that was about to come. On 25 June, in one of the most disingenuous letters ever to issue from the Secretary's office, Stoddert wrote to Talbot that in looking through the records he could not find any indication that the Captain had actually received a commission. Stoddert knew very well that such a document had never been sent and this was his point. If Talbot could not produce a dated commission from 1794 his case for seniority over Truxtun was impaired. For months Stoddert had done everything he could to avoid dealing with the seniority relationship of Talbot and Truxtun. Now, when he finally had to confront the issue, he employed a lame stratagem that fooled no one.[37]

Talbot exploded when he read the letter and his new commission. He was to rank from 1798, not 1794. In the words of the Secretary, "It places you after Barry, Nicholson and Truxtun." Unacceptable. He returned the commission to the Secretary and so informed the President. Adams was perplexed. What he failed to appreciate was that during his long absences from Philadelphia members of the cabinet, Stoddert included, had grown accustomed to acting on their own, often without fully informing the President. As Secretary Stoddert wrote to Captain Truxtun:[38]

> *I do not think you need to be under the least uneasines on the subject of rank. The Heads of Departments all concur in my opinion that you must rank from 1794 - Talbot from 1798. I have not laid my correspondence*

*with Talbot before the President tho I have sent him a Commission for
Talbot dated 1798. He will not like to interfere at all.*

Stoddert was wrong. Not only did Adams support Talbot's position,
he was horrified at the thought of the Captain resigning his command at a
moment when he was desperate to get *Constitution* to sea. On Monday 8 July,
when Adams learned that Talbot was leaving the service, he wrote to him
"Your Refusal to accept the Commission has ruined all my design." He asked
Talbot to meet with him and pleaded that "If you cannot come here I would
meet you any where." That Thursday evening Talbot was the President's
guest at his home for dinner.[39]

To that dinner Talbot brought copies of all the correspondence that
had passed between him and the Secretary concerning his appointment and
rank. Many of these were letters Stoddert had kept from the President.
Adams asked Talbot to leave the letters that he might read them and come
to a judgment on the issue.

Adams did come to a judgment, and it was not one to please Stoddert.
In a 3000-word letter he told the Secretary "In the case of Captain Talbot, I am
perfectly clear, that he has been a captain in the navy of the United States
from the time of his appointment, in 1794, to this hour." Whether or not he
actually held such a commission in his hands was irrelevant. He was, Adams
told Stoddart, well aware of the "censures" that would be cast upon him. He
also knew that his decision would likely cause Truxtun to resign, but so be it
because, as the President admonished his Secretary, "it is right."[40]

On the same day that Adams dispatched this letter to Stoddert he
informed Talbot of his decision. That afternoon, "amidst the joy and good wishes of many thousands of good federalists," *Constitution*, "making a beautiful and
noble figure," left Boston bound south for Norfolk enroute to the West Indies.

Stoddert was left with the unhappy task of informing Truxtun of the
President's decision. True to his word, the self-described petty despot resigned
from the navy. Well, sort of. After a few weeks at home in Perth Amboy, New
Jersey, with his family Truxtun had second thoughts. He finally decided that
he preferred to be at sea and made some discreet inquiries to Stoddert. The
Secretary, wanting very much to have such an able commander back, told
Truxtun that the department never officially accepted the resignation.
Truxtun returned—vowing, of course, and the Secretary agreeing, that he
would never serve under Talbot.[41]

Notes

1   George Washington Talbot to Silas Talbot, 14 June 1798, B4 F14 STP.

2   Of all the children George seemed to delight most in informing his father of the misdeeds of his siblings, Theodore in particular.

3   Samuel Smith to Silas Talbot, 10 March 1798, B1 F5, Collection 151 STP; Theodore Talbot to Silas Talbot, 3 October 1798, B1 F1, Collection 151 STP; and Theodore Talbot to Silas Talbot, 16 November 1798, B1 F1, Collection 151 STP.

4   Cyrus Talbot to Silas Talbot, 28 October 1797, B4 F11 STP.

5   Cyrus Talbot to Silas Talbot, 1 March 1798, B4 F13 STP.

6   George Washington Talbot to Silas Talbot, 28 July 1796, B3 F4 STP; George Washington Talbot to Silas Talbot, 14 June 1798, B4 F14 STP.

7   For an overview of the period see Alexander DeConde, *The Quasi-War: The Politics and Diplomacy of the Undeclared War With France, 1797-1801* (New York: Charles Scribner's Sons, 1966).

8   George Washington Talbot to Silas Talbot, 14 June 1798, B4 F14 STP.

9   Michael Palmer, *Stoddert's War: Naval Operations During the Quasi War with France, 1798-1801* (Columbia: University of South Carolina Press, 1987), 74-75.

10 For a description of this affair see Peter P. Hill, *William Vans Murray, Federalist Diplomat: The Shaping of a Peace with France, 1797-1801* (Syracuse, New York: Syracuse University Press, 1971), 55-58.

11 Richard Kohn, *Eagle and the Sword* (New York: The Free Press, 1975), 211-214.

12 Quoted in James Morton Smith, *Freedom's Fetters: The Alien and Sedition Laws and American Civil Liberties* (Ithaca, New York: Cornell University Press, 1956), 15.

13 *Statutes at Large* 1:552-54.

14 SecNav to Silas Talbot, 20 September 1798, DQW, 11:428.

15 The best analysis of the business activities of John Brown and his brothers may be found in James B. Hedges, *The Browns of Providence Plantations*, 2 vols. (Cambridge: Harvard University Press, 1952).

16 SecNav to Silas Talbot, 29 August 1798, DQW 1:351; SecNav to Silas Talbot, 20 September 1798, DQW 1:428.

17 Theodore Talbot to Silas Talbot, 4 September 1798, B1 F1, Collection 151 STP; Theodore Talbot to Silas Talbot, 3 October 1798, B1 F1, Collection 151 STP; Theodore Talbot to Silas Talbot, 16 November 1798, B1 F1, Collection 151 STP.

18 Silas Talbot to George Washington Talbot, 8 November 1798, B5 F1 STP.

19 Cyrus Talbot to Silas Talbot, 19 September 1798, B4 F15 STP.

20 Cyrus Talbot to Silas Talbot, 11 December 1798, B5 F4 STP.

21 SecNav to Fletcher, 25 September 1798, DQW 1:452.

22 Names were assigned to the six frigates at various times. I have given their names here simply to ease identification.

23 The issue of rank weaves through a good deal of the Secretary's correspondence with his Captains and the President. This correspondence may be followed in DQW.

24 SecNav to Alexander Hamilton, 6 February 1799, DQW 2:313; Truxtun to SecNav, 20 March 1799, DQW 2:516-17.

25 Silas Talbot Account with the United States, B5 F6 STP.

26 Silas Talbot to George Washington Talbot, 30 December 1798, B5 F4 STP.

27 George Washington Talbot to Silas Talbot, 3 January 1799, B5 F6 STP; Silas Talbot to George Washington Talbot, 5 January 1799, B5 F6 STP; and George Washington Talbot to Silas Talbot, 8 January 1799, B5 F6 STP.

28 Truxtun to SecNav, 20 March 1799, DQW 2:516-17.

29 SecNav to Hamilton, 6 February 1799, DQW 2:313; SecNav to Hamilton, 3 May 1799, DQW 3:131-32.

30 SecNav to Silas Talbot, 2 May 1799, Adams Papers, reel 395; SecNav to Hamilton, 3 May 1799, DQW 3:131-32; Silas Talbot to SecNav, 7 May 1799, Harold C. Syrett, ed., *The Papers of Alexander Hamilton,* 27 vols. (New York: Columbia University Press, 1960), 23:117n; Silas Talbot to SecNav, 17 May 1799, Adams Papers, microfilm, reel 395.

31 SecNav to Silas Talbot, 29 May 1799, DQW, 273.

32 Extract from log of USS *Constitution,* 5 June 1799, DQW 3:309.

33 For Adams's position in this matter see his long letter to SecNav, 23 July 1799, DQW 3:528-32.

34 Adams to SecNav, 7 June 1799, DQW 3:312.

35 SecNav to Adams, 25 June 1799, DQW 3:399-400.

36 SecNav to Stephen Higginson, 19 June 1799, DQW 3:369; SecNav to Silas Talbot, 27 July 1799, DQW 3:554.

37 SecNav to Silas Talbot, 25 June 1799, DQW 3:401.

38 SecNav to Truxtun, 3 July 1799, DQW 3:463.

39 Silas Talbot to Adams, 3 July 1799, Adams Papers, reel 395; Adams to Silas Talbot, 8 July 1799, Talbot Papers, RIHS.

40 Adams to SecNav, 23 July 1799, DQW 3:528-32.

41 Eugene S. Ferguson, *Truxtun of the Constellation* (Baltimore: Johns Hopkins University Press, 1956), 178-87.

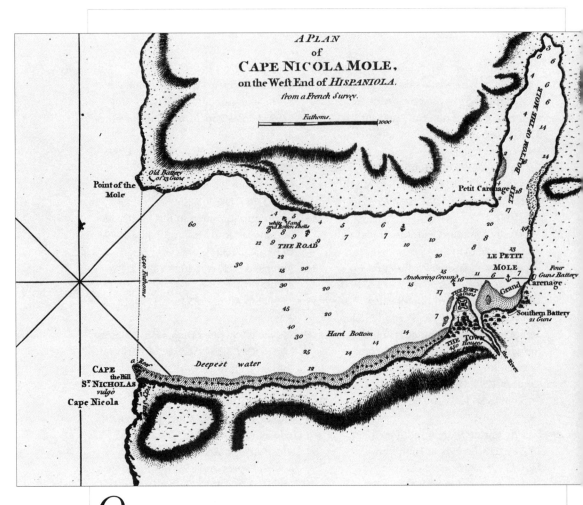

*O*NE OF THE principal ports on the western shore of Hispaniola was Mole St.
Nicholas, shown here in a 1794 chart. It
was here that Silas Talbot tracked down
Admiral Sir Hyde Parker when in the
West Indies to represent impressed
American seamen in 1797, and it was
here that he re-provisioned Constitution
in December 1799.

(Judy Beisler photo, Mystic Seaport Museum, MSM 95-4-7)

Chapter Eight

Quasi War

A s *Constitution* cleared Cape Cod's Race Point, her crew went to work snugging the frigate down for the cruise to Norfolk. From the quarterdeck Talbot watched as officers and men stood to their stations. Despite the command presence, this new Captain was a bit uneasy. It had been more than 20 years since he had had charge of a warship, and he had never sailed anything like this mighty frigate. Nor was he comforted by the thought that it was an open secret that Stoddert, Truxtun and others thought he was a soldier at heart and thus no seaman.

As he stood by the wheel Captain Talbot gazed along the spar deck and took the measure of his ship. This deck stretched forward nearly 200 feet. From the knightheads the bowsprit stabbed forward another 65 feet. Just under the bowsprit and above the cutwater was a graceful figurehead. It was Hercules "standing on the firm rock of Independence resting one hand on the fasces, which was bound by the genius of America and the other hand presenting a scroll of paper supposed to be the *Constitution* of America with proper appendages, the foundation of Legislation." Close to the bulwark, lashed down behind closed gunports, Talbot could count two dozen stubby carronades. These pug-nosed cannon, short of range but powerful, fired a 32-pound shot. One deck below were 30 larger brethren, the main battery of fire-belching long guns, each capable of delivering a 24-pound shot. They too were hunkered down behind closed gunports.[1]

Through the complicated weave of rigging, Talbot cast his eye up. Rising from the neatly holystoned deck were three fir sticks, the mizzen, main and foremast, each of them composed of four parts, the lower mast, topmast, topgallant and royal. The mainmast, tallest of the three, was nearly 220 feet above the deck. Where the lower and topmast joined on each mast were platforms—fighting tops. From this lofty perch marine sharpshooters were stationed in battle to fire down on an enemy's deck. When not crowded with marines, the tops were home to the topmen, sailors sent aloft to handle the frigate's sails. At right angles to the masts were at least a dozen yards from which the frigate set an acre of canvas that could push her ahead at a maximum speed of 12 knots.

To man these guns and sail this ship, Talbot had a crew of nearly 500 men who lived in a crammed world later described by Herman Melville as an "oaken box." According to Melville, it was in this box that "the sons of adversity meet the children of calamity, and here the children of calamity meet the offspring of sin." For the great seaman-author, who had sailed as one of the sons of adversity in *Constitution*'s sister frigate *United States*, the navy was an "asylum for the perverse, the home of the unfortunate."[2]

Talbot would have understood Melville's colorful description. He was a horny-handed seaman himself—a man who had come in through the hawse. He knew the kinds of sailors likely to swing their hammocks on the berth deck, and he held no romantic notions about their character or conduct. To keep order in this floating asylum Talbot relied upon the naval regulations and their enforcement by the strong hands of his officers. Chief among those were the ship's four Lieutenants and the Captain of Marines. In appointing Isaac Hull to be *Constitution*'s first Lieutenant, the President did the ship and Talbot a great favor.

The 25-year-old Hull was the son of a respectable Derby, Connecticut, family. Going to sea as a young man, he had traded to the West Indies aboard some of his father's vessels. He rose to command just in time to suffer capture by French privateers. It was then that he decided to enter the navy, and with the help of his uncle William Hull, a prominent soldier of the Revolution, he managed to secure a lieutenancy in March 1798. He had served on two cruises aboard *Constitution* under Nicholson and was now on his third trip aboard the frigate. Hull had a reputation for being good natured and well liked by both officers and men. From the point of view of a Captain who had not been to sea in 20 years, nor ever commanded a vessel the size of *Constitution*, Hull's most valuable contribution to the cruise was his well-known skill as a seaman and ship-handler.[3]

Constitution's second Lieutenant was Robert Hamilton, a cousin to Talbot's mentor and defender, Alexander Hamilton. The former Treasury Secretary had introduced his cousin to the Captain some months before in New York. Talbot took his cue and recommended young Hamilton to Stoddert, who was quick to endorse the choice. Ironically, by the time the appointment was made, Adams and Hamilton were at odds, and if the President had enjoyed a free choice, it is likely this Lieutenant would have seen early retirement. On the other hand, both Talbot and Stoddert had outstanding political debts to Alexander Hamilton, and finding his cousin a berth aboard *Constitution* was a convenient way to discharge the obligation. Sensing the uproar his intervention might raise, Adams made no objection.[4]

Rounding out Talbot's quartet of Lieutenants were third Lieutenant Isaac Collins and fourth Lieutenant Edward Boss. The latter came aboard with his son Edward, an acting midshipman. Unlike Hull and Hamilton, neither of these Lieutenants had much in the way of experience commanding men at sea. Talbot was wary of them. Collins seemed too fond of drink and Boss had a reputation for being a "quarrelsome alcoholic." Talbot could only hope they would earn his confidence.[5]

In addition to her crew of 450 seamen, *Constitution* also carried a contingent of approximately 50 marines commanded by Captain Daniel Carmick. Although Talbot was a bit stale leading men at sea, he had, albeit some years past, at least done so. He had never commanded marines.

Marines aboard sailing warships were in an unusual and sometimes uncomfortable position. While they shared the seaman's "oaken box," in bearing, uniform and function they lived in a world deliberately walled off from their fellow travelers. In battle they took positions in the fighting tops and fired down on the enemy. They led boarding and shore parties. When not engaged in combat, the marines acted as the ship's policemen, a role that won them few friends among the seamen. What the marines did not do was participate in handling the ship. In the words of Captain Carmick, his men would "do no kind of work that will Tar their Cloathes."[6] Carmick's imperative was an inheritance from Britain's Royal Navy, upon which the Americans modeled themselves. Indeed, the pejorative term "sogering," meaning to shirk work, was a corruption of the word "soldiering" which sailors in the British Navy used to describe marines. American bluejackets viewed their marines with equal disdain.

The tender relations between marines and seamen could also invade the wardroom. According to naval regulations, the commander of the marine detachment reported directly to the Commandant of Marines in Philadelphia. It was an arrangement that could well lead to the ship's captain, a despot in his own right, feeling that his authority was being circumvented and abridged. Fortunately for life aboard *Constitution*, Talbot and Carmick were able men who held one another in high regard. They were careful to tread lightly in those delicate areas of divided command.

Captain Carmick's command capacity was soon to be tested. When he reported aboard *Constitution* in Boston he was shocked at what greeted him. He described the men of his detachment as a "shabby set of animals" who "could not shoot a musket or march across the deck."[7] The source of such incompetence was Samuel Nicholson. Throughout his command Captain Nicholson had never allowed the marines aboard *Constitution* to drill. To Captain Carmick's great relief, Talbot quickly agreed to allow him to drill the men and do whatever else was necessary to get them into fighting condition. While others aboard the frigate might not have agreed, the slow passage from Boston to Norfolk was just what Carmick needed. It provided him time to organize a seagoing boot camp. In his report from Norfolk to the Commandant of Marines on 18 August, Carmick noted that, while the men were still not as fit as he required, they had improved greatly upon their scandalous state of only a month before.[8]

As *Constitution* sailed into Lynnhaven Bay, she passed *United States* and *Insurgent* outward bound. Talbot knew they were on their way to stations in the West Indies. He was determined to join them there as quickly as possible. His first task was to fit a new bowsprit from the stores collected at Norfolk. With an impatient Captain barking at them, the carpenters finished that task with alacrity. After taking on additional stores and a few more men, including a marine drummer, *Constitution* departed Hampton Roads on 26 August. Talbot's orders were to proceed directly to Cayenne, a port on Cayenne Island in French Guiana, where, according to the Secretary, "the French have some large Privateers which harass considerably our Trade to Surinam."[9] Cayenne, however, was only a stopover point where *Constitution* could wait out the waning days of the hurricane season. By mid-October 1799, Stoddert expected Talbot to be away from there and on station off the island of Hispaniola where the Secretary told him he should "remain the whole Winter & perhaps longer."

Stoddert had a dual purpose in sending Talbot first to Cayenne and then to Hispaniola. By keeping *Constitution* on the move he was keeping her away from her sisters *United States* and *Constellation*. There was a fair argument for keeping these frigates together as a force incomparably stronger than anything the French might be able to present; however, both Adams and Stoddert decided that the greater advantage was to be had by dispersing vessels over a broader area. The official justification was tactical—that is, three frigates on independent command could sweep and secure a broader area. The political justification was just as compelling. Stoddert would have been mad to put these scorpions—Barry, Truxtun and Talbot—in the same bottle. No area of command was large enough to accommodate these men. They had to be kept apart. The Secretary managed this separation by putting Talbot to the south while keeping Barry cruising off the coast until he was ready to be dispatched to Europe on a diplomatic errand. As for Truxtun, he was ordered to the windward station far from Hispaniola. From a naval perspective the plan was seriously flawed, but under the circumstances Stoddert had little choice.

Unlike the slow sail from Boston to Norfolk, *Constitution* caught a fair breeze that carried her swiftly down towards Cayenne. Three weeks out of Norfolk, at latitude 18°46′ and west of Guadeloupe, *Constitution* took up the pursuit of a suspicious vessel. Within a few hours the fast frigate was able to overtake and board *Amelia*, a Hamburg merchant ship that had been captured only ten days before by a Frenchman. Talbot took her as a prize, and after putting a crew aboard he ordered her off to New York to the care of his son and agent. To George, he wrote "I stand pledged for your good conduct. I know you will not deceive me."[10] With that business tidied up, Talbot resumed his course to Cayenne.

Constitution cruised off Cayenne only briefly. Talbot was already overdue at Hispaniola and he wished to hurry there. Furthermore, he found that the situation in the region had taken a turn for the better. In August the British had occupied Guiana, and while the port of Cayenne was still in French hands, it was under close scrutiny by British squadrons, lessening the need for an American presence. Talbot made a 72-hour reconnaissance in the area and then sailed north for Guadeloupe. He passed the island on the 8th of October and a week later came up on the eastern end of Hispaniola.

For three days Talbot kept within 20 miles of the northern coast as he made his way westward toward Cap François and a rendezvous with Dr. Edward Stevens, the American consul.[11]

Encountered by Columbus on his first voyage, Hispaniola had a long and tragic history. Within a few generations of their conquest the Spanish invaders managed to devastate the land and destroy the native population. For the most part the Spanish only settled the eastern end of the island, leaving the western portion sparsely inhabited. This lack of population proved to be an invitation for interlopers, and by the end of the seventeenth century, French settlers had arrived from nearby Tortuga island as well as from other French possessions in the West Indies and settled in fair numbers along the western shore. In 1697, by the Treaty of Rijswijk, the western third of the island was ceded officially to France and renamed Saint Domingue. Under French rule the new colony prospered. Hundreds of thousands of slaves were imported to labor on very lucrative plantations that grew sugar, coffee, cocoa, indigo and cotton. By the eve of the French Revolution two thirds of France's overseas investments were on this island. At the same time the population of Saint Domingue was approximately 556,000. Of that number 500,000 were slaves.[12]

In the summer of 1791, inspired by the thundering rhetoric of the French Revolution, the slaves of Saint Domingue rose in rebellion. Thus began a struggle that ended, in its first phase at least, in February 1794 when, in order to keep the island loyal, the government in Paris abolished slavery.[13] The following year, by the Treaty of Basel, Spain ceded the eastern portion of Hispaniola to France. But at that time French forces were not able to take possession of their new colony. The army of the republic was busy conquering Europe, and the navy was confined to port by Britain's Royal Navy.

With Spanish authority gone and the French not yet arrived, affairs on Hispaniola were confused and uneasy. It was a tinderbox made even more dangerous by the presence of more than half a million newly freed slaves. These men and women were ostensibly citizens of the republic, but the Saint Domingue government was still in the hands of white planters. The points of friction were many. What most people feared on the island was the outbreak of a race war. For the Americans the situation was especially awkward. As a slave-holding society, the United States was reluctant to deal with, let alone support, a black government. On the other hand, following the age-old dictum that "the enemy of my enemy is my friend," it made sense to encourage any group resisting French authority.

In the near-anarchy brought on by the loosening of foreign control on Hispaniola, two remarkable men came to the fore—André Rigaud and Toussaint L'Ouverture. Rigaud's connections were with the mulatto elite of the island, and thence to France, whereas Toussaint led the black faction. Within a short time these two men and their armies were involved in savage fratricidal war. Toussaint's power centered in the north, while Rigaud's forces commanded the south of the island. In 1798, as part of the diplomatic break, the U.S. Congress had suspended all trade with France and her dependencies. What would soon become the new nation called Haiti, despite its confused state, was still technically a colony of France and was therefore included in the American embargo.

Haiti's distress served the interests of both the United States and Great Britain. In the initial stages of confusion on the island, the English, seeing an opportunity to strike at the French and take a strategic position in the West Indies, had actually invaded. The invasion turned out to be folly, particularly because it became apparent that as much could be gained diplomatically as militarily and at a significantly lower cost. Under the astute direction of General Thomas Maitland, the British forces withdrew—but not before concessions were extracted from Toussaint which would allow British trade with areas under his control and a commitment from the black General that he would make no attempt against the island of Jamaica.

America's interests in Haiti were akin to Great Britain's, and Toussaint was anxious to secure American favor. In November 1798 he wrote secretly to President Adams and offered to accept any reasonable terms the President might offer if the United States would end its embargo. Adams was agreeable. Trade with Toussaint would help distress the French while at the same time filling American ships and pockets. There was more than the usual amount of cynicism to be found in these arrangements. Toussaint had no illusions that the slave-holding power to the north would embrace his cause, and many in the American administration were less than enthusiastic about entering any agreement with a former slave. Nonetheless, cooperation served both sides. The deal was struck. Adams would allow trade and Toussaint would not permit the French to use his ports.[14]

Talbot was aware of the contradictions in his new nation's relationship with Toussaint, and his feelings were complicated by his own attitude toward slavery. With him aboard the *Constituton* was William Roberts, the Jamaican slave he had owned for several years. Talbot also knew a good deal about Hispaniola and the West Indies. He had, after all, lived and traveled in these islands for two years. It is likely that the President shared his thoughts with the Captain on American interests and policy in the West Indies when Talbot made his visit to Quincy in 1799, for it was precisely at this time that Adams was preparing a proclamation opening Toussaint's ports to American trade. Some Americans wanted to do even more to help Toussaint, and perhaps themselves. Stephen Higginson, the navy agent in Boston, had 4,000 Prussian muskets in his warehouse which he had not been able to sell. He proposed to ship them to Toussaint on board *Herald*, a U.S. Navy vessel bound for Hispaniola. Stoddert said no; he was not prepared to sell arms to a black insurgency.[15]

From off Cap François Talbot sent a message to Consul Stevens asking for the latest intelligence. A friend of Alexander Hamilton's, Edward Stevens had been posted to Haiti for the specific purpose of assuring Toussaint of American support. Indeed, at the time of Talbot's arrival Stevens was away from the Cap negotiating with the General.

While Talbot waited for the Consul's return, he went about the business of establishing his authority. Although his station included all the waters off Hispaniola, and other nearby islands, for practical purposes the area of action was at the western end of the island where trade as well as Toussaint's forces were concentrated. Talbot's squadron consisted of *Boston*, a small frigate of 28 guns under the command of the very able Massachusetts Captain George Little; *General Greene*, another small frigate with Christopher Perry of Newport in command; and the brig *Norfolk* commanded by William Bainbridge. Later, Talbot's force was augmented by the ship *Herald*, whose Captain Charles Russell had been informed bluntly by the Secretary that his charge was "one of the oldest Vessels in Service, and has been so unfortunate as never to have been in Action nor to have captured any thing." Stoddert expected more. In addition, two smaller auxiliary vessels, the schooner *Experiment* and the brig *Augusta*, joined at the end of the year.[16]

Protecting commerce, lending support to Toussaint and chasing privateers kept Talbot and his Captains busy. It also presented the "Commodore" with certain problems.[17] Covering such a vast area argued for spreading out the force, yet rumors were circulating that the French had dispatched several armed vessels to the island. Under those circumstances Talbot took seriously the risk of dispersing his vessels. Although he eventually felt compelled to send his subordinates to cruise at a distance, for reasons of command and control he kept his own ship near Cap François. It was a sound decision, but it removed *Constitution* from a good deal of the action. And even in his own area at Cap François Talbot found himself isolated from the local action, since the deep draft of his frigate kept him offshore and unable to chase the shallow-draft privateers that were nibbling at trade.

Constitution's draft was not the only reason Talbot cruised offshore. Early in November, when Stevens finally came aboard to visit, the consul laid before Talbot the delicate political situation. He told the Captain that while the arrival of the American squadron brought great comfort, it also introduced potential problems. The appearance of foreign warships in the harbor might ignite hostile feelings and result in violence. It would be best, he suggested, if Talbot kept his vessels out of port and away from the coast.[18]

Talbot had no quarrel with Stevens's request. He had no wish to introduce himself or his squadron into the confusion that passed for local politics. On the other hand, he did have to support his ships. Stoddert had promised to send provision vessels but their arrival was unpredictable. Talbot knew from experience how fragile the health of a crew was in tropical climes. Stoddert might be able to forward biscuit and salt horse, but to keep his men healthy Talbot needed fresh provisions and ample good water. These could only be secured ashore.

Out of a welter of worries over politics, health and resupply, Talbot fashioned an ingenious system for support. Initially he thought he could rely on Nathan Levy, the navy agent at Cap François, to send out provision vessels. In this, as in so many other ways, Levy proved feckless and whined that he could not find a single vessel to send out. Talbot then decided to importune passing American merchantmen for supplies. When that failed, as a last resort he sent one of his smallest vessels into port to ferry out fresh meat and produce. By late November *Constitution* had been at sea for nearly one hundred days without dropping anchor. While Talbot was able to replenish his fresh food stores from Cap François, albeit with difficulty, getting water was another problem. When the frigate left Norfolk she stowed below 200 tons of water. Since arriving on station Talbot had managed on occasion to take in some replacement casks, but even under the best of circumstances transferring casks of water, each weighing several hundred pounds, from one vessel to another at sea, was difficult and slow. In a hot climate, and with a crew of 500 thirsty men, *Constitution* needed water and plenty of it.

Dry water casks finally convinced Talbot to leave his station and sail west to Mole St. Nicholas. The Mole was one of the best harbors in all of the West Indies. It had deep water, faced on the Windward Passage, and was surrounded by lofty mountains. For some time the British out of Jamaica had used this "Gibraltar" as a forward position from which to protect the approaches to Jamaica, and this had been one of the places on the island that British forces had occupied. Had it been left up to Admiral Hyde Parker, Talbot's old "friend" and still commander at Jamaica, British forces would still be there. It was General Maitland who had ordered withdrawal over the Admiral's objections. Parker was a naval officer who had trouble seeing over the beach and could not understand that, however impregnable the Mole looked from the sea, landward the port was vulnerable.[19]

On Sunday afternoon 2 December 1799, for the first time in 100 days, *Constitution* dropped anchor. Talbot wasted no time getting to the business at hand. In less than a week he took aboard 191 tons of water, discharged 15 seamen whose terms of service were up, overhauled the rigging, and brought aboard four bullocks for the ship's mess. Sunday morning about dawn *Constitution* hove short on her anchor cable, took a pilot aboard and headed for sea. With her casks full she now drew more than 22 feet as she laid a course back towards Cap François. Once underway Talbot announced to the crew that henceforth water would be rationed.[20]

Constitution resumed her routine of offshore patrol. During this time Talbot kept up a frequent correspondence with Stevens, and contrary to the customary relationship between naval officers and diplomats, Stevens and Talbot came to hold one another in high regard and friendship. Just after Christmas, as he was preparing to visit Toussaint, Stevens wrote to the Secretary of State with praise for his naval friend.[21]

> *I have had several Interviews with Capt. Talbot since I wrote*
> *you last. I find him so candid - so prudent & liberal that I am*
> *convinced that he will do every Thing that can contribute to the*
> *good of the Service & for supporting the Dignity and Interest*
> *of the U. States. It is a happy Circumstance for me to have a man*
> *of his Character to cooperate with. I shall see him again as soon*
> *as I return from the West & shall do every Thing in my Power*
> *to assist him in his operations during his Continuance on this*
> *Station.*

Talbot's "Continuance on this Station" remained dependent upon his capacity to supply his squadron. Stoddert understood Talbot's plight. To help the situation, early in December the Secretary ordered the storeship *Elizabeth* to sail in convoy with the brig *Augusta* to Cap François. *Elizabeth*'s cargo was consigned to agent Levy who, according to Stoddert, was to see to its distribution among Talbot's little fleet. Sending supplies down from the States solved the problem of being forced to buy local goods at exorbitant prices. But how to get these foodstuffs from the supply vessels on board *Constitution*? Stoddert and Levy simply assumed that *Constitution* and her squadron would have to come to port, whatever the political consequences. Talbot had a different plan.

On the last day of 1799 *Constitution* was jogging back and forth about 20 miles off Cap François. The breeze was light and the sky cloudy. At dawn her lookout called to the deck announcing a strange sail to the N N E. As he had done dozens of times since his arrival in these waters, Talbot intercepted the stranger and ordered the vessel to heave to and stand by to receive a boarding party. It was *Elizabeth*. Talbot made a bold decision. Instead of allowing the storeship to pass into Cap François and offload her cargo, and then go through the difficulty of finding ways to get the stores aboard his vessels, Talbot decided to organize an underway replenishment.

Supplying a vessel at sea is a tricky business. No captain in the United States Navy had ever tried it before; nonetheless, Talbot was determined that he would keep his command at sea and not lose valuable time, or get mired in shoreside politics, by coming into Cap François. At ten in the morning *Constitution* and *Elizabeth*, both lying to, began the difficult chore of hoisting hundreds of barrels and casks out of *Elizabeth*'s hold, over the side, and then gently lowering them into *Constitution*'s boats. The two vessels tried to remain as close as possible, but ships lying to need considerable space between them lest they collide, and so the transfer needed to be made in ship's boats. The boats came alongside the frigate where these same cumbersome barrels and casks had to be hauled aboard and stowed below. It was heavy work. Talbot and his crew were blessed with a kind sea and an overcast sky. Men from *Elizabeth* and *Constitution* labored for a steady twelve hours well into the night, working by the dim light of shipboard lanterns. Work resumed in the morning, and by late evening *Constitution* had taken aboard tons of provisions, including:[22]

260 barrels of bread
75 barrels of beef
75 barrels of pork
15 barrels of Indian meal
10 barrels of flour
30 barrels of potatoes
4 tierces of rice
8 barrels of cheese
1 tierce of peas
1 cask of peas
6 kegs of butter

After dark the winds continued calm but a heavy swell drove down from northward and forced Talbot to suspend operations. The swells increased during the night, but by dawn the sea had calmed enough to allow *Constitution* to continue replenishment. By four in the afternoon the job was completed. *Constitution* resumed her patrol off Cap François.

As the father of American underway replenishment, Silas Talbot helped give "legs" to the United States Navy. By resupplying at sea ships could remain on duty for prolonged periods of time, an operation Talbot pioneered and one in which the modern U.S. Navy excels. Talbot himself continued and improved on this technique. In February he rendezvoused with a supply vessel out of New York under convoy of the brig *Richmond*. The seas were less kind in this instance and the operation dragged on for three days. In April another store ship arrived and the process was repeated. To supplement these major resupplies from home Talbot also took on smaller amounts of stores from vessels captured by other members of the squadron. Silas Talbot deserves great credit for keeping his ship at sea. For the 366 days of his command he kept his frigate at sea for 347 days, a remarkable feat in any navy in any age.

Victuals and water were not all that was needed to keep a ship of war at sea. Wooden ships are lively, almost living things. They need constant care and adjustment. Henry Wadsworth Longfellow, whose own uncle Henry Wadsworth was killed while serving aboard *Constitution* during the Barbary Wars, caught this sense of life when he described the moment of a ship's launching:[23]

She starts, - she moves, - she seems to feel
The thrill of life along her keel,

And, spurning with her foot the ground,
With one exulting, joyous bound,
She leaps into the ocean's arms!

Constitution's leap had been problematical. She had what her former Captain and best historian, Tyrone Martin, has described as a "shakey shakedown." Her bowsprit worked so much as to threaten opening the bow, her foremast was sprung and in general her tophamper showed signs of weakness. Eighteen months later, to his great distress, Talbot discovered that despite considerable work the frigate still had serious problems aloft. On Saturday 14 December the carpenter reported that upon inspection he had discovered that the fore topmast trestle trees were sprung. Talbot ordered the fore topmast brought down and replaced with a new one. At the same time another crew working aft was busy taking down the old spanker mast and putting up a new one.

The foremast and spanker were irksome but not critical problems. They could be fixed at sea. Three days later a serious problem arose when the officer on watch noticed about noon that the mainmast "laboured very much about 10 or 12 feet below the Tressletrees." Closer examination revealed that the mast was checked—that is, cracked—in several places. Lest it go over the side in the next heavy blow, Talbot ordered the carpenters to attend to the problem immediately. At sea the only possible solution was to "fish" the mast. Fishes were splints attached to broken or weakened spars to reinforce them. The carpenters spent several days fashioning two oak fishes, each 32 feet long, which were then attached to the weakened portion of the mast by woolding—that is, wrapping the fish tight to the mast with heavy cordage. By 8 January the repair job was finished and Talbot was confident his mainmast would hold.

In the new year the war between Toussaint and Rigaud heated up. Toussaint's forces began to move south to seize Rigaud's bastion at Jacmel. Key to Toussaint's success was control of the Gulf of Gonave, a huge bay 80 miles broad at the mouth and nearly 100 miles deep that opened onto the Windward Passage. Notorious for its frequent and sudden calms, these waters were a rich hunting ground for Rigaud's privateers. Almost as soon as a merchantman's sails went slack for want of a breeze, swift row barges bristling with armed men came out to rob and ravage hapless victims. Rigaud's marauding hampered Toussaint's move south while it also harassed

American trade. In the new year Talbot ordered two of his squadron, *Augusta* and *Experiment*, over to the Gulf to protect American commerce. Their presence served the interests of America and Toussaint L'Ouverture.

During her cruise in the Gulf, *Experiment* captured the schooner *Amphitheatre*. She was fast and armed and offered Talbot an opportunity he could not afford to lose. Ever since coming on station he had been frustrated by *Constitution's* inability to get into the action. About all he had been able to do was to jog off Cap François and watch as his smaller vessels went in pursuit of an elusive enemy. Their modest success was encouraging but not very profitable. As an old privateersman Talbot's concerns were never far removed from prize money. As Commodore of the squadron he was entitled to a five percent share in the value of captures made by members of his squadron even when he was not present. As Captain, however, he could take a fifteen percent share of any captures *Constitution* made. Talbot wanted prizes, and in *Amphitheatre* he saw his vehicle.

Talbot ordered *Amphitheatre* to sail in consort with *Constitution* off the north coast in the vicinity of Montechristi. To command her he appointed a very able young Lieutenant from *Experiment* named David Porter. With profit in mind, Talbot crafted his orders to Porter with great care.[24]

> *To prevent any mistake that may arise in case any prizes*
> *should be taken by the Amphitheatre or the Constitution while*
> *you have the command of her. You are to understand, that the*
> *crew of the tender you command is to be considered as a part of*
> *the crew of the Constitution, and that if any prizes are taken*
> *by either in company or separately the effects are to be divided*
> *as if taken by the Constitution, as if you and your crew were*
> *really on board her, yourself sharing in the class of my*
> *Lieutenants, and the other part of your crew to share as if on board*
> *the Constitution.*

Talbot insisted on putting this in writing since, according to him, he had been much abused by one of his captains who had reneged on a verbal agreement to share prize proceeds. That Captain, George Little of Boston, had taken a particularly rich prize, *Les Deux Anges*. Talbot asserted that he and Little had verbally pledged to share all prizes on the same basis as had Talbot and Porter. Little had a different view. He denied having ever agreed to such a thing. Talbot would never suffer this to happen again. In the meantime he wrote to son George in New York and told him to prepare for litigation against Little.[25]

With *Ampitheatre* as his consort, Talbot laid plans for a rich capture. For some time he had been aware that farther east at Puerto Plata a former British vessel, now the French letter of marque *Sandwich*, was loading cargo for France. It was a tempting target, but there was a complication. Although the entire island had been ceded to France, the eastern two thirds was still under Spanish authority. Spain was neutral and so too was Puerto Plata.

As he pondered his strategy, happy news arrived. *Ampitheatre* had made a successful attack against some small French privateers. In the course of the battle she had been damaged and was unable to pursue the fleeing French. To aid her, Lieutenant Isaac Collins had been sent from *Constitution* with two armed boats. Collins caught up with his quarry and during the melee an American sloop, *Sally*, had been recaptured. *Sally* fitted nicely into Talbot's plan, since before her capture she had been a routine visitor to Puerto Plata and could enter the port without causing alarm. If Talbot moved quickly before news of *Sally*'s capture reached Puerto Plata, he might be able to fill her with his men, then get her into the port and alongside *Sandwich* without causing any suspicion.

Talbot turned to his first Lieutenant, Isaac Hull, to command this cutting-out expedition. For all the fame that was to be his, Isaac Hull always held that this command was one of his greatest moments.[26] Hull took with him about 80 men along with Captain Carmick and his Lieutenant William Amory. The men from *Constitution* stayed silently below as *Sally* came into port. Her American Captain, Thomas Sandford, a familar figure at Puerto Plata, had been "persuaded" to stand on deck and discourage any suspicion from shore. About ten in the morning *Sally* eased over towards *Sandwich*. *Sally* came up on her starboard side, and as she made contact Hull, Carmick, Amory and 80 screaming men, armed with cutlass and pistol, scrambled over the bulwark. Within minutes *Sandwich* was secure. Next Hull sent a party off to spike the four cannon in a small fort overlooking the harbor. Now came the hardest part—preparing *Sandwich* for sea. It took Hull and his crew more than twelve hours to clear the decks, set up the rigging and bend sails, but by midnight *Sandwich*, escorted by *Sally*, caught the land breeze and headed for her rendezvous with *Constitution*. Talbot greeted Hull with high praise and congratulated Amory and Carmick. Meanwhile the Spanish authorities were preparing a strong protest over this violation of neutral rights. Although the prize was bravely taken, ultimately the courts would decide if it was legal.

Sandwich's capture on 11 May came at a time when Talbot was again concerned with the condition of his vessel, particularly the mainmast. Over time not even the ingenuity of *Constitution's* carpenters could stay the forces of nature working against a flawed spar. Talbot was keeping a careful eye on it, and on 4 July he wrote to Higginson in Boston to report that, while repairs were holding, the mast was giving way and needed to be replaced. Ten days later the matter turned critical. During the first dog watch Lieutenant Hull reported that the mast was inclining forward.

No time could be wasted. The maintopmast had to come down. Doing it while underway was impossible. Talbot had no choice but to head for Cap François. Within 48 hours of Hull's report *Constitution* arrived at the Cape and her carpenters went to work. It took a week of heavy work to get the masts and rigging down, repaired and put back in place.

Soon after dropping anchor *Constitution* was visited by General Moise, the local commander and Toussaint's adopted nephew. He extended an invitation to dine. Talbot accepted, and on the afternoon of 16 July a party of officers from *Constitution* went ashore. Joined by Lieutenants Hamilton and Collins, Captain Carmick, the frigate's surgeon, Doctor Peter St. Medard, and the purser, James Dublois, Captain Talbot presented himself at the General's quarters. The scene turned bizarre.[27]

Lieutenant Isaac Collins was a drunken fool who on this hot July day had begun tippling long before the first toast was offered at the General's table. As the meal went on and the wine flowed, the Lieutenant alternated between boisterous talk and falling asleep. He downed glass after glass of wine, his tumbler in one hand, the other clutching the decanter. Talbot asked Carmick to quietly remove Collins. Carmick drew back. This officer who had swept over *Sandwich's* deck was reluctant to challenge a fellow officer. It must have been a very long lunch for everyone. Finally Collins stumbled out into the street. Talbot ordered Carmick and Hamilton to take him back to the ship. It was not easy. Collins kept pushing them away and falling in the gutter, all the time cursing Hamilton as a "damned Scotch bugger." They finally got him back to his cabin but that was not the end of it. Collins had stowed some liquor in his quarters, and the next morning when the Captain summoned his Lieutenant the steward could only report that the officer could not get out of bed. Talbot sent St. Medard to examine Collins. The man was indeed drunk, the Doctor reported, and were he to continue in this condition, his life might well be in peril.

It took Collins three days to recover. When he finally sobered up, he wrote a pleading letter to Talbot begging forgiveness and ascribing all his difficulties to his neglect to eat breakfast on the 16th. Talbot was neither persuaded nor amused by this pitiful excuse. He told the Lieutenant he had only two choices—resign from the service or be put under arrest. Alcohol abuse was widespread in the naval service. Drinking was hardly frowned upon, and by regulation every seaman was entitled to a half pint of "spirits" per day or a quart of beer. The overserved Lieutenant might well have expected Talbot to relent, for Collins's sin lay not so much in getting drunk as in doing it publicly. On 28 July Collins wrote another plaintive letter. This time he did not mention breakfast but instead told his Captain that he was in heavy debt and that dismissal from the service would ruin him. Talbot held firm, and on 4 August Isaac Collins resigned from the service.

While *Constitution* was repairing at the Cape, her sister *Constellation* arrived with orders from the Secretary. *Constitution* was to come home. Stoddert gave Talbot the welcome news while at the same time telling him what "great satisfaction" his conduct had given him and President Adams. Anxious to leave, and pleased to know that his welcome would be a warm one, Talbot prepared to sail.[28]

At three in the morning *Constitution*'s crew walked round the capstan to heave up the anchor. At dawn two pilots came aboard and the ship set sail. While the entrance at Cap François was deep, it was also narrow, at its widest not more than half a mile. The frigate had almost cleared the harbor when a sudden change of wind came on from the north. The breeze put the ship aback and her stern struck a reef. For nearly an hour she banged on the rock; but finally after some guns were moved forward and the anchor was set she came free and got under way. Fortunately, the grounding did no damage. *Constitution* was bound home to Boston.[29]

Notes

1 The best histories and descriptions of *Constitution* are Tyrone Martin, *A Most Fortunate Ship* (Chester, Connecticut: Pequot Press, 1980) and F. Alexander Magoun, *The Frigate Constitution and Other Historic Ships* (Salem, Massachusetts: Marine Research Society, 1928).

2 Herman Melville, *White Jacket,* 1850 (New York: Oxford University Press, 1990), 379.

3 Linda Maloney, *The Captain from Connecticut: The Life and Naval Times of Isaac Hull* (Boston: Northeastern University Press, l986) is by far the best and most complete biography of Hull.

4 Hamilton to Silas Talbot, 20 August 1798, B4 F15 STP.

5 Michael A. Palmer, *Stoddert's War: Naval Operations During the Quasi War With France, 1798-1801* (Columbia: University of South Carolina Press, 1987), 174. See also the several references to these officers in Christopher McKee, *A Gentlemanly and Honorable Profession: The Creation of the U.S. Naval Officer Corps, 1794-1815* (Annapolis, Maryland: U.S. Naval Institute Press, 1991).

6 Carmick to Major Commandant William Burrows, 19 August 1799, DQW 4:91-92.

7 Carmick to Burrows, 29 July 1799, DQW 3:480-81.

8 Carmick to Burrows, 18 August 1799, DQW 5:90-91.

9 Stoddert to Silas Talbot, 27 July 1799, DQW 3:553-54.

10 Silas Talbot to George Washington Talbot, 15 September 1799, B6 F1 STP.

11 The day-to-day movements and activities aboard *Constitution* may be followed in the appropriate volumes of DQW as well as in The Journal of Silas Talbot, USS *Constitution*, 14 December 1800-15 June 1801, Peabody Essex Museum; *Constitution*, Journal, 1 December 1798-15 February 1800, inscribed "Peter St. Medard," USS *Constitution* Museum; and Log, USS *Constitution*, 6 December 1798-20 October 1800, *Constitution* Museum.

12 These convoluted politics are best examined in Carolyn E. Fick, *The Making of Haiti: The Saint Domingue Revolution from Below* (Knoxville: University of Tennessee Press, 1990). The geographical designations can be confusing. In dispatches, and elsewhere, the island is variously referred to as Saint Domingue, Hispaniola and Haiti. For the sake of consistency I will use the term Hispaniola. Today the western end of the island is the Republic of Haiti. The eastern portion is the Dominican Republic.

13 Decree of the Convention on 16 Pluvoise Year II (4 February 1794).

14 John Adams, A Proclamation, 26 June l799, *A Compilation of the Messages and Papers of the Presidents, 1789-1908,* comp. James D. Richardson, 10 vols. (Washington: Bureau of National Literature and Art, l908), 1:288-89.

15 DQW 4:209-10, 235.

16 DQW 4:192.

17 At the time of Talbot's service the U.S. Navy did not use the rank of Commodore either officially or custom-

arily. After his naval service Talbot enjoyed being referred to as "Commodore."

18   DQW 5:461.

19   Palmer, *Stoddert's War*, 153-54.

20   For a thorough examination of *Constitution's* logistical problems see Tyrone Martin, "Underway Replenishment, 1799-1800," *American Neptune*, 46:159-64.

21   DQW 4:570.

22   DQW 4:590-91.

23   *"The Building of the Ship,"* in *The Poetical Works of Longfellow* (Boston: Houghton, Mifflin Company, 1975), 99-103.

24   DQW 5:263-64.

25   Silas Talbot to George Talbot, 5 February 1800, B6 F8 STP.

26   Reports of the expedition may be found in DQW 5:500-506.

27   Accounts of this episode and related correspondence may be found in Talbot, Memorandum, 17 July 1800; Collins to Silas Talbot, 20 July 1800; Silas Talbot to Collins, 20 July 1800; Collins to Silas Talbot, 28 July 1800; and Collins to Silas Talbot, 4 August 1800, all in B7 F5 STP.

28   DQW 5:510.

29   DQW 6:169.

*A*T ANCHOR IN PORT, Constitution
displays the jack on her bowsprit and,
with gunports opened, shows off 12
of her 24 carronades and 15 of her
30 long guns. The two other frigates
in her class were President, *launched*
in 1800, and United States, *launched*
in 1797.

(Courtesy Peabody Essex Museum, Salem, MA)

Chapter Nine

End of War — End of Service

Pushed by a warm summer breeze and carried along by the Gulf Stream, *Constitution* made her way northward. Talbot put in briefly at Charleston where, as a favor to Toussaint, he had agreed to deliver a distinguished passenger. General Augustus Joseph Michel, along with several other French officers, had been sent to Hispaniola by Napoleon. With his usual presumption and arrogance the First Consul expected that they would take key roles in the government of the island. Toussaint thought otherwise and suggested that the visitors were not welcome. His mission on the island at an end, Michel asked if Talbot would bring him to Charleston where he might visit relatives before continuing on to France. It was a pleasant voyage, with the amiable company of the French officers enlivening the wardroom mess. Within a few days *Constitution* was passing between Morris and Sullivan Islands and making her way up the channel into Charleston. She remained only long enough to set the Frenchmen ashore.[1]

Early on the morning of 24 August *Constitution* came around Race Point and entered Massachusetts Bay. She signaled for a pilot, and within a few hours the frigate was at anchor in President Roads. Talbot wasted no time. His plan was to discharge members of the crew whose enlistments were expired, then reprovision stores and, most importantly, replace the tophamper that had caused him so much trouble in the West Indies. All this was to be accomplished as quickly as possible so that he could get back to Hispaniola without delay.[2]

Talbot's passion for a quick turnaround was driven in part by a desire to serve the nation, but there was also his old appetite for prizes. To the Captain's embarrassment the tour around Hispaniola had been a great financial disappointment. Not only had few prizes been taken, but even the ones captured had proven unrewarding. *Amphitheatre*, for example, was described as tired and worn out in the service and of little value. As for *Sandwich*, the most valuable capture of the entire cruise, she was declared an illegal prize. Puerto Plata was deemed neutral Spanish territory, not a proper place for Americans to take prizes. *Sandwich* was to be returned to her owners. Adding to these woes was the distressing news that while prize money was short, legal fees were not. Much of the scanty proceeds from *Amphitheatre* were being eaten up by the court and lawyers.[3]

After getting repairs underway, Talbot left *Constitution* in the able hands of Isaac Hull and headed for New York and Philadelphia to see his family and tend to business. The reception was bound to be a bit chilly. He had been more attentive to his ship than to his wife. As she had done before during her husband's long absences, Becky had spent a good deal of her time in Philadelphia. When she got word that *Constitution* was putting in to Boston she hurried home. She need not have rushed.

Becky was annoyed. She had married a gentleman farmer who had then turned politician and had now become a sea rover. For three out of the last four years he had been on duty in the West Indies. She had not bargained for this style of life. Adding to her annoyance was the fact that while she wrote often to her wandering husband he rarely replied. As if to underscore this callousness, when *Constitution* arrived in Boston, Talbot, instead of rushing home, lingered with his ship and took up matters that could well have been attended to by Hull and the other lieutenants. Becky resented what she saw as the Captain's indifference, and in a somewhat testy letter to her husband, sent to him while he was in Boston, she referred sarcastically to his "long expected visit." She also took the occasion to let him know that her sister Susan in Philadelphia had sent up a marvelous silver tea urn. It cost one hundred pounds and was so splendid that all her friends thought it could only have been given to her by her husband. Of course it was not.[4]

Having scolded her husband for his behavior, Becky next addressed the behavior of young Henry. As a ten-year-old boy is wont to be, he was, according to his mother, "as wild as a Colt untamed." His regular school was on vacation, so to keep this colt corralled she had enrolled him by the week with a local woman who agreed to keep him busy and out of mischief. He needed the strong hand of his father. Where was he? Henry's stepbrothers went unmentioned. Indeed, Becky rarely had much to say about her stepchildren.[5]

News of Cyrus, George and Theodore was, as usual, mixed. Since George handled much of his father's business during his absence, he was the most frequent correspondent. George was the family informer. He relished passing on tales about Cyrus and Theodore, particularly the latter, who seemed of all the children to lead the most interesting life. If we are to believe George, Theodore had left Princeton behind him but had not left his bad habits there.

Like many young college graduates with indulgent parents, Theodore was far more interested in finding ways to spend money than to work for it. Ostensibly he was studying law in New York City with William Harrison; yet he spent more time relaxing in the New Jersey countryside than studying in the city. His excuse for these long absences was his health. He suffered from some sort of infection that caused a painful inflammation in one of his eyes. However bothersome this affliction may have been, it seemed to interfere only with work and not play. Theodore enjoyed what brother George referred to as a "propensity for pleasure."[6]

After recuperating from his eye problems, Theodore returned to New York where, in order to save money, he decided to board with his mother. It was not a happy household. Becky found Theodore's behavior unbecoming. Partying and playgoing occupied his evenings, and during the day he was often seen riding about town in grand style with reprobate company. All this cost money. Becky estimated he spent at least twenty dollars per week, probably double his salary, and it was a mystery to her where he found the money.

George thought he knew where his wastrel brother got his money. He checked first with his father's associates to discover that none of them had been underwriting Theodore. Nor did it seem that any of Harrison's clients had been tipping Theodore, as was the custom for law clerks. That left only one possibility. Theodore had fallen in with evil company and was probably borrowing money. A few more inquiries revealed that he had taken up with one of the city's most notorious high livers —Anthony Ackley. Theodore had been often seen in his company at the most disreputable places.[7]

Naturally George felt obliged to inform his father of Theodore's behavior, especially since the Captain's allowance to Theodore was helping to fund his son's good times. Ironically, at the very moment George was posting his version of the news to Talbot, Theodore was also writing to his father. The two versions are not reconcilable. Respectful, pious and subdued, Theodore's letters are the model of a son-to-father correspondence—not a hint of anything amiss or other than news of fine progress in his profession and character. He was, he assured his father, reforming his life. He had even joined a literary society in order to improve himself during his leisure time.[8]

Unctuous letters to his father notwithstanding, Theodore was not happy at Harrison's. The pay was pitiful and the tips a clerk often received for filing client papers were not forthcoming. Harrison, to Theodore's detriment, had eschewed private practice in favor of more certain government work. Theodore wanted out. He tested the waters by soliciting advice from his brother-in-law George Metcalfe. Metcalfe told him he was a fool even to think of leaving. Theodore did not consult George. Indeed, except to pick up his allowance, Theodore rarely visited his brother.[9]

Late in the spring of 1800 Theodore's world began to unravel. He learned that someone had written to his father and informed him of the real situation in New York. He suspected George but could not be certain. Faced with the risk of losing his father's patronage, Theodore leaped into action. He requested that several of his father's closest associates, including Richard Harrison and Abraham Skinner, write favorably of his character. To further demonstrate his repentance and new-found virtue, when his stepmother left for a visit to Philadelphia, Theodore took up residence with brother George, who reported to Talbot that "He is behaving well."[10]

While Theodore's self-indulgence must have troubled Silas Talbot, his other children did not leave him without care. George, following the example of his father, married a woman pregnant with his child, Maria DePeyster Banecker. She delivered a daughter in March 1800. As for George himself, he narrowly escaped death during the winter when he was struck with the "putrid sore throat." On the bright side, Betsey and George Metcalfe were doing well in Albany, where Metcalfe's law practice was growing and he was investing in real estate.

Cyrus, the eldest, and like his father a naval officer, was earning a fine reputation in the service. After commanding *Richmond* on a short cruise along the coast, he wrote to the Secretary indicating that he would prefer to be an officer on a large vessel rather than commander of a small one. Stoddert agreed and posted him to the frigate *United States* under the command of John Barry. Of all his children, Cyrus was most like his father, and the two were particularly close. Each had pledged to the other to care for his family should either not return from sea.[11]

Henry—Becky and Silas's only natural child—was quite different from his stepbrothers and stepsister. Living in a household dominated by his mother's social routines, and indulged by his father's prosperity, he was growing up in a world softer and more subtle than that of his siblings. He had earlier written to his father:[12]

> *My dear Papa*
> *I received your letter with a great deal of pleasure but I have*
> *all this winter gone to bed very early and get up as soon as the*
> *fire is made. I wash my face and hands well every morning.*
> *I don't miss going to school and learn as fast as I can. I have*
> *got fat red cheeks now. Mama says she wishes my dear Papa*
> *could see how handsome I look in my fur cap half boots and*
> *great coat. ... Mama sends her love to you. She has been very sick*
> *but is better now.*

Captain Talbot remained aboard *Constitution* for three weeks tidying up affairs. Finally, on the morning of 11 September, with William Roberts following to mind the luggage, he made his way over to Thacher's Tavern on Boston's State Street to catch the stage to New York. In the Captain's absence Lieutenant Hull was in command. Talbot left him one last order—"no women of ill fame must be allowed to take shelter on board the ship." With that parting shot Talbot took his leave, promising to return as soon as possible.[13]

It took nearly four days to cover the 220 miles between Boston and New York. The inconvenience of being jostled, bounced and bruised in a swaying coach was hardly to be tolerated. It was worse than any voyage he had endured at sea. Not even the beauty of the New England fall could compensate for the indignities of travel. If he had the luxury of time—and no letters from home to make him anxious—he probably would have elected to take passage on a coastwise packet, but wind and weather made such trips unpredictable. Although uncomfortable, the coach had the advantage of being fast and reliable.

On the first day the party made it to an inn just south of Providence. After breakfast the passengers climbed aboard the coach which rolled on through Norwich, Connecticut, down along the Thames River for a stop at New London, and then followed the shoreline to cross the Connecticut River on a ferry at Saybrook. There they put up for the night. Day three brought Talbot to Rye, New York, where he supped and slept—but only briefly, for the stage pulled out at three in the morning in order to make an early arrival in the city.

It was an exhausted and disheveled Silas Talbot who presented himself at Becky's door. It had been more than a year since they had seen one another, and whatever his condition, and however she felt about his tardiness, she was glad to have him home. Her joy, however, was whisked away by her husband's brusque announcement that he could stay only a week. Duty called in Boston. Becky was saddened and angry. After a year apart, one week seemed pitiful. There was barely enough time to see the boys and not enough time for Betsey to get down from Albany. Furthermore, Becky knew that most of Talbot's waking hours during these precious days would be eaten up by tending to a year's backlog of business, including household accounts, investments and the maddening tangle of affairs resulting from prize cases. Henry was disappointed too. There was so much he wanted to know about his father's adventures and so little time to learn. The week went by very quickly.

Having endured the stage to New York, Talbot opted for a more comfortable return to Boston by sea. The sea, however, was fickle. On the morning of 23 September he boarded a packet bound for Providence. She made her way up the East River and onto Long Island Sound where a strong east wind and a driving rain made the trip particularly miserable. Once the vessel rounded Point Judith, the wind shifted and it had to beat its way up the length of Narragansett Bay to Providence. After a day or two in Providence, Talbot took the stage to Boston and was back on board *Constitution* by the first of October.[14]

On the same day that he returned to his ship, Talbot reported to the Secretary that the frigate would be ready to sail on the first of November. As usual in the business of getting ships ready for sea, that prediction was optimistic. Rerigging took longer than anticipated and it was proving difficult to recruit seamen. The previous cruise had been a great disappointment for those who hoped for prize money. New recruits, suspecting that a second cruise would yield no better, were reluctant to sign on. Indeed, some of those already pledged to the ship deserted. But with the aid of local authorities, a relentless Lieutenant Isaac Hull tracked them down and sent them back on board where they were welcomed with "one dozen at the gangway."

Finally, after a delay of six weeks, *Constitution* got to sea on 14 December. Her destination was once again Hispaniola. This time, however, her orders were somewhat different. It had never been John Adams's intention that the unpleasantness with France should erupt into full-scale war. Although he was under considerable pressure from the more extreme elements of his own party, Adams refused to commit the nation to anything so dangerous. Sensing that the French too were reluctant to take such a step, in February 1799 Adams took a courageous stand. Without consulting his cabinet, most of whom would probably have objected, he nominated William Vans Murray, then United States minister to Holland, to be minister to France, thus restoring diplomatic relations which had been broken since the infamous XYZ affair. Opposition was fierce. Adams held his ground and in the end compromised only by agreeing to send a commission of three men rather than one minister to negotiate with the French. Talks between the American commissioners and the French got underway in March.[15]

Negotiations bogged down over a variety of complicated issues, particularly the question of indemnities for vessels seized illegally. Finally on 13 September the Americans called upon the French to sign a temporary convention that would simply end hostilities, leaving the outstanding complicated issues for future solution. On 30 September that convention was signed.

Although details of this agreement took several weeks to arrive in America, the hope that peace was near influenced the administration as orders were prepared for Talbot. Crafted at a moment when matters were hopeful yet still uncertain, the Captain's instructions were necessarily ambivalent. He was told to proceed to the Hispaniola station. Maintaining good relations continued to be a priority, but attacking the French was not. He was not to seek out the French, nor was he to spend time cruising in search of privateers. His task was to protect commerce by providing convoy escort.

Talbot could not have been pleased as he read his orders. His previous cruise had been most disappointing, but at least he had had the opportunity to take prizes. That he did not take more was simply bad luck. Following these orders he was in a situation where it would be virtually impossible to capture prizes unless a hostile vessel was foolish enough to come right up under his guns and offer itself as prey.[16]

On 14 December *Constitution* took the tide and fell down Boston harbor. In President Roads she was joined by the schooner *John* out of Gloucester bound for Cap François. Together they cleared Cape Cod and took up a course for Hispaniola.[17] Perhaps it was the rumor that this would likely be an unprofitable voyage that irked the crew, or it may have been the foul weather of the winter North Atlantic. For whatever reason, *Constitution's* crew was restless in December 1800. Three days out the Captain stopped the grog ration for twenty men who were absent during the mid watch. At least one man, however, still missed the message, and on Christmas Day Thomas Compton, a known troublemaker who had already spent several days in irons, was flogged for absenting himself from his watch. In barely a week Talbot had encountered nearly as much trouble out of the forecastle as he had seen during an entire previous voyage that had lasted a year.

If the crew's behavior caused some concern, so too did the frigate herself. *Constitution* plowed through heavy seas as she fought her way south and, according to her Captain, she rolled so badly that her gunports were often underwater. This was not the first time one of *Constitution's* commanders had experienced difficulties with the sailing qualities of the frigate. Samuel Nicholson had also had some problems. Talbot was cautious. He remembered the checked mast on the previous cruise, and he ordered the carpenter to visit each masthead every day and to "examine everything aloft that was of wood." The sailing master was to sound the hold every half hour. The boatswain was to check the rigging every day. And all lieutenants, midshipmen and sailing masters were to keep an "exact account of the ship's way and report daily to the Captain and not consult with each other."

On 19 December *Constitution* spoke a vessel bound from France. From her Talbot learned that "peace was made with France." He continued south. The Captain and his officers tried to put the best face on it, but everyone aboard now knew how little promise of profit this cruise held for them.

On 29 December Cap François came into sight. Two days later *Constitution* spoke the frigate *Congress*, Captain James Sever. Sever came aboard to pay his respects and remained for dinner. Talbot explained the latest diplomatic and political situation to Sever and asked for the most recent local intelligence. Sever reported that Toussaint continued to consolidate his control over the island and that the French were scarcer than ever. Sever also told Talbot that Consul Stevens, his wife and family were in fine health although Stevens himself was plagued by gout. They were all, according to Sever, looking forward to visiting *Constitution* and seeing their old friend again.

During the dinner Sever queried Talbot about *Constitution* and her sailing qualities. His own command *Congress*, a smaller sister to Talbot's frigate, had been launched at Portsmouth, New Hampshire, in August 1799. As the evening wore on and the wine flowed, there may have been a bit of boasting and perhaps a friendly challenge or two as to who had the faster ship. No captain could leave such a question unanswered, and there was only one way to prove one's self. Sever and Talbot agreed to race. The next morning at 7:00 the two frigates took the wind and set off. The race lasted four hours. As might have been expected *Constitution*, having the advantage of greater size, won handily. The next day *Congress* took leave and sailed for her station, a cruise track between Turks Head and Puerto Rico. *Constitution*, as was her wont, remained tacking off the Cape.

On 21 January Stevens came aboard. The consul and Talbot brought each other up to date on affairs. Stevens described Toussaint's continuing success on the island and his own desire to leave for home. His gout, aggravated by climate as well as his frequent indulgence at lavish diplomatic dinners, was kicking up. Besides, with Toussaint nearly triumphant and the war with the French over, he saw little reason to remain. Talbot agreed. As the two men chatted, talk turned to politics and the future.[17]

When Talbot left America, the nation was in the throes of electing a new president. The election was in a mess. After the states had selected their electors and these gentlemen had cast their ballots, it was clear that no one candidate had a sufficient majority to be elected. As prescribed by the Constitution (Article II sec. 1) the decision went over to the House where the vote would be by state. The choice was between the two top candidates, Thomas Jefferson and Aaron Burr. Jefferson, the Democratic Republican, found few friends in the Federalist ranks, including Silas Talbot. Burr, however, was known as a false and conniving man who could never be trusted. As the nation awaited the result of the election, Becky wrote to her husband describing the uncertainty of events. She, like the Captain, despised Burr.[18]

> *Who is to be President is the general cry in all Company.*
> *Burr it is supposed with the subtlety of a Fox will overreach*
> *both parties and come in triumphant. He has already declared*

> *what he means to do when at the head; a glorious substitute*
> *for General Washington. He may look down and say my poor*
> *Country how fast it has degenerated.*

Fortunately for the republic, after a month and 35 ballots in the House, Jefferson won on the 36th vote. The nation was saved from Aaron Burr. With peace near there was bound to be a demand to lay up the ships, and Jefferson, a man known for economy, was certain to agree. The future of the navy was in doubt.

Constitution remained on station but there was little left to do. In the weeks before returning home she did not take a single prize. The quasi war with France was over. As the days dragged on the crew saw little purpose in jogging along the western shore of Hispaniola. Their resentment found vent in various forms of misbehavior. To keep good order Talbot found himself punishing men on nearly a daily basis.

While *Constitution*'s Captain worked to maintain discipline and keep his ship and squadron in fighting trim, affairs in Washington were also turning. On 4 March Jefferson took the oath as President. His inaugural address was intended to calm the fears of his enemies. He told those few who crowded close to hear him that "We are all Federalists. We are all Democrats." Many of the new President's Federalist critics were pleased and comforted by this conciliatory speech. They still worried about his dangerously democratic ideas, but at least they no longer viewed this intellectual Virginian as the devil incarnate.

Among those who felt relieved at the gracious beginning of Jefferson's presidency was Benjamin Stoddert. Although a firm Federalist, he held the new President in high regard, and the President returned the compliment. Indeed, Jefferson may well have wished that Stoddert remain, for a time at least, as Secretary. Stoddert had other plans. On 31 March he resigned. Among his last acts as Secretary was to order the recall of the West Indies squadrons under Barry and Talbot.

For Talbot the recall could not have come soon enough. His discipline problems were growing worse. On 22 April the sailing master complained to him that a seaman had refused his order and that when he tried "to force him to a compliance" the seaman "collared" him and threatened his life. The seaman got 12 lashes.

At the very moment that punishment was being meted out on the

spar deck, mutinous mutterings were overheard by a midshipman who hastened to inform the Captain. No time was wasted, and within minutes
another seaman was receiving 12 lashes "laid on at the gangway." On 3 May
two more seamen got 12 apiece for "absenting themselves from watch," and
on the same day Moses Davis, "a young lad," got six lashes. For a commander who had prided himself on using the cat so little, these sanguinary scenes
were distressing. The sense of relief could almost be tasted when news arrived
of the recall. On 25 May *Constitution* put Cap François over her stern and
headed north for home. On 14 June Talbot recorded in his journal "moored
ship before the town of Boston."

The next few weeks were filled with a hectic round of paying off seamen, reckoning accounts and preparing reports for the Secretary. In the
midst of this duty and diligence came some joy when son Cyrus presented
himself. Several months before he had been transferred from the frigate
United States to take command of the sloop-of-war *Warren*. He had brought
her home to Boston a few weeks earlier, where at the order of the new administration she was to be laid up and sold. While his sloop was being stripped
Cyrus took a few days off to visit Dighton. There he heard the news of his
father's arrival, and so hurried to Boston.[19]

Cyrus and Silas had much to talk about—there was family news to
catch up on as well as news of their naval careers. In an effort to save a few
ships for the navy on the day before he left office, President Adams signed
The Peace Establishment Act which reduced the number of vessels in active
service from 33 to 13 with a corresponding reduction in personnel.
Henceforth the service would rank 10 Captains, no Master Commandants
(the rank held by Cyrus), and 36 Lieutenants. Both Talbots stood high in the
eyes of the President and the Secretary. Silas Talbot was retained in service
and ranked third. Cyrus, on the other hand, was asked to remain not at the
rank of Master Commandant, which no longer existed, but at the lesser rank
of Lieutenant. It was, Secretary Stoddert assured him, regrettable, but
nonetheless required by law. Stoddert, still on duty as Secretary of the Navy
until a replacement was named, urged Cyrus to stay in the service. Father
and son talked it over, but for the moment made no decision.

Constitution had not enjoyed a thorough overhaul since her launching nearly four years previous. After long and arduous service in tropical
waters she was in need of considerable attention. Her hull, despite its copper
sheathing, had suffered attack from silent armies of marine life so abundant

in southern waters. Above the waterline, Caribbean sun, wind and water had done their best to eat away at the hull and rigging. As reports on the ship's condition came to Talbot's cabin, he realized that if he stayed aboard he would likely be in for considerable port time. And then what? Even if Jefferson did not lay the frigate up, as his parsimonious nature might incline him to do, the most likely scenario was a mission to the Mediterranean where trouble was brewing with Tripoli. Long days in port and then an even longer deployment overseas seemed to be in prospect.

Had Becky been consulted about her husband's future (there is no indication that Talbot ever wrote to her about his concerns) she would have been quick in her response. Although her husband was absent, his business and other involvements were not. She wanted him out of the service and back in New York. She was, she told him in a particularly direct tone, tired of dealing with the parade of men who came to her door with business that was in his domain.[20]

By September 1801 Talbot had made his decision. On the 8th of that month he forwarded his resignation to the Secretary, who responded with a letter that pleased the Captain with its praise for his services but then jolted him in its refusal to grant a final favor. By the provisions of the Peace Establishment Act "deranged" officers—that is, those who were dismissed from the service—were entitled to four months pay. Talbot had applied, and to his utter dismay he was now told that since he had left the service voluntarily he was not entitled to payment. Silas Talbot took his departure from the navy burdened with that same sense of betrayal he had felt 20 years earlier when leaving the Continental service.[21]

Cyrus decided to wait a while before resigning. There was still a chance the Navy Department might keep him in the rank of Master Commandant. He knew that a squadron was forming up for the Mediterranean, and there might be a command for him on that station. Cyrus was right, but only in part. In November the Secretary offered him command of the schooner *Enterprise*. He had command of a vessel but only as Lieutenant, not in his old and higher rank of Master Commandant.[22]

The offer from the Secretary reached Cyrus while he and his wife were in Dighton. *Enterprise* was a small vessel, too small for an officer with Cyrus Talbot's seniority and experience. He was inclined to reject the offer but decided to withhold a decision until he had a chance to travel to New York and talk with his father.

The elder Talbot was restless. After spending the last three years at sea in an unpredictable and exciting world, the Commodore had a lot to get used to. The thought of sitting out the rest of his life in New York City was bothering him. Theodore was studying law, and despite the occasional lapse into his old bad habits, it was clear he was bound for the life of a city lawyer. George was deep into his own business and family affairs and was doing reasonably well. Betsey, of course, was upstate, happily married and content. Young Harry was bouncing from tutor to tutor, but within a few years he would be off to college. From a family perspective things seemed to have settled down. The Talbots had done well; they were genteel and decidedly middle class. Yet for the elder Talbot it was a bore; the Captain needed something more. In Cyrus he saw his opportunity for another adventure.

Shortly before Christmas, Cyrus arrived to visit his father in New York. He had not yet responded to the offer of command of the schooner *Enterprise*. Father and son agreed that a vessel like *Enterprise* was too insignificant a command for an officer of Cyrus's experience and reputation. Silas may also have pointed out that the squadron bound for the Mediterranean was likely to spend a good deal of its time convoying and blockading. As they both knew from experience, such duties suffered the twin evils of being both dull and unprofitable since the chance of taking prizes while sailing off a harbor mouth or playing shepherd to lumbering merchantmen was severely limited. Cyrus came to a decision. He politely rejected the Secretary's offer and resigned. Since he technically had been deranged—he was, after all, prevented from remaining in the navy at his former rank—the Secretary informed him that he was entitled to four months pay. His father's reaction to his son's better fortune is not recorded.[23]

On the beach, both Talbots were ready for new projects. While neither had gotten rich serving in the navy, they had put away respectable sums. As senior Captain and Commodore, the elder Talbot, in two cruises, had probably accumulated prize money to the tune of $20,000 or more. Cyrus had pocketed much less, perhaps in the range of a few thousand dollars. Nonetheless, they were sailors with money.

Investing in trade held no appeal. Silas had never been keen on mercantile endeavors, and now with Europe in turmoil he was less likely than ever to be drawn into such ventures. Although he had speculated a bit in Vermont land, Cyrus had so little experience in anything but seafaring that he looked to his father for guidance. As usual, Talbot's compass needle swung round to a course marked land. This time the scale of speculation was beyond anything he had ever tried before. He would find his fortune, as well as his son's, in the developing frontier.[24]

Talbot's interest in western land had begun shortly after the Revolution and focused on the western part of Virginia in the region of Kentucky. In June 1787 while on a visit to Philadelphia Talbot bought nine tracts of land in Virginia's Jefferson County (later part of Nelson County, Kentucky). He had never seen these lands nor did he know much about their resources. It had been an act of pure land speculation, and during his years in the West Indies he had paid little or no attention to the investment. Now Talbot took a new interest in his western lands, and so did Cyrus. Like thousands of Americans, father and son saw in the west a chance for a new beginning.[25]

A few years after this first purchase, and following the Johnson Hall experience and his two years in the West Indies as impressment agent, Talbot took another, albeit much smaller, speculation in western lands. In 1788 Congress had agreed to provide land warrants to soldiers who had served in the Revolution. The size of the grant depended upon rank. As a Lieutenant Colonel, Talbot had been awarded 450 acres. The lands were all located in a 4000-square-mile tract in the Northwest Territory known as the United States Military District. The location of the lands within the District was determined by lottery, and in 1796 Talbot drew 400 acres east of the Muskingum River in the southeast section of the District and a separate 50-acre parcel about 70 miles distant. As with Kentucky, the Ohio lands were meant for speculation.

By the time Captain Talbot returned from his second cruise, land fever was running high. In addition to the giveaway for veterans, Congress had also liberalized provisions for purchasing public lands. In May 1800 the Harrison Land Act reduced the minimum purchase from 640 acres to 320 and gave purchasers four years to pay while offering an 8 percent discount for cash payment. These developments were a further incentive to the plans of father and son. With large tracts of land to be had at bargain prices, and with nothing else to do, the Talbots looked west.

Notes

1   DQW 5:490; Memorandum, 6 August 1800, B7 F5 STP.

2   DQW 6:284.

3   DQW 6:274-75, 320.

4   Rebecca Talbot to Silas Talbot, Fall 1800, B7 F16 STP.

5   Rebecca Talbot to Silas Talbot, Fall 1800, B7 F16 STP.

6   George Washington Talbot to Silas Talbot, 1 July 1799, B5 F15 STP.

7   George Washington Talbot to Silas Talbot, 8 March 1800, B6 F10 STP; George Washington Talbot to Silas Talbot, 22 March 1800, B6 F11 STP.

8   Theodore Talbot to Silas Talbot, 4 April 1800, B6 F12 STP; Theodore Talbot to Silas Talbot, 18 January 1800, B6 F7 STP.

9   George Washington Talbot to Silas Talbot, 22 March 1800, B6 F11 STP; George Washington Talbot to Silas Talbot, 23 April 1800, B6 F14 STP.

10   George Washington Talbot to Silas Talbot, 20 June 1800, B7 F2 STP; Richard Harrison to Silas Talbot, 21 June 1800, B7 F2 STP; Abraham Skinner to Silas Talbot, 21 June 1800, B7 F2 STP; James Halley to Silas Talbot, 22 June 1800, B7 F2 STP; Theodore Talbot to Silas Talbot, 22 June 1800, B7 F2 STP; and Theodore Talbot to Silas Talbot, 27 August 1800, Collection 151, B1 F1 STP.

11   Cyrus Talbot to Silas Talbot, 12 June 1799, B5 F 10 STP.

12   Henry Talbot to Silas Talbot, Winter 1800, B5 F10 STP.

13   Journal kept by Silas Talbot, B7 F 9 STP; Silas Talbot to Isaac Hull, 11 September 1800, B7 F 8 STP.

14   Talbot recorded his trip in his journal, B7 F8 STP.

15   For a detailed discussion of the peace negotiations, see Peter P. Hill, *William Vans Murray, Federalist Diplomat* (Syracuse, New York: Syracuse University Press, 1971) and Alexander De Conde, *The Quasi War: The Politics and Diplomacy of the Undeclared War with France, 1797-1801* (New York: Charles Scribner's Sons, 1966).

16   SecNav to Silas Talbot, 18 November 1800, B7 F12 STP.

17   During this cruise Talbot kept a journal. Much of the information concerning this cruise is taken from this source. Journal kept by Silas Talbot on board *Constitution*, 14 December 1800-15 June 1801. Peabody Essex Museum, Salem, Massachusetts.

18   Rebecca Talbot to Silas Talbot, 10 January 1801, B8 F1 STP.

19   Rebecca Talbot to Silas Talbot, 10 August 1801, B8 F10 STP.

20   SecNav to Silas Talbot, 21 September 1801, B8 F11 STP.

21   DBW 1:622.

22   DBW 2:18.

23   Deed, 29 October 1801, B9 F12 STP.

24   Nelson County Deed Book—Book 1:96. Bardstown, Nelson County, Kentucky.

25.   Bounty Land Warrant 2133, National Archives, M 829 RG 49, v 218:28

A BIG BOX WITH another box mount-
ed on it, the western rivers flatboat,
with its sweep oars forward and awkward rudder astern, looks impossible
to manage. Yet this was the workhorse
of pioneer travel and transport during
the first half of the nineteenth century
on downstream trips on the Ohio,
Mississippi and Missouri. A boat like
this took Silas, Cyrus and Alice Talbot
down the Ohio from Pittsburgh to
Louisville.

(Courtesy Filson Club Historical Society)

Chapter Ten

Westward Ho to Kentucky

Although intrigued by the promise of western lands, Talbot was not so foolish as to put all his money into a single enterprise. He was cagey enough to appreciate the wisdom of diversification and a balanced portfolio. To that end he bought a considerable amount of stock in the newly formed Columbian Insurance Company. He also took shares in the recently chartered Bank of the United States and purchased some city real estate as well. He bought lots and buildings in New York City both for speculation and for rental income. Becky added to the family fortune, too. Through her family she inherited real estate in Philadelphia from which she derived rents.[1]

Talbot was hardly alone as an Ohio and Kentucky landholder. Promises of free land for veterans, and cheap land for everyone else, persuaded thousands of land-hungry Americans to trek along crude roads and float down rivers to settle territory west of the Appalachians. Between 1790 and 1800 the newly admitted states of Kentucky and Tennessee nearly tripled in population while the Ohio Territory grew at an even faster rate. The men and women of the new nation went west out of a medley of motives. The Talbots were no different. Silas sought profit. Cyrus wanted a future.

Through the winter of 1801-2 father and son laid plans for the western venture. Like many speculators, Silas Talbot planned to settle his land with other people. He was in the real estate business. He had no intention of removing permanently to Kentucky. Becky would never leave her friends and family in the east, and Silas had done all the frontier farming he cared to do in Johnstown. Cyrus and his family, on the other hand, would settle the land. They would be the harbingers of what he hoped would be a flock of others flying west.

Among those Talbot hoped to entice west was Isaac Hull. Talbot's resignation had been a shock to Hull. He admired Captain Talbot and hoped that he might continue to serve under him as senior Lieutenant aboard *Constitution*. The Captain's departure coupled with the Jeffersonian reductions in the service set the young Lieutenant adrift. In a melancholy mood, uncertain about the future, Hull wrote to Talbot in mid-January 1802. He told his former Superior and mentor, "I fear that there never will be any permancy in the navy and am almost discouraged and think of leaving in the spring."[2]

Talbot had always been fond of his Lieutenant. Hull was a highly competent officer and a jovial shipmate. He would be good company and a great help in Kentucky, and so Talbot wrote asking him to come along. Hull's problem was that he had very little money. For him, as with all who sailed in *Constitution*, prize money had been short. Furthermore, the Lieutenant's family in Derby, Connecticut, never prosperous, looked to him for assistance. For both financial and personal reasons Hull could not go west. He wrote back to Talbot:[3]

> *I assure you nothing would give me so much pleasure as*
> *to make a journey with a family I so much respect, and*
> *nothing should prevent my going but the want of funds*
> *sufficient to get me a comfortable settlement in that country.*
> *I feel how happy three or four such families as your sons must*
> *be settled down for life within a few miles of each other where*
> *they would have nothing to trouble them but their family*
> *concerns and what pleasure they must take in visiting each*
> *other with their families. The very thoughts of the journey*
> *give me pleasure and the more I think of it the better I like it.*

Although Hull disappointed Talbot with his refusal to move west, in another matter he greatly pleased his friend and mentor. Talbot's slave, William Roberts, shortly after *Constitution* arrived in Boston, had disappeared. In Massachusetts slavery was illegal, and there were antislavery peo-ple in Boston eager to protect runaways. Never a compliant servant, Roberts had waited long for his opportunity. Talbot was furious, both with Roberts, who had somehow managed to get ashore. and with those who were hiding him. He would have led the search himself were it not for his need to return to New York. He left Hull with orders to find Roberts.

Hull placed an advertisement in the local papers and spread the word that cash was being offered for those who could help. It worked. On 29 December Roberts was captured and thrown into jail in the town of Dedham, just a few miles south of Boston. When Hull showed up to claim his Captain's property, more difficulties arose. Roberts claimed to be a freeman. The jailer, apparently an antislavery man, refused to surrender Roberts. For the time being, all that Hull could do was collect proof for his claim and ask the jail-er "not to suffer any black people to Se him (Roberts) for fear of them putting him up to something of that kind as there are people enough in Boston that would be glad to get him clear." Poor Roberts did not get clear. Hull proved his case and within a few weeks the Lieutenant packed William Roberts off to Talbot in New York.[4]

In his letter Hull had referred to Talbot's sons. Were George, Theodore and Henry planning to join in the western venture? For certain Cyrus was going west. George, however, was deeply rooted in New York. Henry was young, still in school, and his mother wouldn't let him out of her sight. It may have been that Silas planned to take Theodore along, just to get him out of the city and its vanities. Despite his promises to improve his life, Theodore continued to pursue law casually and pleasure assiduously. His pursuits were not cheap. The bills came in waves across his father's desk—lodgings, din-ners, carriages, travel, books and sundry other expenses. Theodore himself complained that his legal mentor Harrison, with whom he remained despite feeling ill served, gave him little to do and tutored him not at all. Silas saw Theodore as a prime candidate for a trip west, where he would find countless opportunities for developing useful skills.

From Theodore's perspective, life on the frontier (i.e., danger and deprivation) held no attraction. The challenge of Kentucky could not hold a candle to the pleasures of New York. He would not go. In late March, as Talbot settled his accounts in preparation for the trip to Kentucky, he record-ed an expense of $528 for law books. He was buying Theodore a library. Five days later he recorded ruefully in his daybook:[5]

> Theodore Talbot
>> *To money paid to him and for and on account of him Extra*
>> *Expenses for about ten years back great part of which was*
>> *unnecessary and all beyond what I have laid out on my*
>> *other children which I compute to be at least $1000*

Time and again Theodore tried his father's patience. Each time, however, Silas gave in, paid the bills and listened as his son promised to reform. Talbot loved and cared for all his children, even this prodigal.

While preparing for his Kentucky trip Talbot was approached by a hack writer named Ben Taylor who sought to write his biography. Although Talbot was well known as Captain of *Constitution*, it was the rising mythology of the Revolution that intrigued Taylor. The death of Washington in December 1799 had unleashed a torrent of adulation for the founding fathers and renewed interest in the heroes and exploits of the Revolution. Taylor, who was clearly a better salesman than writer, saw in Talbot's war record material for a best-seller. He made arrangements with a bookseller on Broadway, Hocquet Caritat, to market the book.

Caritat was a French émigré who had arrived at New York in 1797. Devoted to the principles of the Enlightenment, Caritat established himself as a publisher, bookseller and general patron of the arts. He would bring literary culture to New York. Just how he reconciled a fawning biography with his high literary standards is hard to judge. That he approved a writer like Taylor suggests that Caritat the publisher won out over Caritat the philosopher.[6]

Talbot, flattered by the proposal, consented on condition that the story end with the Revolution. Taylor agreed; no one, it seems, was much interested in the years after the war.

Taylor's problem was time. In a few weeks his chief source of information was off to Kentucky. Over the weeks that remained, between packing and winding up his business affairs, Talbot spent many hours with Taylor reviewing the years of the Revolution and his role in the war. Talbot saw in this biography his chance to take a place in the pantheon of revolutionary heroes.[7]

By mid-April the Talbots were ready for Kentucky—some of them at least. Becky, of course, would not be going, and neither would Theodore nor George. Cyrus, his wife Alice and their two-year-old daughter, named for her mother, were the only other family members venturesome enough to head west. They, along with Talbot and his unhappy slave William Roberts, got underway.

The route west went first to Philadelphia, where Becky left the group to remain with her family during her husband's absence. After some final goodbyes the Talbots headed for Pittsburgh along the well-traveled overland route via Reading and Bedford. Understanding how difficult the trip was likely to be, the migrating Talbots had packed lightly. Shortly before leaving New York Cyrus sold several lots of furniture. Cash was far more portable than tables and chairs, and whatever they might need in Kentucky could be purchased once they arrived.[8]

At Pittsburgh they boarded a flatboat bound downriver. Their destination was the town of Louisville several hundred miles downstream. For two sea rovers accustomed to a trackless and fearsome ocean, the Ohio must have seemed strangely tame. They passed long stretches of wild countryside with only an occasional sign of settlement. For Alice Talbot, who had not known much beyond the tiny world of Dighton, these scenes were both grand and frightening. The Ohio River was nothing like the tiny Taunton.

On 11 May, after nearly a month of travel, the Talbots reached Louisville where everyone went ashore. Louisville was located at the falls of the Ohio. Above and below the settlement the river was navigable, but to continue their trip in either direction travelers had to portage through the town. It was a bustling place with about two hundred buildings scattered close to the river. The streets were filled with boatmen and folks heading west and south. For the Talbots, however, Louisville was the last stop before Bardstown. After offloading their belongings, they made arrangements to stay overnight at a local tavern. In the morning they set off on the 35-mile trip overland to their new home.[9]

Although slow and long, their flatboat voyage had been reasonably comfortable. The same could not be said for the road trip to Bardstown. First came the problem of finding suitable conveyance. Regular stage service between Louisville and Bardstown had not yet been established, so Talbot had to scout around at the local liveries to find his own transportation. He hired a wagon and loaded it up with family and baggage, and at dawn the pioneers got underway, bouncing along on a trail that barely deserved to be called a road. The countryside was pleasant, rolling hills laced with small streams. Occasionally along the way a small farmhouse and a few outbuildings came in sight. The road got busier as the family drew near the town.

Like all of Kentucky, Bardstown was a young place. It was first settled by pioneers from Pennsylvania and Virginia who came into the region on either the Ohio River and its tributaries or the Wilderness Road and its branches. First called Salem, the town underwent a name change about 1780 when Patrick Henry, Governor of Virginia (the region called Kentucky was at this time still part of Virginia), granted 1000 acres of land in Salem to William Bard, a Pennsylvania surveyor. The change became official in 1788 when Virginia incorporated the town under that name. Four years later when the state of Kentucky was established, Bardstown became the shire town for Nelson County in the new state.[10]

Although organized politically and open for settlement for some years, Kentucky had seen its prosperity postponed by the continuing threat of Indian attack. Mad Anthony Wayne's victory against the Indians at Fallen Timbers in Ohio in August 1794 broke their hold over the Northwest Territory and opened the way in the following year for the signing of the Treaty of Greenville, which set boundaries between the nations. Fallen Timbers and Greenville brought stability and peace along the frontier.

Peace and land drew thousands of people west, and because of its status as county seat, Bardstown soon became the leading town of the region. Located less than a mile north of Beech Fork, a tributary to the Salt River, Bardstown sat astride a network of important trails and roads in an area known for its good land. As his family entered the settlement, the first sight that caught Talbot's eye was the large county courthouse. Near the courthouse was the old Stone Tavern, probably the first place they stopped. Scattered through the town were an assortment of lesser buildings, but even some of these were made of stone and were not unimpressive for a frontier community.[11]

Talbot stayed in Bardstown with his son, daughter-in-law and grand-daughter through the summer and into the early fall. The hills, farms and streams were reminders of his years in Johnstown. Even the crops were alike, for here as in New York wheat and corn were the mainstays. What he didn't miss was the backbreaking work a farm required. Talbot may have wished to stay longer in Bardstown, but he knew that he had to begin his trip home before winter blew in. As he prepared to leave he made some final arrangements with Cyrus. He sold his son "Horses, Wagon, Harnesses, Wheat, Household Furniture, Shays & Harness together with one Negro wench." In return Cyrus agreed to pay his father $2400 whenever his father demanded it. Talbot also agreed to sell Cyrus 10,000 acres for $5000 with the same arrangement for payment. Having seen his son settled, Silas left late in October for home.[12]

It was a long trip home and it would be by a different route than the journey out. Going upstream against the Ohio was impractical so Talbot would have to ride east to Harrodsburg where he could join the Wilderness Road that would take him into Virginia. The air was turning chilly and all along the trail the leaves were showing brilliant hues, but the visual joy could not compensate for the physical discomfort of the journey. Although only 51, the years had not been kind to Silas Talbot and he could feel the damp and cold in his bones. Not only did nature seem to conspire against Talbot, so too did his fellow travelers. Somewhere along the way between Bardstown and Philadelphia, perhaps at one of the wretched taverns that accommodated wilderness travelers, his trunk was broken into and looted. Late in November a somber and tired Kentucky land speculator arrived at his wife's lodgings in Philadelphia. It was a relief to be home. He stayed the winter in Philadelphia, enjoying the society of his wife and her friends.

Having been away so long and so often, Talbot had not been able to keep up with son Theodore's social life, if he could ever keep up with it. Unbeknownst to him, and apparently to Becky as well, Theodore had a serious love interest. In a strange twist of fate she was none other than the widow Elizabeth Truxtun Cox, daughter of Talbot's old rival Thomas Truxtun.

For obvious reasons Theodore had been careful to keep his romance quiet. Not even brother George, the family informer, had caught wind of Theodore's secret. The Truxtuns lived in Perth Amboy, New Jersey, and this may explain Theodore's frequent visits to that neighborhood. Commodore Truxtun, despite his arrogance in naval matters, was known ashore as a most affable man. He and his wife kept a well-appointed home where Theodore found love and fellowship. Commodore Truxtun knew long before Commodore Talbot about this courtship and gave his wholehearted approval. Commodore Talbot took a different tack.

Theodore was anxious about his father's reaction. He loved his father and had no wish to anger him, particularly at the risk of incurring his financial displeasure. Somewhat gingerly he informed his father of his plans to marry. Talbot minced no words. He made it clear that he strongly disapproved of such a match. Having run aground on this course, Theodore decided to back off and try to reach his father through other channels. He wrote to his stepmother for her help. Becky understood the history between Talbot and Truxtun; it was a career rivalry she had lived through. She also understood that these young lovers ought not to bear the burden of their fathers' differences. Theodore asked his stepmother if she would act the peacemaker. Becky spoke to her husband, and a few days later Theodore wrote to his father, once more explaining the situation and asking his blessing. He told his father how delicate the situation was, and that since Commodore Truxtun approved the match he expected Talbot to do the same. If Talbot did not approve, Truxtun might well feel offended and a rift between the two families might be the result. Theodore reminded his father that more than love was at stake here. Having lived on the margin of success for so long, a well-placed marriage such as the one now offered would give him the chance to move ahead.[13]

Despite his son's pleadings Talbot would not be moved. Near the end of April he wrote to Theodore and detailed in very strong terms his opposition to the match. He stayed away from any personal assault on the Commodore or his daughter; instead he launched into an attack on Elizabeth's late husband, calling him a thief. The attack unnerved poor Theodore. Left no other alternatives than surrender or defiance, Theodore uncharacteristically chose to fight. He told Silas that under no circumstances would he convey the objections expressed in his father's letter to the Truxtuns. It would, he wrote, "create useless pain and severely wound the feelings of their daughter." Whatever his father's sentiments, Theodore was determined to marry Eliza.[14]

The wedding took place on 2 June 1803 at Pleasant View, the Truxtun home in Perth Amboy. Becky was present, as was George and his wife. The senior Talbot refused to attend. Instead he went west to Bardstown. He was, he said, bored with life in New York and Philadelphia. At least in Bardstown his days were filled with useful activity. In that frontier place he may even have found some opportunity to practice or teach his old skills with stone. Furthermore, although he was reluctant to say it, he had decided to have nothing more to do with his son's affairs. The marriage, it seemed to him, was so much like what Theodore had done in the past—wrong-headed and frivolous. Left unsaid was his wish to avoid any contact with his old foe Commodore Truxtun. Following their marriage Theodore and Eliza went to live in New York City, and Theodore prepared to launch his career in law.[15]

Arriving back in Bardstown in June, accompanied as usual by William Roberts, Talbot found that Cyrus had taken ill. Within a few days

William came down with the same fever, but soon both William and Cyrus were back to health.[16] William was a problem. He had made clear his intention to be free, and there was no reason to believe that he was more willing to remain in bondage in New York than he had been in Boston. Although New York still held slavery legal, the bordering states of New England and Pennsylvania had abolished the institution. With free states next door, and rising antislavery sentiment within its borders, it was clear that slavery in New York was doomed. Indeed, by 1800 New York City had more free black citizens than slaves. Free and slave living side by side in the same community produced an anomalous situation fraught with tension. Adding to the pressure on slaveholders was an act for Gradual Manumission passed by the New York State legislature in 1799. By the provisions of this act all children born to slave women after 4 July 1799 were free. Males were to be free when they reached age 28 and women age 25. The act did not free any current slaves.[17]

Gradual manumission was seen by slave and slaveholder alike as a prelude to abolition and created an atmosphere in which it was increasingly difficult to sustain obedience. Some New Yorkers dealt with the difficulty by negotiating with their slaves. They promised them freedom after a limited period of bondage with the thought that a few years of good service was better than a runaway slave. Others, contrary to the provisions of the law, sold their slaves south where the institution was firm and the market good.

Talbot understood that keeping a slave in New York, particularly one as restless as William, created more problems than it was worth. To avoid it all he took William to Bardstown. Kentucky was and would remain a slave state. Silas left his slave with his son. What happened to William Roberts after that is uncertain. Whether William remained with Cyrus as a slave forever or in bondage for a set time is not known. What is clear is that Silas Talbot was no longer comfortable with keeping a slave in New York.

When Talbot left New York Becky had not been well. To her husband she wrote that her illness had persisted throughout the summer and that she had gone to live with her sister Susan in Philadelphia. What Talbot did not know was that Becky's health was deteriorating rapidly. According to her doctors she was suffering from dropsy, most likely a form of heart failure. As Becky slipped further, her sister and friends grew alarmed. Aware of her condition, Becky asked that Henry, who was then at school in New York, be sent to her side. George, who in his father's repeated absences had become the center of the family, made arrangements to ride with Henry to Philadelphia.

It was too late. Before either son or stepson could get to her side, Becky died on 26 September in Susan's home.[18]

A letter from his old Philadelphia friend Josiah Hewes brought the melancholy news to Talbot. That he had not been by his wife's side at the end must have weighed heavily on him. As soon as he read the letter he left for home. By late November Talbot was in Philadelphia seeing to his wife's estate. She left everything to him, including real estate, fine furniture and two particularly elegant Philadelphia-made silver services, one for tea and the other for coffee, which had come down through the Morris family. These were so special that Talbot put them away in a New York bank vault.[19]

As Talbot passed a lonely winter in New York, more bad news arrived. During his stay in Kentucky, true to their pledge, Taylor and Caritat had brought out the biography. In typical nineteenth-century style the book was burdened by a sonorous title:

> An Historical Sketch to the End of The Revolutionary War
> of the Life of Silas Talbot, Esq. of the State of Rhode Island,
> Commander of the United States Frigate, The Constitution
> and of an American Squadron in the West-Indies.

The book had hit the New York market with a pronounced thud. The print run had been overly generous, and in Caritat's back room was a large supply of unsold copies. An unalterable belief of every failed author is that his book's poor performance is a result of the publisher's ineptitude. Taylor was no exception. He and Caritat enjoyed the kind of relationship characteristic of nineteenth-century publishing—hostility seasoned with suspicion. As soon as he could Taylor was visiting Talbot's home to let him know how poorly Caritat had served them both. A few weeks later Taylor brought even worse news. The pittance that had been earned had been allegedly stolen by Caritat. The publisher had fled with the cash, leaving behind an ample supply of bound books and unbound sheets.[20]

Talbot was depressed. With Becky gone there was even less to keep him in the east. He longed for Kentucky. There he found purpose, excitement, something new and vital being created—a great contrast to the predictable routines of city life. As the weather improved Talbot couldn't wait to head west. Indeed, on this his third trip he left earlier than he ever had before. He was on the road by early April.

Talbot's decision to go west came in the face of an offer to take command at sea again. For those who could navigate the politics and waters around Hispaniola there was money to be made in trade to the troubled island. Who could manage such a venture better than Talbot? Recognizing his knowledge and skill, a group of Philadelphia merchants headed by John Murray approached the former Captain to take a share and command a vessel ordered to Hispaniola for coffee. More than coffee seems to have been on their minds, however. Murray proposed that the vessel would carry 20 guns and a crew of 60 men. They may well have intended, should the coffee market prove disappointing, to parlay trade into a bit of privateering under the flag of Talbot's old acquaintance Toussaint L'Ouverture. Affairs were still "confused" in those waters and almost anything was possible. For Talbot the offer came too late. He was committed to return to Bardstown, for one thing, and his taste for harum-scarum adventures seems to have declined. The prospect of going back to the Caribbean with all it entailed—long days in a miserable and sickly climate, as well as endless tedium awaiting developments—was not what he wanted. This Captain had retired. He put the oar over his shoulder and headed inland.[21]

Before he left, however, there was one piece of unfinished business that required attention. Becky's death had made Talbot conscious of his own mortality. He was 53 years old and time had not been altogether kind to him. His life had been hard. Campaigns in the Revolution, years of intermittent seafaring, months in prison and long assignments in the tropics had all taken a toll. So too had an unseen enemy—Doctor McCarthy's mercury prescriptions. Talbot decided that he must secure the future, and in March 1804 he drew up his last will and testament.[22]

After the usual pious preliminaries Talbot made certain specific bequests. To Cyrus he gave his portrait "taken in the uniform of the American Navy during the Revolution." To George he bequeathed the family bible and his gold watch. To Henry he gave all the silver plate, including presumably the silver in the vault, recognizing that this plate had originally been "the property of the said Henry's Mother." To his grandson and namesake, Silas Talbot Metcalfe in Albany, he left $1000 to be used for his education.

Talbot made no specific bequests to either Theodore or Betsey. The reason was the same in both cases. Each of them had previously received considerable support from him. Talbot had loaned Betsey and her husband a sizable amount of money to build their home in Albany. Theodore had been on the receiving end for years and deserved nothing more, and even though the old Captain had reconciled himself to the Truxton connection, he still resented the match.

Having disposed of specific pieces of property, Talbot then decreed that the remainder of his estate, personal and real, be distributed among his children, with certain provisions. Henry, the youngest and now a favored child, was to be given $2000 more than any of the others. The extra money was to be used for education. Again, as with the plate, Talbot justified this act "because my property hath been considerably increased by the property of the said Henry's Mother." Theodore and Betsey also came in for special consideration, but of a slightly different kind. Their shares in the estate were to be taken by the executors and invested in New York City real estate in such a manner that neither they nor their heirs would be able to sell it. For good reason Talbot did not trust Theodore's judgment, and in Betsey's case he apparently wanted to prevent George Metcalfe from having any direct control over her inheritance.

After stipulating what he was giving to his children, Talbot closed by indicating what he was owed by them. In every case save Henry, who was too young to owe any debts, each of the children, according to Talbot's carefully reckoned accounts, owed him money. Cyrus was the chief debtor. Between old accounts accrued during his misfortunes in the mid-nineties and his new Kentucky debts he owed his father $22,134.50. Betsey was assessed $5,750 for the Albany house. The seemingly ever-insolvent Theodore owed $5,425.87, and finally George had a debt of $5,500. Although we may never know, the accumulated debts of each of the children may well have exceeded the value of their share. Talbot was aware of this possibility, and so he inserted into the will a proviso that any debt owed beyond the recipients share of inheritance was automatically discharged upon his death.

Talbot's trip west and south in the spring of 1804 took him from New York City down to Philadelphia and thence west on the turnpike through Reading, Carlisle, and Bedford, and on to Pittsburgh, where he caught a boat to Louisville. Debarking at Louisville Talbot crossed the last 35 miles overland. It took the usual month or so, but by the middle of May he was back with Cyrus and his family.

Summer and fall passed quickly. On this visit Talbot stayed late into the season and did not leave for New York until near the end of November. Among those who awaited his arrival home was 13-year-old Henry. With his mother gone his attachment for his father had grown deeper. Talbot had left him under the care of Samuel Hay at a local Episcopal Academy. During his school holiday Henry decided to go up the Hudson and visit Betsey. It was a pleasant visit but a hard trip. Henry hated sailing but he loved to write to his father, and his letters are by far the most playful and endearing of the whole family. A good example is a letter he wrote to his father from Albany.

For years Henry had heard his father rail against President Jefferson. It was Jefferson's economy that had driven both Silas and brother Cyrus out of the navy. The same economy that had prompted the President to lay up frigates had also led him to build small gunboats. Fifty or sixty feet in length with one or two guns, these cockleshells were stationed along the coast to protect America from seaborne attack. Talbot thought it was a ridiculous idea and was wont to share his opinion with anyone who would listen. Henry had heard his father often on the subject. In early September a hurricane swept up the southern coast and tore through Savannah and Charleston. Gunboat number one (Jefferson's boats had numbers not names) was torn from her moorings and deposited high and dry in a cornfield on White Marsh Island, Georgia. Jefferson's opponents delighted in the image of the President's gunboat dumped in a field. In its 17 October issue the Connecticut *Courant* wrote, "Let her rest there, and she will grow into a ship of the line.... Should this new experiment in agriculture succeed, we may expect to see the rice-swamps of Carolina and the tobacco fields of Virginia turned by our philosophical Government into dry docks and gun-boat gardens."

Henry saw the reference and took the opportunity to tweak his father a bit about gunboats and his own dislike of sailing: "If ever I should be a sailor I should go in one of Mr. Jefferson's gun boats that goes on dry land in case of a storm." Talbot was amused by the reference to Jefferson. He may have been less amused by Henry's disdain for sailing.[23]

Some things never change. As soon as Talbot got home Henry came to embrace him, George came by to enlist his support in an ambitious business venture, and Theodore showed up to borrow money. George was in partnership with Richard King. Together they had a one-quarter share in the ship *Superior* bound for Canton. By 1805 New York's China trade was profitable and well-established, but its high profits were accompanied by enormous risks. To reduce the risk and monitor the investment George decided to sail aboard the ship himself, probably in the role of supercargo—that is, the person responsible for the conduct of business during the voyage. Departure was set for mid-May, and George was so confident of success that he asked his father to join in the enterprise. Surprisingly, given Talbot's generally negative attitude toward mercantile activities, he agreed to join and invested $9,000.[24]

George's investment had a reasonable chance of producing a return; Theodore's scheme was just another loan. When Theodore came forward with his request for help, Talbot responded, but he had far less hope that anything might come of it. Theodore needed $1000 just to get by. He and Elizabeth had just had a son. As the elder Talbot knew to his regret, and as Theodore was just learning, children are not cheap. Theodore's new expense, coupled with the cost of establishing himself as a lawyer, had overwhelmed the young family's precarious finances. His plea brought a typical patriarchal reply—money and a lecture.

Talbot's lecture was a reprise of the one he had been delivering to Theodore since his student days at Princeton. According to his father Theodore's lifestyle was extravagant and frivolous. His new home was furnished too elegantly. And why, for example, was it necessary for his son to have two servants? Would not one do? Censoriously the father reminded Theodore that this was not the first time he had needed financial help. He referred pointedly to a time when Theodore had been saved from financial embarrassment by brother George.

Theodore wasted no time in accepting the money, but it took him nearly five months to respond to his father's lecture, and then only when the old man was far away in Bardstown. Indeed, rather than confronting him directly, even in writing, Theodore began the letter with the information that some people in New York gossiped that he did not care for his children because he was away so much. Theodore quickly assured his father that he did not believe this, and whenever anyone mentioned such a thing in his presence he disabused them of the notion.

Theodore also pointed out that his father was rewriting family history in a way, as usual, that favored George and damned him. It was not true, he said, that George had bailed him out of financial difficulty. In this instance at least, since George was in China, he could not be summoned to give testimony. As for his extravagance, Theodore made no excuse—living in New York was expensive. Rents were high and two servants were the absolute minimum to keep Elizabeth from "drudgery." Despite what his father said, according to Theodore his home was "parsimonious" in the extreme and had none of the trappings it was alleged to possess.

Yes, it was true, Theodore admitted, that his education had been cost-ly—but had his father spent any more on him than he had on the other children? He did not think so. He concluded his letter with a melodramatic plea, characteristic of the age and typical of him.[25]

It moistens my eyes while I write to you that I should be denied
a moment unmindful of and thankful for the constant and
unremitting affection kind care of a Parent whom I have always
regarded with love and respect or that I should forget the
example of one whose personal exertions alone have raised
him into the esteem and regard of the world.

Even in distant Kentucky, where every letter from home was wel-comed and devoured, this epistle must have seemed tiresome. It was all so familiar.

Silas Talbot was back in New York in late fall. He had made his last visit to Kentucky. He was too old to continue the commute, and while life in New York might still seem boring and full of pretense, for a man of Talbot's age it was a safer and more comfortable place to be than a town on the Kentucky frontier.

The winter of 1805-6 was a dull time for Talbot, made even worse by the knowledge that come spring and summer he would still be in New York. The days crept by slowly. On a few occasions the city somnolence was inter-rupted when, phoenix-like, some old unsettled business, even from as far back as the Revolution, returned. These were nearly all the same—usually a sailor accusing Talbot of not having paid him his prize money. The claims were a nuisance without any serious consequence. Talbot did belong to the New York Marine Society, the Library Society and the Society of the Cincinnati, but he seems to have been only nominally interested in any of these organizations.

In September 1806 the Talbots rejoiced at the return of brother George from China. The trip had been a success and George finally seemed to have found financial security. George's good fortune was short-lived. The continuing struggle between France and England was once more shaking America. The problems were many: British connivance with the Indians in the west to disrupt American settlements; continuing harassment of American trade on the high seas; the desire on the part of some Americans to expand into Canada and Florida; and once again that most emotional of all issues—British impressment of American seamen.

Jefferson responded by threatening economic retaliation. In April 1806 the President announced that unless the British ceased their violations of American rights, particularly impressment, a ban on British imports would be imposed. Before any such measure could take effect the British blundered badly. On 22 June 1807 the British frigate *Leopard* intercepted the American frigate *Chesapeake* bound for her station in the Mediterranean. Reliably informed that British deserters were aboard the American frigate, Captain S. P. Humphreys of the Royal Navy demanded permission to come aboard *Chesapeake* and make a search. *Chesapeake*'s commander, Commodore Samuel Barron, rightly refused. *Leopard* fired on her, and in a matter of minutes the American frigate was a shambles. The British came aboard and removed four crewmen.

The *Chesapeake-Leopard* incident hurled America and England to the precipice of war. Fortunately, Jefferson was too wise to allow his country to be provoked into a war it could never win. Instead of sending an answer to the British through the muzzles of American cannon, he decided to strike at them through trade. The President proclaimed a total embargo. All American ports were closed to all foreign trade.

The embargo was devastating to merchants such as George Talbot. He, his father and others involved in trade howled at the pain being inflicted upon them by their own government. They had no love for the British; quite the opposite, they wanted the nation to respond to this insult with force. And men like the Talbots felt it was Jefferson's fault that this could not be done. His ruinous policy of disbanding the army, laying up the navy, and building puny gunboats instead of frigates had left America so impotent that its only response to being bullied by John Bull was self-imposed punishment in the form of an embargo. It was a scandal and a humiliation.

Although he was saddened by his country's inability to defend itself by other than economic means, Talbot could at least take some comfort that his personal policy of not investing in trade, other than George's China venture, had again proven wise.

Notes

1 Receipt, 30 shares Columbian Insurance Company, B8 F12 STP.
2 Isaac Hull to Silas Talbot, 15 January 1802, B8 F13 STP.
3 Hull to Talbot, 29 January 1802, B8 F13 STP.
4 Hull to Talbot, 15 January 1802, B8 F13 STP; Linda M. Maloney, *The Captain from Connecticut: The Life and Naval Times of Isaac Hull* (Boston: Northeastern University Press, 1986), 61-62.
5 Daybook, B9 F17 STP.
6 George G. Raddin, *Hocquet Caritat and the Early New York Literary Scene, 1796-1803* (Dover, New Hampshire: Dover Advance Press, 1953).
7 Ben Taylor to Silas Talbot, 27 January 1802, B8 F13 STP.
8 Sale of furniture ordered by Col. Talbot, 7 April 1802, B9 F17 STP.
9 Tavern bill in Louisville, 11 May 1802, B9 F17 STP; Josiah Espy, "A Tour in Ohio, Kentucky and Indiana Territory in 1805," Ohio Valley Historical Series, VII (1871).
10 L. Collins, *Historical Sketches of Kentucky,* 2 vols. (Covington, Kentucky: Collins and Company, 1878), 1:644; William Allan Pusey, *The Wilderness Road to Kentucky* (New York: George H. Doran Company, 1921), 23.
11 Sarah B. Smith, *Historic Nelson County, Its Towns and People* (Bardstown, Kentucky: GBA/Delmar, 1983), 311-20.
12 Receipt, 26 October 1802, B8 F14 STP.
13 Theodore Talbot to Rebecca Talbot, 1 April 1803, Collection 151 ; Theodore Talbot to Silas Talbot, 4 April 1803, Collection 151; Theodore Talbot to Silas Talbot, 11 April 1803, B8 F15 STP; and Theodore Talbot to Silas Talbot, 29 April 1803, Collection 151 STP.
14 Theodore Talbot to Silas Talbot, 29 April 1803, Collection 151, STP.
15 George Washington Talbot to Silas Talbot, 31 May 1803, Collection 151; Theodore Talbot to Silas Talbot, 15 June 1803, Collection 151, both in STP.
16 Silas Talbot to Rebecca Talbot, 17 July 1803, B8 F15 STP.
17 For a discussion of slavery in New York, see Shane White, *Somewhat More Independent: The End of Slavery in New York City, 1770-1810* (Athens, Georgia: University of Georgia Press, 1991).
18 Josiah Hewes to Silas Talbot, 27 September 1803, B8 F15 STP; George Talbot to Silas Talbot, 28 September 1803, Collection 151, STP.
19 Daybook, October 1803, B9 F17 STP.
20 Ben Taylor to Silas Talbot, 28 August 1806, B8 F18 STP.
21 John Murray to Silas Talbot, 2 April 1804, B8 F16 STP; Silas Talbot to Murray, 10 April 1804, B8 F16 STP.
22 The will is in B8 F16 STP.
23 Connecticut *Courant,* 17 October 1804; Henry Talbot to Silas Talbot, 17 November 1804, B8 F16 STP; Spencer C. Tucker, *The Jeffersonian Gunboat Navy* (Columbia, South Carolina: University of South Carolina Press, 1993), 77.
24 Silas Talbot to George Talbot, 16 March 1805, B8 F17 STP; George Talbot to Silas Talbot, 27 March 1805, Collection 151, STP.
25 Theodore Talbot to Silas Talbot, 27 August 1805, B8 F17 STP.

*N*EW YORK IN THE new century,
shown here from idyllic Brooklyn
Heights in 1802, was the aging
Commodore's home from 1804 until
his death in 1813, ten years that
included business ventures, visits
from his children and grandchildren,
and a tempestuous third marriage.
(Mystic Seaport Museum, MSM 54.163)

Chapter Eleven

A Miserable Marriage

Having decided to give up the annual trip to Kentucky, Silas Talbot settled down to the life of a sedentary urban gentleman. It was a life he had once disdained as boring and wearisome, but to a man of his accumulated years and declining health it seemed comfortable and pleasant in 1806.[1]

Since Becky's death George had been living in his father's house on Vesey Street between Broadway and Greenwich. When Talbot returned from Kentucky he stayed first with George and his family, and then he and Henry moved a few blocks west to 311 Greenwich Street overlooking the Hudson. They spent a year there and then bought a house on Chambers Street parallel to and one block south of Vesey.[2]

Although Henry lived with his father on Chambers Street he was away a good deal of the time at school, and even when he was in the house his shy and withdrawn manner made him less than exciting company. In addition to Silas and Henry, the retired Captain's household included several servants, not slaves, who saw to the cooking, cleaning and personal needs of the Talbots.

The house on Chambers Street was a fairly ordinary city dwelling with two floors, a garret, and a small garden in the back. Talbot knew from the moment he moved in, however, that he needed to enlarge it. While the house might be comfortable for himself and his son, it was far too small for properly entertaining friends and relatives, and so he bought the lot next door at number 77. Soon 75 and 77 Chambers Street were abuzz with the confusion and noise of construction as workmen doubled the place's living space.[3]

Talbot was delighted to see his home enlarged and improved, and as an old builder himself he saw to every detail. His years with Becky and her high-style Philadelphia friends had introduced him to furnishings and conveniences unknown in his previous life. He ordered the best, including pieces made by Duncan Phyfe. The expense of his expanded home and its furnishings put enough of a strain on the budget that Talbot had to call in some old notes. Fortunately his debtors had the cash and could deliver.[4]

The addition could not be finished too soon. Guests were already making plans to visit. Since he knew he could no longer undertake the trip west, it was Talbot's hope that Cyrus would come east. Indeed, Cyrus wrote his father that in the summer he would be at New York. Summer also promised visitors from Albany.[5]

Talbot always felt a special closeness to Betsey. He loved her dearly and had watched her mature into a lady admired by all. Despite her somewhat inauspicious birth, she was the child that had caused him the least grief and had brought him the greatest joy. Betsey's most precious gifts to her father were grandchildren. Talbot was particularly fond of the two oldest—his namesake Silas and the younger sister Maria.

He wanted both to come to New York. At first his son-in-law wrote that only Silas would be coming. Maria, he suggested, was "not very skilled in domestic affairs." Silas, on the other hand, was eager and ready to visit. Indeed, it was George Metcalfe's design that grandfather might even take young Silas under his wing and see to his education. The Commodore was keen to help.[6]

By springtime George was still of a mind that Maria ought not to go, but it was no use. Betsey, Maria and probably grandfather Talbot all insisted that Maria ought to make the trip as well. And so on 14 May Silas and Maria said farewell, boarded a Hudson River sloop alone and sailed down to the city. The trip would have been pleasant and quick—leaving early in the morning they probably arrived on the city's west side sometime the next morning. From there they might have walked the few blocks over to Chambers Street.[7]

The summer passed quickly. Talbot enjoyed the company of his grandchildren and he spent long hours taking them around the city to see relatives and friends. He may even have taken them on the ferry over to New Jersey where Theodore was living and practicing law. Henry was home from school and Maria developed a fondness for her young and bashful uncle. They were not far apart in age and enjoyed one another's company.

Late in August it was time for the grandchildren to return to Albany. Against current and wind, the trip upriver was more difficult than coming down and it took their sloop four days to make the passage. As soon as she could, Maria wrote to her grandfather telling him what a wonderful summer it had been and asking if he would send her a lock of his hair by which she might remember him. She also asked if Henry could come to Albany for a visit.[8]

Talbot missed the grandchildren as summer became autumn. The house seemed empty without them. He banished his loneliness with the consolation that soon his home would be filled again. Cyrus was coming, and even though he was traveling without his family, it was a reunion to be anticipated with pleasure. Having enjoyed Cyrus's hospitality so many times in Kentucky his father was anxious to return the favor and hear the news from Bardstown.

Cyrus too was looking forward to the visit. He had not been east in nearly four years, and aside from his father he had not seen any of his family in that time. His departure, however, would have to wait until much of the harvest was finished. By mid-September his crops were well on their way to harvest, and it promised to be a very good year. He wrote to his father that "our Crops of Hay, Wheat and Rye have been abundant and our Prospect for a good Crop of Corn is flattering."[9]

With matters in Bardstown under control, Cyrus left for New York on 25 September. He was pressed for time. He had to be back in Kentucky before winter set in. Since the trip took a month each way that meant leaving New York almost as soon as he arrived. The trouble was so great for a time so short that Cyrus must have had a compelling reason to make the trip. In all likelihood that reason was concern over his father's health.

Not only was Cyrus's timing poor, but so too was his itinerary. Like most inexperienced travelers he was overly ambitious. He left Bardstown and struck out on horseback for Pittsburgh nearly 400 miles away. From Pittsburgh he rode east towards Harrisburg, but just short of the town he struck a more northerly course into the Susquehanna Valley. Apparently

Cyrus was going first to Albany and then to New York City.

Unfortunately, Cyrus only got as far as Tioga, a small settlement on the New York-Pennsylvania line 160 miles from New York City and 120 miles from Albany. It had taken him 26 days to get that far. The trip had cost more than he planned, and he was running out of money. Finally there was the calamity of a horse that could go no farther. With a sick horse, and no money to buy another, Cyrus could not risk going on to New York. Neither could he start back for Kentucky. He settled for wintering in Tioga. With the arrival of spring he was needed back home. Sadly he had to write to his father that instead of coming to New York he was bound home to Kentucky.[10]

The news that Cyrus could not come to New York was disheartening, and it was made even worse when he added in his letter that he would not again attempt such an arduous journey. Talbot knew that it was unlikely he would ever see his son. The winter of 1807-8 was unpleasant for many others in New York. Jefferson's embargo had shut the port, leaving ships laid up and hundreds of men idle. Merchants were especially hard pressed, and Federalists were outraged. George Metcalfe wrote from Albany how much he and his associates hated the embargo and despised Jefferson. Even in the west, where the President's measures found some support, complaints were heard. Cyrus, a former naval officer inclined to fight and now struggling to make a living as a farmer in the heart of a region strongly pro-Jefferson, couched his opinions carefully. He told his father only that he had much sympathy for those suffering in the ports.[11]

Talbot was not much concerned with the sufferings of others in New York. He had his own woes. He had not been well for some years, and the damp cold of the New York winters did nothing to improve his health. It was while he was ill, lonely, and emotionally vulnerable that he decided to marry again. It was a colossal blunder.

His betrothed, Elizabeth Pintard, was born in Ireland about 1760. As a young woman she moved to Funchal, on the island of Madeira, where she met John Marsden Pintard. Born in New York in 1760, John was the son of Lewis Pintard, and a member of one of New York's most respected merchant families. Although supporters of the American cause during the Revolution, the Pintards, like many international traders, were eager to reestablish ties with their former English partners after the war. As soon as word arrived in the spring of 1783 that peace was in the offing, Pintard went off to seek his fortune in Madeira. He went there, in part, to act as agent for Searle and

Company of London in the wine and salt trade and in part to work on his own account. Pintard did well and was soon an important supplier of fine wines for many of the new nation's notables, including Jefferson and Madison.

Funchal was a listening post for American interests. As an outpost of the Portuguese empire, Madeira was in close communication with Lisbon and the whole of Europe. Its location along the sea route to Gibraltar also made it privy to news of all the world's trade with the Mediterranean. Given Funchal's position, and Pintard's connections, it is not surprising that in October 1783, only a few months after his arrival in the islands, he was appointed American consul.[12]

In Funchal John Marsden Pintard fell in love with Elizabeth. They were married on the island in 1785. Over the next dozen years the Pintards remained in Madeira with occasional visits to family in New York. But the marriage proved to be unhappy, and by 1797 the Pintards arranged a divorce. Elizabeth agreed to renounce all "wifely claims" and in return Pintard agreed to pay her the handsome sum of £3,000 in three equal installments at six-month intervals. Should either of them forfeit the bargain, a penalty of £10,000 was assigned to the aggrieved party.[13]

John and Elizabeth signed this agreement at Funchal on 17 August 1797. Even though neither of them planned to remain on the island, getting the divorce in Madeira was essential since under New York law the only acceptable grounds for granting a divorce was adultery. Neither Elizabeth nor John Marsden alleged such unbecoming behavior.[14]

Both Elizabeth and John made their way to New York after the divorce. It soon became apparent that John could not afford to live up to his part of the bargain. Elizabeth hounded him but it was no use. In the meantime, having fallen into debt herself, she dragged the impecunious Pintard into court. The Court of Chancery found in her favor and compelled Pintard to place a $10,000 security. The amount was far beyond what John Marsden could pay. Under the circumstances all that he could do was to throw himself on his father's mercy. Lewis Pintard was a man of considerable wealth who had great concern for the family honor. He agreed to pay Elizabeth £100 per year for life if John Marsden would pay another £50 under the same terms. The son agreed and a deal was struck. Then the hapless John Marsden fell into arrears again. Elizabeth, however, saw the wisdom of ignoring the default; any move she might make against the son could imperil the regular arrival of support from the father. Indeed, until the day she died, thanks to Lewis and his executors, Elizabeth Pintard received her £100 a year.[15]

Elizabeth's connection to the Pintards drew her into the same social circles in which Talbot moved. It was a world of teas and suppers, not on the scale of elegance that the grand families enjoyed but characteristic of an urban upper middle class. Talbot met and liked Elizabeth. She was social, garrulous, and still closely connected with the better families of the city despite the divorce and its aftermath. She offered what Talbot seemed always to be seeking—status. Talbot was aware of Elizabeth's previous marriage, but her divorce was legal and accepted and presented no problem. His only concern was whether the rumors of Elizabeth's financial problems were true. She assured him that she would bring no debts to the union.

A divorced woman in early nineteenth-century America was in an awkward position. Elizabeth was an odd fit in New York City's social puzzle. She was neither a spinster nor a widow, the usual situation for an unmarried woman of her age. Marrying Talbot offered renewed respectability. Although he had nothing to compare to the wealth of the Pintards, Talbot possessed a good name, a modicum of fame and a comfortable living.

On Thursday evening, 19 May 1808, Elizabeth and Silas were married by the Reverend Dr. Rodgers in the First Presbyterian Church. As befitted the age and previous marital experiences of the couple the service was simple and discreet.

The event came as a surprise to the Metcalfes in Albany and the Talbots in Bardstown. Indeed, George Metcalfe read about the marriage in the newspaper before his father-in-law took the time to write and tell him the news. It is not even certain that the nearby sons George, Theodore and Henry knew much at all about the event. Talbot may have been reluctant to tell his children his plans for fear that they would not approve. Already there had been some discussion in the family that because of his health he should move in with one of them. Such a discussion suggests apprehension that the aging Commodore might be incapable of managing his own affairs. Marrying Elizabeth might have been Talbot's way of answering his children's concerns and simultaneously reasserting his own independence.

The newlyweds settled into domestic life on Chambers Street. To satisfy Elizabeth, Talbot finished off the house and ordered more furniture from Duncan Phyfe. Just as the furniture arrived, so did sad news from Albany. Young George Metcalfe was not a good swimmer; nonetheless, he enjoyed going down to the river and jumping in with his friends to frolic a bit. Towards evening on Friday, 17 June, he made his way down to the Hudson alone. He removed his clothes and piled them carefully on a spot by the river's edge. He then went into the water. As the daylight faded, his father and mother began to worry. They asked Silas to look for his brother. All that Silas found was the pile of his brother's clothes. Immediately the alarm went out and the hunt began. By the light of morning the searchers found the body of George Metcalfe.[16]

For Silas Talbot the grim news from Albany could not have arrived at a worse time. Just as the world of the Metcalfes was full of grief and regret, Silas's own life, thanks to his new wife, was in emotional turmoil. Since we know Elizabeth Pintard Talbot only through the eyes of her husband, hardly an unbiased observer, judgments on her character should perhaps be tempered. But however exaggerated Silas's version of events might be, there is no doubt that she was an extraordinary person in disposition and demeanor. What is equally certain is that Talbot was a fool to marry her.[17]

Less than a week after taking their vows, the domestic war began when Elizabeth told her new husband that on several occasions during her previous marriage she had threatened to murder John Pintard. She planned, she said, to shoot him and then turn the pistol on herself. Five days after exchanging vows, and for apparently no reason, at least according to her husband, Elizabeth launched into the most amazing repertoire of Billingsgate that had ever come to his ears. Words exploded from her mouth that he had rarely heard in the forecastle or around an army campfire. He was, she screamed, "vile," "low-born" and a "whore master." At first her eruptions came once a day, then twice a day, and finally she swung her verbal broadsword at him three times a day.

As quickly as Elizabeth flew at Talbot with equal speed she could retreat. Whether it was a quirk of her mental illness or simple cunning, Elizabeth calculated the distance to the precipice carefully and never rode over the edge. After each burst of verbal savagery she recanted, came to her husband and literally fell on her knees to beg forgiveness. She was, she said, helpless to stop herself. It was as if demons possessed her. Should she ever again feel the evil coming on, she promised to dash herself with cold water and then lock herself in the garret until the demons departed.

If not ranting at her husband she was often spying on him. When gentlemen came to Silas on matters of business she would close the parlor door and then bend over and listen through the keyhole. Whenever Talbot wrote letters she snuck up to his back and peered over his shoulder. One day when he left the house to make a brief visit to son George only a few blocks away she went nearly berserk. Although he was gone less than an hour, when he came through the door she came flying at him and accused him first of having spent his time in a grog shop. When that seemed to have little effect she raised the stakes and let loose that he had been in a Negro whorehouse. If he could spend his time in such ways, she said, then she could too. That night, according to Talbot, he got no rest, fearing what she might do to him in his sleep.

Each new day seemed to bring more misery. One warm Sunday afternoon Elizabeth asked Talbot to go with her on a "frolic" over to New Jersey. Talbot declined, pleading fatigue. This caused Elizabeth to announce that she would go into the street if necessary and find a man to go with her. She went as far as the front door and then relented.

That afternoon, after being out for a bit, Talbot returned to find his front door locked. Rarely did anyone in the neighborhood lock their doors. He had no key with him and had to wait several minutes until his wife answered his knocks. She finally opened the door, took him by the arm and quickly hustled him out to the garden at the rear of the house. Since she had never spent much time in the garden, Talbot thought her behavior a bit strange until he realized that after they had gone out the back of the house someone, presumably a man, may have gone out the front. This incident returned to his mind when a few days later he learned from a neighbor that he had seen Mrs. Talbot sneaking out of her house at night and slinking over to a house of ill fame where she remained for several hours.

If Talbot doubted Elizabeth's fidelity, she certainly doubted his. Right to his face she accused him of sleeping with other women. His response was that he was too old. She, who should have known the truth of that defense better than anyone else, responded by hitting him three times in the face "causing much discharge of blood." A few nights later she assaulted him in bed. She intended, in Talbot's words, "to put an end to my existence."

If Talbot's accounts are to be believed, then it must be wondered why he continued to endure it. Why did this hero of the republic, a man who had faced down death many times, not move to rid himself of this madwoman? Did he enjoy being a battered husband? There are two parts to the answer.

The first is simply that divorce, the most logical remedy, was not a reasonable option. New York State had one of the most restrictive divorce laws in the United States. Adultery was the only grounds for securing a decree, and even if both were guilty of the sin neither would want such a thing to become public. It was a standoff.

The second restraint was financial. Early on Elizabeth had raised the prospect of being amenable to a separation, not divorce. But her price was high—$10,000. As matters worsened in the household, however, with behavior that tended to undermine her position, Elizabeth's price came down. Talbot probably calculated that the longer he waited the less it would cost him. In the fall Talbot decided upon a course of action that seems odd. He decided that he and Elizabeth should leave New York. He proposed that they move to Fairfield, Connecticut, more than 40 miles up the coast. He had some friends there, Samuel Smedley and Joseph Squires, from the days of the Revolution. He planned that he and Elizabeth would lodge with Squires. In such new surroundings, and with others watching (she only went crazy in private), Talbot believed that his wife would enjoy some kind of conversion to sanity.[18]

The couple got as far as the tavern at Kingsbridge, where the road to Connecticut crossed over the Harlem River. That night they went to bed in the same room, but before retiring Talbot bolted the door. In the morning the bolt was still in place but his money was not. In the dark someone had taken $150 out of his pockets. Elizabeth vehemently denied that it was her and demanded that Talbot take her back to New York immediately. After the usual verbal brawl they rode back to Chambers Street.

Talbot was close to a breakdown. He couldn't sleep or eat. His days were spent in deep anxiety and his nights in fear of what Elizabeth might try to do to him. He went to George and Theodore for advice. They put him in touch with an attorney, Josiah Hoffman, who specialized in domestic matters. Hoffman advised his client to leave New York.[19]

Hoffman's counsel was sound. As long as Talbot stayed in New York State he was vulnerable to any legal action Elizabeth might wish to take. Talbot took the advice and went to Fairfield to stay with his friend Squires. Neither Theodore nor George thought Fairfield was distant enough. They suggested that their father go off to Montreal, Europe or Kentucky. Distance might make him "invulnerable" to Elizabeth's attacks. Talbot heeded his own advice; Fairfield was distant enough for him.[20]

From his Connecticut sanctuary Talbot wrote to Elizabeth late in

November asking her to come up and join him. The invitation was also a challenge. He told her she had best not ask him for money for the journey. He thought the $150 she had stolen from him at Kingsbridge was sufficient for coach fare. Elizabeth elected to stay in New York and negotiate an accommodation with a husband who was clearly through with her.

She engaged her own attorney, Thomas Emmet, and sent him to George and Theodore, both of whom detested her. Nevertheless, the sons wanted their father to be rid of this woman as soon as possible. George expressed the tone of the deliberations when he wrote to his father that "no sacrifice of money within reason is too great to enable you to get rid of this woman." A proposal from Elizabeth's attorneys met George's standard: a one-time payment of $1000 followed by £100 per year for life.

Although his sons and his lawyer urged him to accept this arrangement Talbot hesitated. It was not the money. It was a question of what he could expect in return for the payment. Elizabeth refused to give him a divorce. She told him that her friends advised her that "a Woman twice divorced could not expect to hold up her head in Society." After a bit of back and forth they agreed there would be no divorce; instead their arrangement would be what was termed an "absolute separation." Elizabeth's honor remained intact. The financial terms of an agreement finally signed on 21 January 1809 called for Elizabeth to take her leave and in return Talbot agreed to give her the thousand dollars, pay her debts up to $150 and provide her an annual stipend of $250 for the remainder of her life.[21]

Was Elizabeth the harpy portrayed by Silas in his letters? Unlikely. Outliving her husband by nearly thirty years, she became something of a fixture on the New York social scene. She was recognized and honored as the widow of the "Commodore." She was a frequent visitor to her Pintard relatives and was cherished by them as a somewhat odd but loveable and garrulous old lady. Aside from Talbot's lengthy document (written by George or Theodore?), constructed to defend his position, there is no independent evidence to support his charges. Indeed, no one aside from Talbot himself claims ever to have witnessed the violent behavior attributed to Elizabeth.

It is likely that Talbot and his wife did argue and also likely that these episodes were manipulated and exaggerated by George, Theodore and Henry. They knew their father was ill and that Elizabeth was likely to survive him. They also knew that given her history she might be crafty enough to persuade the aging Commodore to change his will in her favor. If that happened she, and not they, stood to inherit Talbot's estate. George and Theodore may have done all they could to separate an ill and failing father from his ambitious wife.

The settlement with Elizabeth left Talbot strapped for cash. He raised some money by calling in another payment on an old loan from his friend George Scriba. That got him over one hurdle, but then he needed to come up with the annual stipend. He solved part of his problem by renting out 77 Chambers Street to the steamboat operator Robert Fulton. The house was too big for him in any case, and the $750 per year rent would go a long way to meeting his expenses.

The arrangement with Fulton worked so well that Talbot shifted some of his other investments, his bank and insurance stocks, to real estate. He bought other properties in the neighborhood that could provide a secure income. Although probably inadvertent, his shift to city real estate proved to be extraordinarily wise, for it provided some insulation from the economic tumult about to break out as a result of the War of 1812.

Talbot stayed in his west side neighborhood, moving down the street to number 133 Chambers Street. He lived there with his housekeeper Roseann O'Brien. With her to watch over him, and with George and Theodore living nearby, he felt comfortable and in touch with the few things he still cared to keep in touch with. The wrenching business with Elizabeth had drained him emotionally, financially and physically and left him with little desire to do more than remain at home, visit with his children and await death. Indeed, the great "iron box" in which he so carefully placed his papers all his life has almost no documents dated after the separation. Among the few late additions is a letter to Cyrus chiding him for allowing himself to be elected to the Kentucky legislature, for, as Talbot could testify from his own experience in public service, his son would "gain but Little and Loose much." In the same letter Talbot tells Cyrus ruefully that he cannot afford to loan him the money he needs. The other item Talbot stowed in the box during these waning years was his will.[22]

In his last testament Silas Talbot insisted that all his children reconcile their debts to him. Each of them, with the exception of Henry, who apparently had yet to leave home or marry, had significant outstanding debts. Cyrus owed the most—$10,836—almost all of it from purchases of Kentucky land from his father. Betsey still had an outstanding debt of $5,750. George owed a modest $5,500, mostly money lent to him for overseas ventures. Theodore, the most profligate of all, actually owed the least —a modest $2,665, mostly for law books.

Having sent out the dead hand to collect the old debts, Talbot still needed to make a few more adjustments in the estate before final distribution. Grandson Silas, always the favorite, got $1,000 for his education. Wife Elizabeth, separated but still dependent, had to be guaranteed $250 per year; and finally Roseann O'Brien, his housekeeper, was granted $250. Once all of these considerations had been attended to, as well as any other outstanding debts, then by Talbot's instructions, upon his death the remainder of the estate was to be divided evenly among his children.

Talbot prepared this new will in January 1813. It was the act of a man who saw death. Six months later, 30 June 1813, he died. The doctor listed the cause of death as "decay." The next day, with the family, a few friends and a delegation from the Society of the Cincinnati present, Silas Talbot was laid to rest in the burial ground at Trinity Church, an unusual place given that the Commodore had long professed to be a Presbyterian and in fact owned a pew in the Presbyterian Church on Cedar Street. He died as he had lived, socially ambitious. Far better to be laid to rest in Trinity's fashionable ground with the notables of New York than to be consigned to anonymity on Cedar Street. As always, Talbot had an eye for good real estate.

Notes

1   Talbot's New York City residences are taken from New York City (Manhattan) Assessments, New York City Municipal Archives, New York, New York.

2   Street locations are taken from Isaac Newton Phelps Stokes, *The Iconography of Manhattan Island, 1498-1909*, 6 vols. (New York: Robert H. Dodd, 1915), vol. 6, plate 64.

3   Daybook, July 1808, B9 F17 STP.

4   Receipts from Duncan Phyfe, 11 April and 20 May 1807, B9 F1 STP; Silas Talbot to George Scriba, 12 January 1808, B9 F2 STP; George Scriba to Silas Talbot, 14 January 1808, B9 F1 STP.

5   Cyrus Talbot to Silas Talbot, 23 March 1807, B9 F1 STP; George Metcalfe to Silas Talbot, 16 February 1807, B9 F1 STP.

6   George Metcalfe to Silas Talbot, 16 February 1807, B9 F1 STP.

7   Elizabeth Metcalfe to Silas Talbot, 11 May 1807, B9 F1 STP; George Metcalfe to Silas Talbot, 13 May 1807, B9 F1 STP; George Metcalfe to Silas Talbot, 20 June 1807, B9 F1 STP; George Metcalfe to Silas Talbot, 24 August 1807, B9 F1 STP.

8   Maria Metcalfe to Silas Talbot, 25 August 1807, B9 F1 STP.

9   Cyrus Talbot to Silas Talbot, 17 September 1807, B9 F1 STP.

10 Cyrus Talbot to Silas Talbot, 21 October 1807, B9 F1 STP; Cyrus Talbot to Silas Talbot, 7 November 1807, B9 F1 STP.

11 Cyrus Talbot to Silas Talbot, 28 February 1808, B9 F2 STP.

12 JCC (1783), 778-80.

13 Court of Chancery P-932, Pintard, Eliza v. Pintard, John M., 2 January 1800, New York County Clerk's Archives (Division of Old Records); other information about the divorce may be from a long statement of 37 pages, either written or dictated by Silas Talbot, concerning his difficulties with his wife. The document is not dated, but from internal evidence it must have been written sometime in the fall of 1809, STP.

14 Roderick Phillips, *Untying the Knot: A Short History of Divorce* (New York: Cambridge University Press, 1991), 142.

15 By 1830 Elizabeth Pintard was receiving annuities from the estates of both Lewis Pintard and Silas Talbot to a total amount of $500. Eliza Noel Pintard Davidson, ed., *Letters From John Pintard to His Daughter, 4 vols.* (New York: New-York Historical Society, 1940), 1:202.

16 George Metcalfe to Silas Talbot, 20 June 1808, B9 F2 STP.

17 The account that follows is taken from Silas Talbot's lengthy account.

18 Elizabeth Hubbell Schenck, *The History of Fairfield, Fairfield County, Connecticut, 2 vols.* (New York: The author, 1889), 2:334-35.

19 Josiah Hoffman to Silas Talbot, 26 November 1808, B9 F2 STP; Hoffman to Silas Talbot, 5 December 1808, B9 F2 STP.

20 Theodore Talbot to Silas Talbot, 2 January 1809, B9 F3 STP; George Washington Talbot to Silas Talbot, 2 January 1809, B9 F3 STP.

21 Theodore Talbot to Silas Talbot, 12 January 1809, B9 F3 STP; Separation Agreement, 21 January 1809, B9 F3 STP.

22 Silas Talbot to Cyrus Talbot, 16 September 1809, B9 F4 STP; Will of Silas Talbot, New York County Wills, 50:605-10.

*S*ILAS TALBOT WAS laid to rest in
Trinity churchyard, Manhattan, on
July 1, 1813. He had been soldier,
sailor, Revolutionary War hero,
prisoner of war, politician, business-
man, country gentleman, U.S. Navy
Captain, and honored citizen of the
republic he helped to create.
(Joseph Gribbins, MSM 95-6-F16)

Chapter Twelve

Conclusion

Silas Talbot was a lucky man. He lived during a time of extraordinary opportunity. Born poor, then orphaned and thrown into the Hobbesian world of the eighteenth century, he had every opportunity—the other kind of opportunity—to disappear. Thousands like him did. Yet he did not. Somehow Silas Talbot not only survived but triumphed. So much, in fact, that his life can be seen as a metaphor for the American dream—a dream of social and financial advancement.

The difference between Talbot and those mudsills like him lies in his own character and the dynamic world around him. Silas Talbot was certainly no saint. He was lustful, sometimes a bit greedy, and he had more than a touch of arrogance. Nor were his moral sensibilities much developed beyond those of his time. He was a slave owner (and so was Thomas Jefferson). And it is unlikely that he will be remembered as a devoted father and husband. He was, in short, a flawed human being. His "flaws," of course, are precisely the things that make him interesting, and it is appropriate to note that one of his flaws was lack of concern for his own safety in escapades and desperate circumstances during the Revolution. He was a wonderfully brash, fearless man.

Matched against his vices are his many virtues. Hard work was no stranger to him. He knew how to lift, haul and plow. He also knew how to learn. Someone in Dighton may have taught him the rudiments of reading, writing and ciphering, but the rest he learned on his own. It was muscle and mind that got him out of the Taunton River valley and into the larger world of Providence. Town life electrified him. It sharpened his senses, awakened his ambition and taught him one of the conventional wisdoms of eighteenth-century American life: property brings status. Talbot wanted status.

Through work, marriage and sound investments Silas Talbot rose in status. Had life gone forward in a predictable fashion he would have emerged as a well-respected tradesman or trader of the middling sort in Rhode Island. Events, however, proved quite unpredictable. That he managed to leap beyond success in Providence is a result of the powerful forces let loose by the American Revolution.

Wars make heroes. The Revolution made Talbot. He was with Washington in Boston. He nearly lost his life on the Hudson. Against overwhelming odds he stood knee deep in the mud of the Delaware defying the British. Sullivan and Gates relied on him in Rhode Island and on Narragansett Bay. Indeed, in the latter theatre he went from being just another Rhode Island infantryman to become a bold privateersman and naval officer. He was both Lieutenant Colonel Talbot of the Continental Army and Captain Talbot of the Continental Navy. No other officer of the Revolution can claim that distinction. With his injuries in the service and bitter experience as a prisoner of war, few other young men of the Revolution suffered so much in support of the American cause.

Service and suffering merited rewards. Talbot and his fellow officers expected a grateful Congress to press upon them the favors of a grateful nation. Even if it had wanted to, Congress could not—at least it could not in the years after Yorktown; victory had been won but financial stability was the next battle. The men in Philadelphia, serving an impecunious and impotent government, embarrassed themselves in the eyes of Talbot and others as they evaded responsibility and remained indecisive, masters of a new order that had yet to take hold.

Although angry at Congress, Talbot had never been dependent upon politicians. If they were powerless, he was not. The war had brought him a good deal of reputation and even a little cash. The war had introduced him to people and opportunities far beyond Rhode Island. He was a young man on the make who joined in the great post-Revolutionary game of speculation.

Talbot's aggressive risk-taking was perfect for post-Revolutionary America. In him was matched risk and sense of opportunity. He was hardly unique; indeed, he was one of thousands of young men of the Revolution out to grab what was available. Land was the resource and investment of choice, and it drew Talbot to Johnstown and Johnson Hall. It provided the platform for his emergence into politics on the side of Federalism, the faction that endorsed good order and nationalism, principles close to Talbot's heart.

Talbot's politics and war record earned him rewards in the new America. They did not come to him by chance. He assiduously sought place and preferment. When threatened, as by Truxtun and Stoddert, Talbot was not reluctant to counterattack and to summon friends and influence to his side. He rarely lost.

Talbot's public advance mirrored his success in private life. Silas Talbot was a calculating man. Is it untoward to suggest that his selection of wives was motivated by more than mere love? The pattern is clear. Anna Richmond of Providence, Rebecca Morris of Philadelphia and Elizabeth Pintard of New York were all women of family and connections far beyond what an orphan from Dighton, Massachusetts, might expect to enjoy. Perhaps it was an ambition to marry well that persuaded him not to engage Elizabeth Arnold. It was the same ambition that blinded him to the perils of marrying Elizabeth Pintard.

Talbot pretended to the landed gentry; Johnstown and even Kentucky stand witness to that. To be a country squire, independent and respected, seems to have been one of his dreams, aside from the intrinsic value of having land. He always felt that investment in land was the only thing that really lasted. Yet if he dreamed of broad acres and a gracious country life, he was happier and more suited to a reality that was urban and bourgeois. He never liked living in the Mohawk River valley, and Kentucky was too primitive and remote.

Much the same may be said for Talbot as seaman and naval officer. Truxtun was right when he described Talbot as a mere privateersman. This is not to suggest that he was not a brave and courageous officer. In that his record speaks for itself. What it does suggest is that Talbot never displayed, or had the opportunity to display, what Admiral William James once described, when writing about Lord Nelson, as the "aces." These were the attributes of the great naval commanders: "moral courage; endurance to resist strain and fatigue; imagination and creative powers for strategical and tactical plans; and fine seamanship."[1] Talbot's career in the Revolution was that of a moderately successful privateersman. In the Quasi War his command of *Constitution*, while competent, was lackluster. It was a performance that in great measure reflected the humdrum duty assigned to him. Unlike his able lieutenant, Isaac Hull, Talbot never really viewed himself as a professional naval officer. His duty on *Constitution* was not an end in itself, nor was it a path to professional advancement. When he left the service he felt no regret and he never looked back.

The American Revolution did not create Silas Talbot. It did not make him brave, ambitious or calculating. All those traits were formed in his rough childhood in Dighton and his adolescence on the Bay. What the Revolution did was release the fetters that held these traits in place. The war was a gymnasium in which he exercised, grew strong and began to understand his own power. To be present at the creation of a new republic was an extraordinary experience. To be one of its builders, as this young Yankee bricklayer was, in the mud of a doomed fort and at sea challenging the ships of King George's empire, was a way to build a better life. The Revolution and its aftermath gave this young man of the Revolution a chance to achieve the kind of wealth and status never possible for people like him before. He was among the first of the new citizens of the new republic to seize its gifts.

1. Admiral Sir William Milbourne James, *The Durable Monument: Horatio Nelson* (London: Longmans Green and Company, 1948), 299.

Index